LOOKING AT LOGISTICS

A Practical Introduction to Logistics and Supply Chain Management

3rd edition

P.M. Price, Ph.D.

N.J. Harrison, M.Ed.

Printed in the United States of America

First Printing: October 2020

Third edition

ISBN 978-1-934231-08-1

Table of Contents

Chapter 1

Introducing the Supply Chain   1

1.1 The Simple Supply Chain and Its Members   2

1.2 Supply Chain Complexity   5

1.3 Supply Chain Flow   7

1.4 Supply Chain Location and Perspective   9

1.5 Internal and External Supply Chains   10

1.6 The Power of the Supply Chain   11

Chapter 1 Review Questions   15

Chapter 1 Case Study   16

Chapter 2

Logistics and Supply Chain Management   19

2.1 Defining Logistics & Supply Chain Management   19

2.2 Looking at Logistics Management   20

2.4 Introducing Supply Chain Management   23

2.5 Supply Chain Management Teams   25

2.6 The Tradeoff Principle and Creating Value in Supply Chains   28

Chapter 2 Review Questions   31

Chapter 2 Case Study   32

Chapter 3

Inbound Logistics: Purchasing   35

3.1 Purchasing and Supply Management   36

3.2 The Five Ws of Purchasing: Who and What   38

3.3 The Five Ws of Purchasing: Where   40

3.4 The Five Ws of Purchasing: When   43

3.5 The Five Ws of Purchasing: Why   44

3.6 The Five Ws of Purchasing Bonus Track: How   47

3.7 The Purchasing Process: Identify a Need   49

3.8 The Purchasing Process: Identify Suppliers 52

3.9 The Purchasing Process: Supplier Selection 56

3.10 The Purchasing Process: Purchase Orders 59

3.11 The Purchasing Process: The Final Steps 61

Chapter 3 Review Questions 65

Chapter 3 Case Study 66

Chapter 4

Inbound Logistics: Warehousing and Inventory Management   69

4.1 Warehouse Management 70

4.2 Case Example: Warehouses in a Supply Chain 73

4.3 Types of Warehouses 74

4.4 Warehouse Layout and Flow 80

4.5 Materials Handling 84

4.6 Inventory Management 89

Chapter 4 Review Questions 93

Chapter 4 Case Study 94

Chapter 5

Outbound Logistics: The Order Cycle and Outbound Goods   97

5.1 Physical Distribution Management 98

5.2 Responding to the Order Cycle 101

5.3 Order Picking 103

5.4 Order Packing 107

5.5 Servicing Marketing's Distribution Channels 108

5.6 What Happens When Goods Are Out the Door? 114

Chapter 5 Review Questions 117

Chapter 5 Case Study 118

Chapter 6

Outbound Logistics: Transportation   121

6.1 Introducing Transportation 122

6.2 Transportation Utility and Tradeoffs 123

6.3 Transportation Basics 126

6.4 Modes of Transportation 130

6.5 Carriers and Third-Party Providers 138

6.6 Intermodal and Multimodal Transportation 142

6.6 The Legal Side of Transportation 144

Chapter 6 Review Questions 147

Chapter 6 Case Study 148

Chapter 7

Logistics Information Systems and Technology — 151

7.1 Defining Information 152

7.2 Information in Logistics 156

7.3 Logistics information Systems 160

7.4 Supportive Logistics Technology 165

7.5 Autonomous Logistics Technology 171

Chapter 7 Review Questions 175

Chapter 7 Case Study 176

Chapter 8

Finance in the Supply Chain — 179

8.1 The Who and What of Finance 180

8.2 Income Statements 181

8.3 The Balance Sheet 186

8.4 Financial Ratios 191

8.5 The DuPont Strategic Model 195

8.6 The Inventory Turnover Ratio 198

8.7 Cost Accounting 199

Chapter 8 Review Questions 207

Chapter 8 Case Exercise 208

Chapter 9

Global Supply Chain Management — 211

9.1 International Market Entry 212

9.2 The Global Supply Chain Environment 216

9.3 Trade Agreements Around the World 222

9.4 International Trade Documentation 225

9.5 INCOTERMS and ISO 9001 229

Chapter 9 Review Questions 233

Chapter 9 Case Study 234

Chapter 10

Customer Service and the Supply Chain

Customer Service and the Supply Chain   **239**

10.1 Understanding Customers and Service   240

10.2 The Customer Experience   243

10.3 Customer Service and Logistics Management   246

10.4 The Marketing-Logistics Relationship   250

10.5 Customer Service Information and Metrics   255

Chapter 10 Review Questions   257

Chapter 10 Case Study   258

Chapter 11

Leading and Managing in the Supply Chain

Leading and Managing in the Supply Chain   **263**

11.1 The People Chain   264

11.2 Management Versus Leadership   266

11.3 Managing Others and Self   269

11.4 Leading Self and Others   274

11.5 Supply Chain Managers and Leaders   278

Chapter 11 Review Questions   283

Chapter 11 Case Study   284

Chapter 12

Strategy and Supply Chain Management

Strategy and Supply Chain Management   **289**

12.1 Strategic Management   290

12.2 Strategy Tools: Refining the Vision   294

12.3 Strategy Tools: External Analysis   297

12.4 Strategy Tools: Internal Analysis   301

12.5 Strategy Tools: Initial and Ongoing Analysis   303

Chapter 12 Review Questions   307

Chapter 12 Case Study   308

Photo and Image Attributions   **311**

Index   **319**

Chapter 1
Introducing the Supply Chain

Every day, we encounter supply chains. Whenever we interact with human-made items in the world around us, we are influenced by the supply chains these items followed to reach us. For example, let's consider the cellphone, something the average user touches 2617 times a day. We depend on our cellphones as communication devices, calendars, calculators, maps, cameras, wallets, bank tellers, fitness managers, shopping centers, movie theaters, gaming consoles, and flashlights. The success or failure of the supply chain of a cellphone and its accessories can impact our lives.

Most of us wake up in the morning to a loud but trusted alarm clock app on our cellphones. They function correctly and get us up when we need to because the phone was part of an effective supply chain. All of its raw materials and component parts reached the cellphone manufacturer on time and in good condition to produce a working finished product. The newly manufactured cellphone then followed a brick-and-mortar or online store's supply chain to reach us in working condition. Our cellphone wakes us up each day thanks to successful supply chains. However, suppose that we want to jazz up our phone and display our fondness for 1980s retro style. After an online search, we find the perfect cellphone case with neon geometric shapes and *Totally Rad* in bubble letters superimposed across the front. However, the day after we purchased and installed this new case, our phone stopped functioning and failed to wake us up one morning, causing us to be late for an important job interview, which left us without an income for an additional three months!

Unbeknownst to us, not all the desired component parts reached the phone case manufacturer because of historically heavy rains, which flooded all major roadways surrounding the factory for a week, which caused the case manufacturer to use an improperly fitting base from another line of cases with similar specifications. Because the base was not an exact match, some cases manufactured had an imperceptible flaw that caused cellphone power cords to pop out of the phone after a few minutes of use. As a result, this flaw in our totally rad new 1980s style cellphone case caused our cellphone to drain its battery, which caused our alarm clock app to fail, which caused us to keep sleeping and miss our interview. We lost the chance of landing our dream job, forever changing our lives due to a simple supply chain failure.

Every day, we interact with thousands of human-made, processed, or harvested items, from the food we eat to the clothes on our backs to the roofs over our heads. The success of our interactions with these items depends on the success of their supply chains.

1.1 THE SIMPLE SUPPLY CHAIN AND ITS MEMBERS

A ***supply chain*** is a company's network of goods, systems, information, and people that connects and moves goods between the company, its suppliers, and its final customers. Supply chains can also move people. In this book, however, we will focus on the movement of goods.

In business and economics, *goods* are tangible manufactured or produced items sold to customers based on their wants or needs. In transportation, *goods* are items a company or person possesses that can be moved, often used synonymously with cargo. Let's keep it simple and define ***goods*** as tangible items that are owned and can be moved.

Anything you see in front of you that is human-made is a good that was once part of a supply chain. The supply chain for Orange-U-Yummy orange juice, for example, would begin with oranges as they are picked and packaged for shipment in a supplier's orange grove in Florida. The Orange-U-Yummy supply chain would then include all the activities associated with transporting and storing the oranges until the juice manufacturer in Oregon receives them. Once the oranges have been squeezed dry and the juice packaged, the supply chain then includes all the activities associated with the handling, storage, and transportation of the packaged juice until it reaches your hometown grocery store, where it is ready for you to purchase.

FIGURE 1.1 - THE SIMPLE SUPPLY CHAIN

A ***simple supply chain***, as shown in Figure 1.1, represents a streamlined representation of the supply chain of a company, its suppliers, and its customers for products such as Orange-U-Yummy orange juice. It spans multiple organizations and begins with the supplier. Also called the *vendor*, the ***supplier*** is a company or person that provides goods or services to another company or individual. In the case of Orange-U-Yummy orange juice, its supplier in Florida, Gator's Groovy Groves, provides the raw materials used in manufacturing the finished product. Orange-U-Yummy has other suppliers, too, such as the companies that provide additional juice ingredients, packaging and shipping materials, and manufacturing machinery. Figure 1.2 represents our simple supply chain from Figure 1.1 based on our Orange-U-Yummy orange juice example, which shows the orange supplier as its supplier.

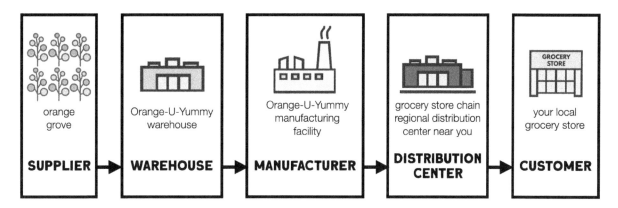

FIGURE 1.2 - THE SIMPLE SUPPLY CHAIN FOR ORANGE-U-YUMMY ORANGE JUICE

Second within our simple supply chain example is a ***warehouse***, a building or area that stores goods. Warehouses could be owned and operated by the supplier, the manufacturer, or the retailer. They can also be owned and operated by a company called a *third-party logistics services provider*, which specializes in various logistics services, such as warehousing and transportation, and provides its services to a range of different and sometimes competing companies. In our orange juice example, the oranges from the supplier, Gator's Groovy Groves, is sent to a warehouse in Oregon that is part of the Orange-U-Yummy manufacturing facility.

Third in our simple supply chain is a manufacturer. A ***manufacturer*** is a company that processes, makes, builds, or assembles a finished product. This company typically utilizes machinery. Work is divided among multiple people across one or more facilities to transform raw materials or unfinished component parts into a different finished product. In other cases, a company may take a natural resource or a raw material and transform it into a sellable raw material or semi-finished good, not necessarily utilizing machinery to transform products. In this case, the company is typically called a ***producer***. Both oil companies and dairy farmers are examples of producers. In our orange juice example, Orange-U-Yummy is a *manufacturer* because it takes raw materials (oranges) and transforms them into a finished product (orange juice) using both machinery and people.

Fourth in our simple supply chain is a ***distribution center***, a warehouse facility where finished goods are sorted, briefly stored, and shipped to wholesalers, retailers, or final customers. Like the previously described standard warehouses within the supply chain, distribution centers may be owned and operated by a manufacturer, retailer, or third-party provider. In our orange juice example, the distribution center could be a regional distribution center for a grocery store chain in our location. While both warehouses and distribution centers store goods, their primary difference lies in their goals. The fundamental goal of a warehouse is to store goods safely, regardless of storage time. A distribution center is also a type of warehouse, but its fundamental goal is to efficiently hold goods for quick movement in, out, and on to the next supply chain segment.

THE CHANGING LANGUAGE OF AMAZON.COM

Some of the most well-known distribution centers you may interact with regularly are those of amazon.com. In 1994, when the company began as an online bookseller, its facilities were called **warehouses**, storing products (books) until shipped to customers. In the 2000s, as it began to add a growing number of products to its online sales, amazon.com changed the name of its locations to **distribution centers**, reflecting a focus on efficient and speedy picking and delivery. Finally, another corporate name change occurred in the 2010s when the label *distribution centers* officially became **fulfillment centers**. Although these facilities are distribution centers, the name change reflected amazon.com's focus on customer service and fulfilling customers' orders.

At the tail end of our simple supply chain is the ***customer***, a company or person who purchases goods or services from another company or person. In supply chains, customers can include *wholesalers*, *retailers*, and *end users*.

A ***wholesaler***, our first type of customer, is a company that purchases goods or services in bulk from manufacturers at low prices and then sells them to retailers and end users at discounted prices. In our orange juice example, Orange-U-Yummy's customer may be C&S Wholesale Grocers, Inc. This company is a real US wholesaler that purchases grocery goods from manufacturers and sells them to independent grocery stores, military bases, and other institutions.

The next type of customer is a ***retailer***, a company that sells a wide range of goods to end users face-to-face in a physical location or virtually through websites or apps. In our orange juice example, a customer for Orange-U-Yummy's entire line of citrus juices could be any of the grocery retailers near you, such as Kroger in the US, Intermarché in France, ParknShop in China, or Wesfarmers Ltd in Australia. As an end user, if you have a hankering for Orange-U-Yummy's orange juice, you would travel to your local grocery retailer and buy a carton or two of juice or perhaps order them online for same-day delivery.

The final type of potential customer in a product's supply chain is an ***end user***, also called a ***consumer***. An end user is the final person or company that uses the product, typically for its intended purpose. In our juice example, the end user in the Orange-U-Yummy supply chain might be a person who loves the company's juice and participates in a direct-to-consumer subscription plan. This happy end user receives two liters of her favorite Orange-U-Yummy juice every week shipped directly from the company's regional distribution center. Another orange juice end user could be a company, Succulent Sam's Steakhouse, that uses Orange-U-Yummy juice to make its salad dressing and marinate its steaks. The restaurant is an end user because it has a bi-weekly standing order for 20 liters of juice from the Orange-U-Yummy regional distribution center. We are also end users of Orange-U-Yummy orange juice when we buy it from our retail grocery store, which means there are two layers of customers in this case: (1) our retail grocery store and (2) us, the ends users buying the orange juice in the grocery store!

1.2 SUPPLY CHAIN COMPLEXITY

In Figure 1.1, we looked at a relatively simple supply chain model. But can supply chains be that simple? In reality, most supply chains for finished products are quite complex. They may involve various suppliers, multiple manufacturers, and a wide range of warehouse and distribution facilities in different countries worldwide. Let's look at a supply chain for a typical large-scale orange juice manufacturer to illustrate this point.

As we mentioned before, an orange juice manufacturer's supply chain begins with fresh oranges, often supplied by Florida-based orange growers. When hurricanes, frost, and other weather events impact Florida orange groves, orange juice manufacturers depend on Brazilian orange suppliers. Other juice ingredient suppliers include: bulk processors in Brazil that provide frozen concentrated orange juice; blending houses in Florida that provide orange pulp and peel oil; and apple orchards in Washington, cranberry farms in Oregon, strawberry farms in California, and pineapple orchards in Hawaii that all provide additional juice ingredients. Orange juice manufacturers also depend on blending equipment machinery and parts suppliers in China and Germany. Finally, orange juice manufacturers need suppliers for the cartons, bottles, jugs, and boxes into which the finished juice is packaged for distribution to end users. Packaging suppliers are typically located close to a beverage company's manufacturing and bottling plants around the world to meet regional and country needs, which include preferred packaging types, container sizes, and label languages. In our orange juice example, the packaging suppliers have located their operations near orange juice manufacturing facilities in Florida.

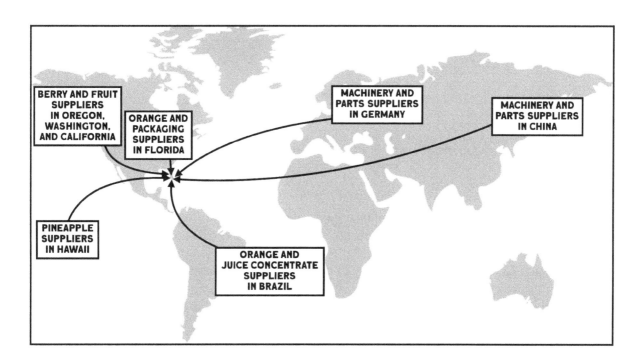

FIGURE 1.3 - INBOUND SUPPLY CHAIN (ORANGE-U-YUMMY FLORIDA MANUFACTURING FACILITY)

Figure 1.3 illustrates the flow of suppliers' goods to one of our orange juice manufacturers' facilities. This flow of goods *to* the manufacturer is called the ***inbound supply chain***. We could also represent the inbound supply chain showing the flow of supplies going to all three of the company's orange juice manufacturing facilities in Florida, the Netherlands, and Japan, which would look far more complicated. Members of the inbound supply chain could change at any time due to machinery improvements offered from new suppliers, customers' changing tastes in desired ingredients and flavors, and external conditions such as weather events impacting supply quantities and prices in different locations from different suppliers around the world.

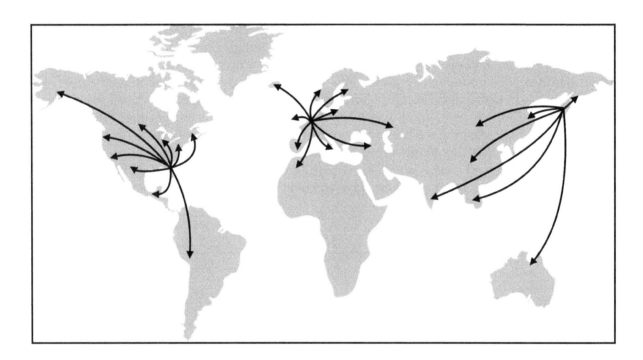

FIGURE 1.4 - OUTBOUND SUPPLY CHAIN (THREE MANUFACTURING FACILITIES)

After our orange juice company manufactures its goods, it distributes them and sends them on their way to happy customers. The orange juice facility in Florida sends its packaged yummy juice to wholesalers and retailer distribution centers across the United States, Canada, and Mexico. Its manufacturing facility in the Netherlands sends juice to wholesalers and retail distribution centers across Europe. Finally, its Japanese manufacturing facility sends packaged juice to retail distribution centers across Japan, Korea, and Australia and directly to consumers throughout Asia. Figure 1.4 illustrates this orange juice flow from the manufacturer's three facilities to wholesalers, retail distribution centers, and end users in each regional market. This flow of goods *from* the manufacturer is called the ***outbound supply chain***.

With various suppliers, manufacturing facilities, retailers, and distribution centers around the world, our once simple supply chain now becomes a complex global supply chain. As shown in the complex supply chain in Figure 1.5, supply chains typically involve many members and span multiple locations.

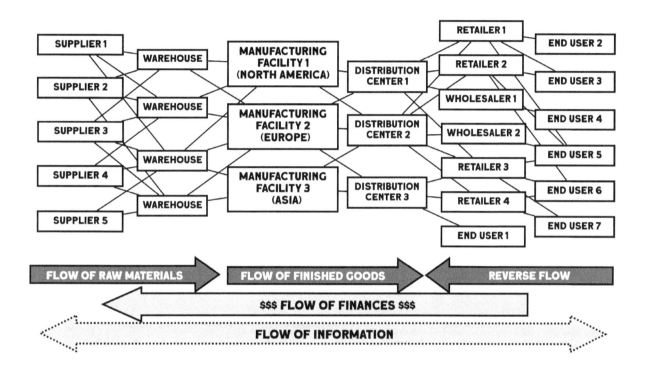

FIGURE 1.5 - THE COMPLEX SUPPLY CHAIN

1.3 SUPPLY CHAIN FLOW

In both the simple supply chain illustrated in Figure 1.1 and the complex supply chain in Figure 1.5, goods flow predictably from left to right toward the end user. These goods flowing in this predictable pattern could be raw materials, semi-finished goods, or finished goods. However, as shown in Figure 1.5, there are also flows from right to left, away from the end user. Let's take a look at some of these flows!

Finances flow from right to left, back up the supply chain. End users pay retailers, retailers and wholesalers pay manufacturers, and manufacturers pay suppliers for goods received. At the same time, information flows both left and right along the supply chain, with members of the chain supplying crucial information to one another to ensure that customers' requirements are understood and met when, where, and how they need them. As we will see in later chapters, information technology systems play a large part in the instantaneous flow of finances and information, creating increasingly efficient supply chains.

It is also quite common for the different customers along a supply chain to return items to suppliers. This ***reverse supply chain*** is the flow of goods and related resources from the customer back to the supplier in a network of support systems, information, and people. Reverse supply chains begin after a product has been sold and delivered to a customer. Goods or related resources flow back to the supplier as product returns, damaged goods to be repaired, or items for recycling or reuse.

Unless you have been satisfied with every item you have ever purchased in your entire life, you have probably participated in a reverse supply chain. When you buy something from a store or an online retailer, sometimes you're just not happy with it. Perhaps the new shoes don't fit, or the curtains look better in the package than they do in your home. With reverse supply chains, you usually have the option of returning it to the seller for a refund. These are all situations where a reverse supply chain begins.

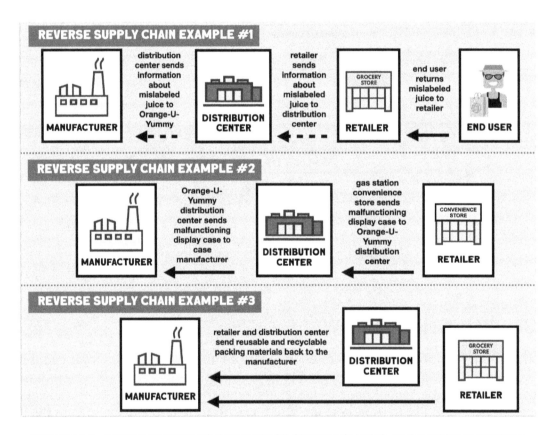

FIGURE 1.6 - THREE EXAMPLES OF REVERSE SUPPLY CHAINS AT ORANGE-U-YUMMY

As shown in the Orange-U-Yummy example in Figure 1.6, there are different types of reverse supply chains. Perhaps you purchased a carton of Orange-U-Yummy cranberry orange juice from your local grocery store and, upon tasting it, you discover that it is actually pineapple orange juice that was packaged incorrectly in the cranberry-orange packaging, so you return it to the retail grocery store, who discards it but informs the distribution center and manufacturer. For another example, let's say that Orange-U-Yummy supplies convenience store and gas station retailers with Orange-U-Yummy refrigerated display cases to store and sell the juice to end users. At your local Gas-and-Go gas station convenience store, the Orange-U-Yummy refrigerated display case stops working. Gas-and-Go sends the display case back to the Orange-U-Yummy distribution center, which sends the case back to the case manufacturer for repair or replacement. In a final example, let's imagine that Orange-U-Yummy has become environmentally conscious. The company has decided to go green by providing recyclable and reusable packing materials for delivery to its wholesale and retail customers, such as grocery wholesalers and grocery retail chains. After these wholesale and retail customers have unpacked the juice that Orange-U-Yummy has delivered, they collect the packing materials, such as cardboard boxes and plastic pallets, and return them to Orange-U-Yummy for recycling or reuse.

1.4 SUPPLY CHAIN LOCATION AND PERSPECTIVE

As shown in our simple supply chain in Figure 1.1 and our complex supply chain in Figure 1.5, multiple companies can be involved in one product's supply chain. We looked at the Orange-U-Yummy orange juice supply chain, but the other companies in the juice chain will have their *own* supply chains. For example, the orange supplier in the previous example, Gator's Groovy Groves, will have its own supply chain with its own suppliers, such as fertilizer and pesticide companies, and its own customers, such as other orange juice manufacturers and grocery store retailers. To help us avoid the confusion of multiple interacting companies with their own distinct supply chains, we need to know precisely which company's supply chain we are addressing.

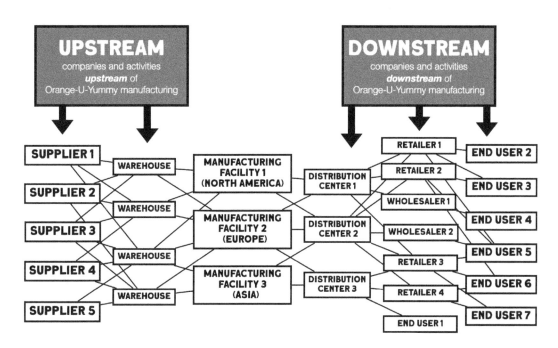

FIGURE 1.7 - UPSTREAM AND DOWNSTREAM IN ORANGE-U-YUMMY SUPPLY CHAIN

It also helps to have language for our location within a supply chain. When companies whose activities occur *before* our company produces and distributes its goods, we refer to them as **upstream**. Companies upstream of our orange juice manufacturer could include suppliers or third-party pre-manufacturing warehouses. When companies whose activities occur *after* our company produces and distributes its goods, we refer to them as **downstream**. Companies downstream of our orange juice manufacturer could include retail distribution centers and wholesaler customers. Figure 1.7 illustrates which companies or activities are upstream and which are downstream, as seen from the perspective of an orange juice manufacturing facility.

Two additional words used to describe supply chains from different perspectives are *demand chain* and *value chain*. These terms are often used interchangeably with *supply chain*, but they reveal something about perspective. **Demand chain** describes a supply chain in which the emphasis is on the final customer or end user's actual demands. When materials are *pulled* through the supply chain based on actual customer demand, rather than the supplier *pushing* materials through the chain according to assumed demand or other criteria, an organization can provide better customer service and control inventory quantities within its chain. The focus is on getting goods to customers when and where they need them in the amount needed, so no extra goods are pushed through the chain, which increases overall costs. In our orange juice example, the amount of oranges ordered from suppliers and the amount of packaged juice produced and delivered to retailers is based on customer demand instead of other factors such as fluctuations in orange prices or factories' abilities to produce more juice.

While the focus of a demand chain is customer demand, the **value chain's** focus is adding value to the final product based on what the customer perceives as valuable and is willing to buy. Value can be added at each stage of the supply chain. In our oranges example, the grower might add value to its oranges by transporting them carefully and quickly from field to factory, perhaps using safer and faster transportation modes. The juice manufacturer might add value by changing juice packaging to make it easier for end users to handle and optimize refrigerator storage spaces. By analyzing all the stages in the value chain, companies can look for opportunities to add more value to goods or reduce current costs.

1.5 INTERNAL AND EXTERNAL SUPPLY CHAINS

In addition to simple supply chains, complex supply chains, demand chains, and value chains, supply chains are also classified as *external* and *internal*. An **external supply chain** represents the flow of goods, information, and finances among *multiple* companies in a product's supply chain. An external supply chain typically includes a company, such as a manufacturer or producer, its suppliers, and its immediate customers, such as retailers. Both the simple and complex supply chains we examined in Figure 1.1 and Figure 1.5 are examples of external supply chains. In the case of Orange-U-Yummy orange juice, the external supply chain would include the flow of goods, information, and finances beginning with orange suppliers at the orange grove and ending with the finished cartons of orange juice on your grocery store's shelves.

Unlike the external supply chain, which focuses on the supply chain activities across *multiple* companies, an **internal supply chain** represents the flow of goods, information, and finance within *one company only*. The internal supply chain begins when a company places an order with a supplier. In the case of Orange-U-Yummy orange juice, as shown in Figure 1.8, the company's corporate headquarters office places orders to purchase supplies or raw materials, such as oranges, and the oranges reach the receiving dock at the Orange-U-Yummy warehouse. It ends when cartons of packaged orange juice leave the Orange-U-Yummy manufacturing facility warehouse or the Orange-U-Yummy trucks used to transport juice to customers. The function within a company responsible for managing this internal supply chain is called *logistics*, but we'll have lots more to tell you about that in the next chapter.

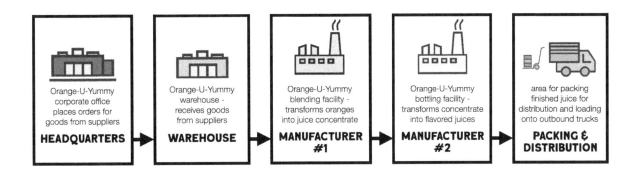

FIGURE 1.8 - ORANGE-U-YUMMY INTERNAL SUPPLY CHAIN

Although a product's internal supply chain resides within one company, it does not necessarily reside within one building or facility. For example, Orange-U-Yummy may receive fresh oranges from twenty different suppliers at its regional warehouse in Florida. It may then send the oranges or condensed juice in refrigerated containers by truck to an Orange-U-Yummy juicing facility in California. After the juice has been produced, blended, and packaged, Orange-U-Yummy may finally send shipping containers of packaged juice cartons to its own regional distribution centers in Los Angeles, Newark, Detroit, Atlanta, Vancouver, and Mexico City. Although widespread, all of these logistics activities are within the Orange-U-Yummy orange juice internal supply chain.

1.6 THE POWER OF THE SUPPLY CHAIN

Companies that manufacture or produce goods are responsible to their owners or **shareholders**, i.e., the people, businesses, or other entities that own shares of stock in a company. The primary goal of most companies is to generate income. Their owners and shareholders expect them to make money. When supply chains are not functioning correctly or if they are poorly designed, they can lose money for a company. Imagine going to your local grocery store to buy a carton of Orange-U-Yummy orange juice but finding the shelves bare because the brand's shipment has not yet arrived at the store. Because you must have your morning glass of orange juice, you find yourself in the precarious position of having to select an alternate brand. Oh no!

But why has your favorite Orange-U-Yummy orange juice not yet arrived? The answer is three simple words: *supply chain failure*. A mistake was made in calculating the amount of dye to order for printing the juice cartons. As a result, cartons were delivered late to the juice manufacturer, which led to a delay in juice production, which led to late deliveries to some juice retailers, which included your local supermarket. This delay not only loses Orange-U-Yummy immediate sales, but it also decreases customer satisfaction and may reduce customers' brand loyalty. This delay allows customers like you to experience a wide variety of other brands of orange juice. You might discover that you like some of them more and choose them in the future, even when Orange-U-Yummy is back in stock. Therefore, a study of supply chains is critical for commercial survival and success in today's increasingly competitive global marketplace.

As consumers, we have come to expect efficient and immediately responsive supply chains. We place orders online and expect same-day delivery and even delivery within the hour. A little more than twenty years ago, online shopping was novel, and supply chains were not as immediately responsive. During the 1999 holiday season, the new practice of online shopping became enormously popular overnight. At the time, the leading US toy retailer, Toys-R-Us, entered into the world of online sales. It told customers that all orders placed by December 10th would be delivered before Christmas. Although considered too long for most goods today, a fifteen-day delivery window was considered very good in 1999.

The *front end* of a retail supply chain system is its ability to receive orders online, process financial transactions, and issue orders to finished goods warehouses for picking. The Toys-R-Us front end could easily handle the massive inflow of customers' requests, and the company had enough inventory on hand to fill the orders. However, the physical **back end** of the supply chain (picking, packing, and transporting customers' orders) was overwhelmed. The new online ordering system worked well, but the company could not physically process and fill the orders fast enough, even though many of its employees worked tirelessly for 49 days straight! As December 25th neared, Toys-R-Us had to send apologetic emails to thousands of its customers, explaining that their orders could not be filled until a week after Santa had returned to the North Pole. Many customers canceled their orders. Customer loyalty levels dropped dramatically, resulting in this fiasco being labeled one of the world's greatest supply chain disasters by various news and business publications.

While the Toys-R-Us supply chain disaster was damaging to its reputation and fiscal health, you've probably heard of an even deadlier disaster caused by supply chain failure. In April 1912, the ocean liner Titanic ran into an iceberg on her maiden voyage across the Atlantic Ocean. Although the Titanic had been called "unsinkable" at the time, 1500 passengers and crew perished when the 41,730-metric ton vessel sank in three short hours. Although the iceberg was the catalyst, a supply chain failure may have caused significant damage to the ship and the colossal loss of life. The ship's builder, Harland and Wolff shipyards in Belfast, Ireland, was building two additional vessels at the time of the Titanic's construction. To keep up with the promised delivery time for the Titanic's launch, the shipbuilder simply could not keep up with the demand for the millions of rivets needed for the construction schedule.

FIGURE 1.9 - RMS TITANIC IN SOUTHAMPTON, ENGLAND PRIOR TO DEPARTURE

Rivets are cylindrical metal fasteners that hold two metal pieces together with a watertight connection because both ends are pounded and flattened into the metal. The shortage of rivets caused Harland and Wolff to order mixed and low-grade materials from multiple suppliers. If the shipbuilder had instead relied on one supplier of high-grade materials, the Titanic would have taken longer to build. However, metallurgic scientists at the US National Institute of Standards and Technology today believe that if the shipbuilder used higher quality rivets throughout, more of the Titanic's hull might have held together when it hit the iceberg. The heads of the rivets would have been less likely to pop off, which would have resulted in a slower sinking with many more lives spared.

In the 21st century, companies are not without supply chain failures, but most know that investment of time, effort, and money in supply chains results in improved customer experiences and reduced costs. Large corporations appoint an executive or vice president in charge of supply chains and invest heavily in related research, information technology, and systems implementation. Former supply chain senior executives and vice presidents are increasingly becoming CEOs of global corporations such as Apple, General Motors, and Intel. Research centers, professional organizations, and entire departments of many top universities worldwide devote themselves to the study of efficient and effective supply chain practices and systems.

13

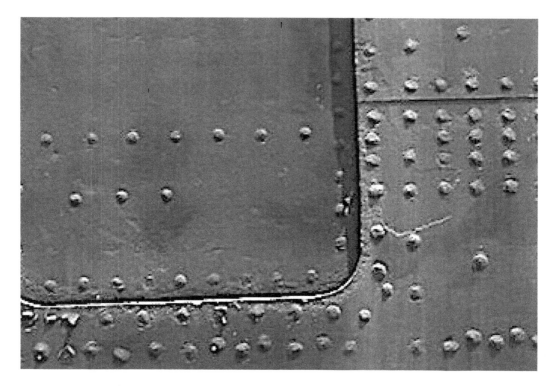

FIGURE 1.10 - EXAMPLE OF RIVETS ON THE HULL OF A SHIP

The study of supply chains is one of the most effective means for companies to gain a competitive advantage in the increasingly competitive global marketplace. In the chapters of this book to follow, we will look at various areas in the necessary and exciting world of logistics and supply chain management.

CHAPTER 1 REVIEW QUESTIONS

1. In your own words, what is a *supply chain*?

2. Look around you right now. What do you see that are examples of *goods*? What do you see that are *not* examples of goods?

3. How are *warehouses* and *distribution centers* related? How are they different?

4. What are the different types of *customers* in a supply chain? Consider a luxury automobile supply chain. What might its various types of customers be?

5. Provide one example of an *inbound supply chain*.

6. Provide one example of an *outbound supply chain*.

7. What is a *reverse supply chain*? Describe one instance when you have initiated a reverse supply chain.

8. Explain the terms *upstream* and *downstream* when used in a supply chain setting. Provide an example with your explanation.

9. A supply chain failure occurred for a well-known ice cream manufacturer when fifty refrigerated cargo containers full of ice cream lost power due to weather-related outages. Ice cream on its way to multiple distribution centers temporarily melted before it refroze. The result was a decrease in product quality because the ice cream became icy instead of creamy. Describe why this might result in both short-term and long-term financial losses for the ice cream manufacturer.

10. What logistics lessons can we learn from the Toys-R-Us incident in 1999 and the sinking of the Titanic in 1912?

CHAPTER 1 CASE STUDY

A SUPPLY CHAIN FAIRYTALE

Once upon a time in the not too distant present in a kingdom called *the Company*, there was an evil stepmother called *the CEO*, whose only concern was keeping the Shareholders happy with good dividend returns. She had two ugly-tempered daughters. One was called *Finance*, and the other was called *Marketing*. Unlike the other evil stepmother of childhood fairytales, our *CEO* also had an ugly-tempered son called *Manufacturing*.

The ugly-tempered sister *Marketing* was preoccupied only with the handsome *Customer*. Nothing mattered to *Marketing* except getting goods delivered and keeping the *Customer* happy, no matter what the cost. *Marketing* didn't care if she made the *Company* poor because she desperately wanted to please the handsome *Customer*. She would often send him what he needed by an expensive golden airplane instead of sending items by the more affordable horse-powered trucks.

The other ugly-tempered sister, *Finance*, had no time for handsome customers. Her true love was money. She wanted to hold onto every penny *the Company* had. *Finance* insisted that *the Company* should do everything at the lowest cost possible. The stingy *Finance* often fought with her frivolous sister, screaming, "We must protect *the Company* and reduce all costs!" to which *Marketing* would cry, "But we need to keep *the Customer* happy! I want to live happily ever after with him!" Both sisters naively thought that reducing costs and maximizing customer service were mutually exclusive.

Adding to the family chaos was the ugly-tempered and very demanding brother, *Manufacturing*. He liked to build and build and build for *the Company*, but he thought he was the fairest of them all and demanded that everything he needed to build should be supplied immediately and upon a silver platter. *Manufacturing* and *Finance* fought long and often because the demanding brother wanted lots of extra materials to be on hand "just in case" *the Company* needed more things to be built. His stingy sister, *Finance*, never wanted him to order more materials than he absolutely needed and insisted that he order the cheapest materials available, regardless of their quality. When *Manufacturing* got his way and won these heated arguments, *the Company's* royal warehouses were overflowing with extra goods, resulting in increased inventory holding costs and a very angry evil stepmother *CEO*. When *Finance* got her way, there were never any extra materials ordered, and the royal warehouses remained almost empty. This pleased *the CEO* because there were no extra inventory holding costs until *the handsome Customer* told *the CEO* that he now needed an additional 500,000 widgets built immediately. Because there were no extra materials available, *Manufacturing* could not begin building widgets for *the Customer* until after the holiday weekend. This displeased *the evil CEO* stepmother greatly.

Manufacturing grew tired of arguing with his stingy sister, *Finance*, and decided to reduce his costs and please the evil stepmother *CEO* by engaging in long production runs, building millions and millions of widgets at a time. While this did reduce production costs, *Manufacturing* naively believed that this would also keep *the Customer* happy by having so many widgets immediately available. However, these millions of widgets were royal blue. The handsome *Customer* told *Marketing* that he was growing weary of royal blue and now wanted all widgets to be awe-inspiring platinum. When *Marketing* told her brother that the next order for the handsome *Customer* must be changed to awe-inspiring platinum, *Manufacturing* flew into a rage, screaming, "We have just started our production run of five million royal blue widgets! I will not change it just because some good looking customer has changed his mind! It will cost *the Company and* my sub-realm too much money!" *Marketing* grew even angrier at her demanding and resistant brother, grabbing him the collar and bellowing into his face, "You WILL change the order to awe-inspiring platinum! If you do not, the handsome *Customer* might leave us for another kingdom, and WE CAN'T HAVE THAT!"

Thus, all was not rosy in the family of our evil stepmother, *CEO*. Now enters the poor stepsister of our story with the mellifluous name of *Cinderella Logistics*. *Cinderella Logistics* was hardworking and fair and kind and just and, well, an all-around perfect person. She knew that the verdant and rich *Company* would shrivel up into a wasteland of hopelessness and despair if her siblings did not stop fighting. She knew what needed to be done, so she rolled up her sleeves and got to work. She decided that, although they were ugly-tempered (and frivolous and stingy and demanding), *Marketing*, *Finance*, and *Manufacturing* were all critical to *the Company's* prosperity. She knew that they all had important needs and concerns, so she decided to put aside family differences and work with them all.

Cinderella Logistics worked with *Marketing* to ensure that all widgets were picked, packed, and transported to the handsome *Customer* to ensure that what he wanted arrived in the right quantity, of the right quality, at the right time, and at the right place, while also being mindful of keeping costs as low as possible. *Cinderella Logistics* also worked with *Manufacturing* to ensure that he had the exact materials he needed in the right quantity, of the right quality, at the right time, and at the right place, while still being mindful of keeping costs as low as possible. Finally, *Cinderella Logistics* worked with *Finance* to minimize inventory holding costs through inventory management.

Through her challenging work with her equally challenging siblings, *Cinderella Logistics* learned an important lesson: minimize all costs associated with all the activities of internal customers (finance, marketing, and manufacturing) while ensuring the right quantity of goods of the right quality are delivered to the external customer at the right time and to the right place with minimum costs and maximum level of service.

The hardworking *Cinderella Logistics* accomplished all of this by listening to her siblings' needs and getting down to work. And she did this without the help of a fairy godmother or some random prince to come to her rescue! She also learned that *Marketing*, *Finance*, and *Manufacturing* weren't so ugly-tempered after all when someone finally listened to them, and the evil stepmother *CEO* wasn't even evil when her headache subsided after all her stepkids stopped arguing.

And they all lived happily ever after... The End?

Chapter 2

Logistics and Supply Chain Management

In Chapter 1, the supply chain was the star. We discovered that everything we see and use in our daily lives involves supply chains, from the food on our table to the table itself. We learned a lot about the members, complexity, flow, structure, and power of supply chains. But isn't this book supposed to be looking at *logistics*? What is logistics, and how is it related to supply chain management? Let's find out!

2.1 DEFINING LOGISTICS & SUPPLY CHAIN MANAGEMENT

Supply chains and logistics have existed for thousands of years. How could the ancient Greek, Roman, and Chinese empires have existed and fed all their citizens without supply chains and logistics? As we know it today, the word logistics originated in the 18th century to refer to moving and supplying French military troops. Since then, the definition of logistics has expanded into the academic and business worlds. In the academic world, *logistics* is the discipline or study of efficient and effective practices to move goods from a raw or unfinished state to a finished state and on to a final customer or end user. Many academics describe it in many different ways, and things can get pretty confusing! Let's instead look at a business definition.

In the business world, **logistics** describes how a company or other organization acquires, handles, stores, and moves goods throughout its internal supply chain. In a company's *internal* supply chain, a lot happens. As mentioned in Chapter 1, a company's internal supply chain begins when it places orders to purchase goods, supplies, or raw materials and then receives them in its warehouse. This internal supply chain ends when goods leave a company's final supply chain facility bound for external customers.

Within most companies, there is a *Logistics Department* or a functional area related to logistics. At Apple, Inc., there is a Logistics and Supply Chain Team that reports to the Operations Department. For Walmart's US division, there is a Supply Chain and Logistics Department. There may also be multiple Logistics Departments across a company, such as the Logistics Departments within the Stores/Retail division for each of the IKEA stores worldwide.

A company's logistics function handles the flow of goods and information into, within, and out from its own company. As shown in Figure 2.1, the logistics function within a company is responsible for many activities, including purchasing, inventory receipt, warehousing, materials handling, order processing, picking, packing, transportation, and the flow of information and finances for these activities. Purchasing, inventory receipt, warehousing, and materials handling are logistics activities in a company's *inbound* supply chain as goods flow *into* that company. Order processing, picking, packing, and transportation are logistics activities in a company's *outbound* supply chain as goods flow *out from* that company. Information flow and financial flow occur in both the inbound and outbound sections of a company's supply chain. We will explore all of these logistics activities in detail throughout this book. Figure 2.1 highlights the chapters in which we'll cover each topic.

FIGURE 2.1 - LOGISTICS ACTIVITIES AND THEIR CORRESPONDING CHAPTERS

2.2 LOOKING AT LOGISTICS MANAGEMENT

Another term you are likely to hear in the world of logistics and supply chains is **logistics management**, which is the planning, implementing, and controlling of logistics activities and practices to meet four categories of end users' or customers' requirements: *time, place, quantity,* and *quality*. From a customer's perspective, this means: *when* they will receive the desired goods, *where* they will receive them, *how many* of each item they wish to receive, and of *what* quality goods must be to be considered acceptable. While logistics management focuses primarily on customers' needs, it also focuses on the company's needs by cooperating with other internal departments and functions, such as Marketing, Finance, Manufacturing, and Human Resources. Boiling it down to one sentence: *Logistics management* is the management of the flow and storage of goods and related information into, within, and out from an organization, spanning and coordinating the multiple departments and functions within that organization that engage in and support logistics activities.

Figure 2.1 highlights some of the key logistics activities in a company's inbound and outbound supply chains. These activities are the ones that are planned, implemented, and controlled within our definition of logistics management. Figure 2.2 provides a model of logistics management in manufacturing and production. The model includes the logistics activities, the immediate focus of these activities, and the flow of goods, finances, and information.

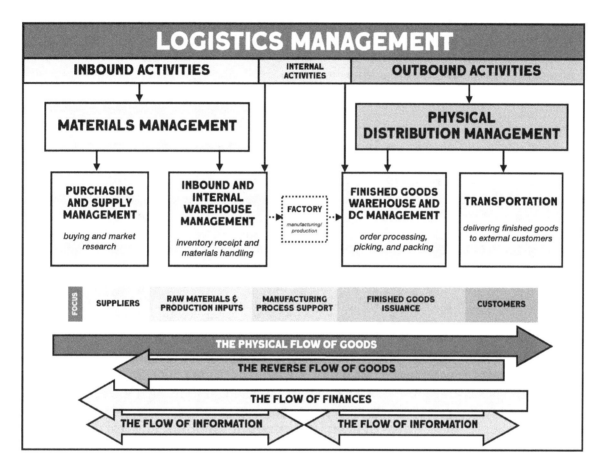

FIGURE 2.2 - A MODEL OF LOGISTICS MANAGEMENT IN MANUFACTURING/PRODUCTION

As previously mentioned, purchasing, inventory receipt, warehousing, and materials handling are logistics activities in a company's inbound supply chain as goods flow *into* that company. **Inbound logistics** includes all the logistics activities at the start of a company's internal supply chain, beginning when orders for goods are placed with the supplier and ending when goods arrive from the supplier. It encompasses both *financial* (purchasing) and *physical* (warehousing) activities. Inbound logistics activities occur throughout a product's more extended complex supply chain. Referring back to our example of a complex supply chain in Figure 1.5 in Chapter 1, all the supply chain members engaged in inbound logistics activities, even after the manufacturing/production stage. For example, in an orange juice supply chain, the suppliers, manufacturers, warehouses, and retailers all engage in inbound logistics activities, including purchasing, receiving, inspecting, and storing incoming goods needed for their portion of the complex supply chain.

Order processing, picking, packing, and transportation are logistics activities found in a company's outbound supply chain as goods flow *out from* that company. Outbound logistics includes all the logistics activities at the tail end of internal logistics management, beginning when an organization produces its finished product and ending when the immediate user receives it. As with inbound logistics, outbound logistics activities occur throughout a product's complex supply chain. Examples of outbound logistics actives within the complex Orange-U-Yummy supply chain include the Orange-U-Yummy supplier sending out oranges to the company, Orange-U-Yummy itself sending out its finished goods of containers of yummy juice, and the retail distribution centers sending out pallets of juice to your local grocery store.

In manufacturing and production, there are two subsets of logistics management related to each inbound and outbound logistics: *materials management*, related to inbound logistics activities, and *physical distribution management*, related to outbound logistics activities. In our Orange-U-Yummy example, the orange juice manufacturer gets the goods necessary to produce its yummy juices by placing orders from suppliers, receiving these ordered goods into the company, and managing storage until goods are needed. In the world of manufacturing and production, management of these inbound logistics activities is called **materials management**. The goal of materials management is to manage inbound logistics activities to ensure that the right raw materials and component parts of the right quantity, quality, and price get to the factory floor at the right time so that manufacturing can begin producing finished goods that customers need.

In our Orange-U-Yummy example, the company sends out its newly manufactured juices to customers by processing orders for juice from customers, picking juice from its refrigerated storage locations, packing juice cartons for shipment, and transporting these packed juices to external customers. In manufacturing and production, management of these outbound logistics activities is called **physical distribution management**. Physical distribution management aims to manage outbound logistics activities to ensure that external customers receive the right finished goods of the right quantity and quality and at the right time and place while minimizing related costs and maximizing customer service. Physical distribution managers can minimize costs by finding the most cost-effective method of shipping. They can maximize customer service by finding the fastest feasible shipping method.

In addition to inbound and outbound logistics activities in manufacturing and production, *internal* logistics activities must also be managed. As a company transforms raw goods or component parts into finished goods, internal logistics activities support the production process, such as storing and moving goods within the same company before and after the manufacturing process. For example, within Orange-U-Yummy, oranges are temporarily stored when they arrive into the company and then moved to the production floor to make new juice. The finished, packaged orange juice is also moved from the production floor to temporary storage or regional distribution centers before moving on to customers.

The model shown in Figure 2.2 focuses on logistics management in a manufacturing or production setting. Although the terms *materials management* and *physical distribution management* are from manufacturing and production, the model of logistics management and its concepts remain relevant in other settings. Companies such as office supply retailers, warehouse and big box stores, and amazon.com receive, handle, and distribute goods but typically do not manufacture them. These companies still need logistics management to plan, implement, and control their logistics activities and the corresponding flows of goods, finance, and information along their internal supply chain.

SUPPLY CHAIN MEMBER	ORANGE-U-YUMMY EXAMPLE	INBOUND LOGISTICS ACTIVITIES	OUTBOUND LOGISTICS ACTIVITIES
RAW MATERIALS SUPPLIER	ORANGE GROWERS IN FLORIDA ORANGE TREE GROVE	Receiving fertilizer and orange picking supplies from suppliers	Delivering oranges to manufacturing facility in right quantity at right time and place
MANUFACTURER	ORANGE-U-YUMMY JUICE PRODUCTION FACILITY	Receiving, inspecting, and storing oranges for juicing	Packaging juice and delivering right quantity of juice to distribution center at right time and place
DISTRIBUTION CENTER/ WAREHOUSE	3RD PARTY REGIONAL DISTRIBUTION CENTER	Receiving, inspecting, and storing finished/ packaged juice	Sorting and delivering right quantity of juice to right retail location at right time
RETAILER	YOUR FAVORITE LOCAL GROCER	Receiving, inspecting, and storing packaged juice for store shelf placement	Distributing juice to paying end user

FIGURE 2.3 - EXAMPLES OF INBOUND AND OUTBOUND LOGISTICS ACTIVITIES ACROSS MEMBERS OF THE COMPLEX SUPPLY CHAIN

Be aware, too, that not all companies, countries, and organizations use logistics management terminology to mean precisely the same thing. Over time, the term *physical distribution management* has begun to become less fashionable. In some settings, it is being replaced with an expanded definition of materials management to include *both* inbound and outbound logistics activities. Therefore, if someone offers you a job as a Materials Manager for $300,000, but you see that the job also includes physical distribution management tasks, don't argue with them over logistics management semantics. Take the job! The primary thing to remember is to understand the concepts and learn the terminology used at your new workplace.

2.4 INTRODUCING SUPPLY CHAIN MANAGEMENT

Now that we have defined supply chains, logistics, and logistics management, let's move on to supply chain management. In a definition from the Council of Supply Chain Management Professionals (CSCMP) edited down to its essence, **supply chain management** is the business discipline and function that: "encompasses the planning and management of ... all logistics management activities" including "coordination and collaboration ... within and across companies."

Management of logistics activities? That sounds like our definition of logistics management! However, logistics management focused on managing and coordinating logistics activities *within one company*. Supply chain management focuses on coordinating logistic activities and collaborating *across multiple companies*. The focus of supply chain management is communication, coordination, and collaboration between *external* supply chain members, such as suppliers, manufacturers/producers, wholesalers, retailers, and third-party logistics service providers.

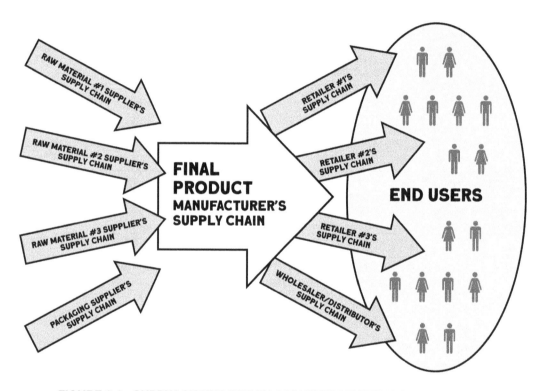

FIGURE 2.4 - SUPPLY CHAINS WITHIN A MANUFACTURER'S SUPPLY CHAIN

Using our Orange-U-Yummy example, the orange juice manufacturer has an internal supply chain. It also has orange, berry, pineapple, machinery, and juice carton suppliers, each with their own internal supply chains. They also have customers, such as grocery retailers, wholesale stores, and beverage distributors who have their own unique internal supply chains. The essence of supply chain management is communication across, coordination throughout, and collaboration among these multiple supply chains to create competitive advantage for the finished product (such as Orange-U-Yummy juice) as it moves toward the end user (juice drinkers like you and me). These supply chains are managed through information sharing and coordinated efforts to minimize costs and maximize customer service within their stage of the complex web of supply chains.

Although logistics is at the core of both logistics management and supply chain management, the primary differences between these disciplines are that:

- ***Logistics management*** is a subset of supply chain management. It is often a function or department within individual organizations.

- ***Supply chain management*** includes logistics management and key business functions, departments, and processes within and across companies.

- Additional business functions and processes involved in supply chain management include marketing, sales, product design, finance, manufacturing, human resource management, and information technology.

- ***Logistics management*** is *internal* and focuses on logistics activities within one company. ***Supply chain management*** is both *internal* and *external* and focuses on logistics activities within one company and across multiple upstream and downstream companies.

However, be aware that different companies, organizations, even individual customers sometimes use these terms interchangeably. One company's logistics might be another company's supply chain management. While we have outlined the most commonly used definitions for both terms in this chapter, make sure to understand how *your* workplace, suppliers, and customers define each *logistics* and *supply chain management*.

2.5 SUPPLY CHAIN MANAGEMENT TEAMS

Most large companies that deal with tangible goods have *Logistics Department* or a similar functional area with "logistics" or "supply chain" in its name. This department helps the company manage increasingly complex supply chains and is responsible for the efficiency and effectiveness of a company's internal supply chain.

However, for an internal supply chain to run smoothly and efficiently, many departments within a company must communicate and cooperate fluidly. A company's supply chain success depends upon the cohesion of its ***supply chain management team***, a group of representatives from the company's core departments that work together to increase the efficiency and effectiveness of a company's internal and external supply chain activities and relationships. The supply chain management team is typically made up of the heads of a company's core departments, such as marketing, finance, manufacturing, human resource management, and logistics, as shown in Figure 2.5. These departments must regularly and openly share information regarding the inbound, internal, and outbound flow of goods. As we will discuss in later chapters, various information technology systems make this information sharing easy and immediate.

The core of the supply chain management team is the **Logistics Department**, responsible for the physical flow of goods and associated information into, within, and out from the company. The Logistics Department bears the ultimate physical responsibility for the success of both internal and external supply chains. The head of this vital department works closely with and depends heavily on the other members of the supply chain management team.

FIGURE 2.5 - THE SUPPLY CHAIN MANAGEMENT TEAM

The **Manufacturing Department** is responsible for transforming raw or unfinished goods received by the Logistics Department into finished or semi-finished products. The head of this department depends on the other members of the supply chain management team. The team ensures that the Manufacturing Department has the necessary materials, employees, information, and finances to begin the production process and take away newly-produced goods to make room for more new finished products.

The **Human Resources Department** is responsible for managing the company's workforce and meeting its needs. This department provides motivated and skilled employees when and where they are needed at all points within the supply chain. A shortage of skilled and motivated employees at any point within the supply chain can lead to costly delays and customer dissatisfaction.

The **Marketing Department** is responsible for the price, promotion, place, and product design of a company's products. The department's ultimate goal is to meet and exceed its customers' expectations. As a member of the supply chain management team, the head of this department must work with team members to set a realistic price for products, factoring in the often substantial supply chain costs. The supply chain management team also works together to ensure that the Marketing Department's goals are met by having products in the right place at the right time in the right quantity of the right quality at a competitive price.

Finally, the **Finance Department** is responsible for financial control within a company, including resource allocation across departments, locations, and activities. Many supply chain decisions rely heavily on information from the Finance Department, especially regarding the amount of company resources available for supply chain activities.

FIGURE 2.6 - BOEING 787 DREAMLINER CLIMATE TESTING AT EGLIN AIR FORCE BASE

Over the past twenty years, some of the most famous supply chain failures have resulted from poor communication between leaders of these five departments and perhaps a lack of a coordinated supply chain management team. One infamous supply chain failure was the Boeing 787 Dreamliner launch in 2009 and the subsequent grounding of all 787s in 2013 because of battery fires onboard. When Boeing began producing the twin-engine aircraft, its *Marketing Department* touted that it would complete them in record time. The *Finance Department* pressed for cost-cutting measures that would increase shareholder value. To achieve these goals, the company decided to outsource up to twice as many *manufacturing* processes as it had done for previous aircraft, even though Boeing had pledged to build the Dreamliner in Seattle. *Human resources* and labor relations problems resulted. Boeing and its manufacturing suppliers also ran into various supply chain problems, unable to acquire the quantity of materials needed at the time needed, leading to costly delays and inferior quality parts. Communication and coordination of a supply chain management team could have prevented these problems, but Boeing introduced its new online communications platform, Exostar, which led to a lack of on-site and face-to-face meetings.

2.6 THE TRADEOFF PRINCIPLE AND CREATING VALUE IN SUPPLY CHAINS

The **core objectives of logistics management** within commercial companies today are to:

- Significantly *reduce* supply chain operating *costs*; and

- *Increase customer service* to the company's customers, including the immediate external customers, the internal customers, and the product's end users.

Often, these two objectives of logistics management are at odds. To increase its customer service levels, a company invariably must raise costs. Conversely, to reduce costs, customer service levels may have to be minimized. Let's consider our Orange-U-Yummy example once again. (This will be the last time. We promise!) Let's imagine that the company wants to increase customer service levels to grocery store retail chains by cutting delivery time from the factory in half. The company also wants to improve customer service to end users by adding a plastic pour spout to the juice for precision pouring. Both of these customer service improvements will cost money. Now let's imagine that, a month later, the Orange-U-Yummy CEO has promised to reduce costs for this fiscal year by 3%. Not only are the new plastic pour spouts scrapped, but the customer service center hours are cut from 24-hours a day to a schedule of 9 am to 5 pm US Eastern Standard Time.

When making logistics decisions and balancing the competing objectives of *reducing costs* versus *increasing customer service*, logistics managers use the ***tradeoff principle***. The advantages and disadvantages of decisions are considered and weighed based on the degree to which they provide: maximization of cost savings, resource use, and customer service level increases.

To minimize cost and maximize customer service, companies analyze and modify their supply chains. As a result, logistics management and supply chain management create substantial value for all involved, including the company's customers, suppliers, and stakeholders. The real value of a product is the customers' perception of it, or more bluntly stated, what they are willing to pay for it. Every stage of the supply chain can add value to a company's product. When realizing a product's value, the company checks to see if any parts of the supply chain could add more value. As we covered in Chapter 1, the supply chain is often called the ***value chain*** in this context when it is outlined and examined in terms of value added throughout each of the chain's stages.

This value created is often called ***utility***, an economics term referring to customers' satisfaction or happiness when consuming a company's goods or services. There are four primary types of utility: *form*, *time*, *place*, and *possession*.

Form utility is the value added to products as their form changes, such as raw materials transforming into finished goods through manufacturing. The Manufacturing Department creates form utility within a company.

Place utility is the value added to products when they are at the right place within the supply chain, from the receipt of raw materials from suppliers to the distribution of finished goods to external customers, when they are at the place *where* customers want them. Place utility is created by the Logistics Department, which helps get products exactly to internal and external customers' desired locations. It also helps companies use preferred suppliers farther away with cheaper or higher quality products.

Time utility is the value added to products when they are available at the time both internal and external customers desire them. Time utility is created by the Logistics Department, which helps get products to customers exactly *when* they want them.

Possession utility is the value added to products when a company creates a desire to possess them in consumers' minds. Possession utility is created by the Marketing Department, which promotes products both directly and indirectly to the organization's customers.

Of these four types of utility, *time* and *place* are the ones added by logistics and supply chain management. Logistics activities add *time* value when it gets products to customers exactly *when* they want them. Amazon.com adds time value in shopping transactions according to individual customers' needs. The e-commerce company allows its Amazon Prime customers to select preferred delivery times, sometimes within one or two hours in some regions. The company also allows customers to choose later, no-rush delivery timeframes for an added value, such as credits to purchase online digital content. During the COVID-19 pandemic in 2020, the company also allowed customers to delay some deliveries. With item delivery delays, more items could be delivered simultaneously, providing the added value of fewer delivery trips to customers' homes when many people were in locations with stay-at-home orders and worried about exposure to the virus from multiple contacts with people.

Logistics activities add *place* value when products arrive precisely *where* customers want them or when procured products arrive from distant or dispersed desired suppliers. Starbucks strives hard to offer place value by ensuring that the same coffee products and cups are found in all of its store locations worldwide. Your Grande Iced Caramel Macchiato will look and taste the same in New York, New Zealand, Ireland, and China!

In some economic utility models, there are two additional types of utility added: *information* and *service*. **Information utility** is the value added to products by having open communication with customers and providing them with the information they need to make informed buying decisions. Information utility may be provided by multiple departments in a company when they offer information customers may regularly need, whether they provide this information directly to customers or to the Sales Department, who liaises with customers as they make their purchase decisions. The Logistics Department can create information utility when providing information to customers and maintaining ongoing transparency about product delivery timeframes. Sometimes the existence or lack of clear information about product delivery dates can make or break a sale!

Service utility is the value added to products by providing high levels of responsive customer service before, during, and after a sale. The Logistics Department can add to the product's service utility by ensuring that customers' delivery needs are met. The right products arrive at the right time at the right place in the right quantity of the right quality. Also, when customers need to return products, the Logistics Department can add service utility. It ensures the return and the reverse logistics process is a seamless one for the customer, like when you receive an order from a company that includes a postage prepaid return shipping label inside the box with your order.

CHAPTER 2 REVIEW QUESTIONS

1. List the logistics activities in an *inbound* supply chain. Select a company that manufactures something you use every day and describe the logistics activities that might occur in that company's inbound supply chain.

2. List the logistics activities in an *outbound* supply chain. Using the same company you used for question number one, describe the logistics activities that might occur in that company's outbound supply chain.

3. What is the difference between *materials management* and *physical distribution management*?

4. Describe the relationship between *logistics management* and *supply chain management*.

5. For a beverage producer like Orange-U-Yummy, what are a few of the many supply chains that must be coordinated in the company's supply chain management?

6. What role does the *Logistics Department* play in a supply chain management team?

7. What role does the *Marketing Department* play in a supply chain management team?

8. Why might the initial failure of the Boeing Dreamliner be described as a supply chain management team failure?

9. What is the *tradeoff principle*, and how is it related to logistics management's two core objectives?

10. Provide two new examples of how a company can provide *time* and *place utility* in its supply chain.

CHAPTER 2 CASE STUDY

A TALE OF TWO (MILITARY) SUPPLY CHAINS

Let's step into our time-traveling shoes to go way back to the origins of supply chains.

For the past few hundred thousand years, our ancestors roamed the land hunting and gathering. Goods were not sold or produced as they are today. They began farming a short 10-20,000 years ago, which led to people staying in agricultural communities and starting to trade and sell what they grew. As a result, the first supply chains formed.

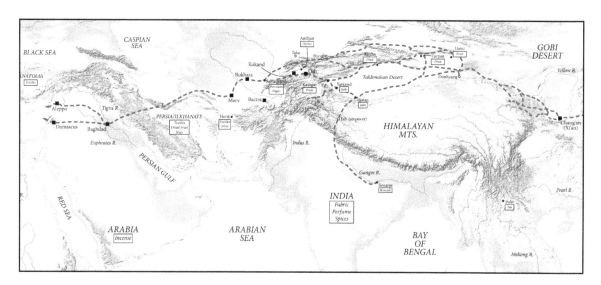

As civilizations grew, they began trading with one another, forming global supply chains. More than 4000 years ago, ancient Phoenicians took to ships and set up supply chains across the Mediterranean and Aegean Seas, trading goods such as wood, linen, metal, glass, dried fish, salt, and wine. A bit further east, civilizations in Kazakhstan and China began establishing land-based supply chains to trade horses, jade, and art. Over the millennia to follow, this grew to become the Silk Road (pictured above), a trade route connecting Asia, Europe, and Africa.

As civilizations continued to grow, they expanded into new lands using military might. Soldiers needed to eat, wear clothing, and be armed, resulting in large camps of support personnel, pack animals, and carts followed each advancing army. This cumbersome support system slowed troops down, and they could only move as fast as their slowest donkey pulling a heavy cart. During his Macedonian reign from 336-323 BC, Alexander the Great used a different means of supporting his 35,000 troops. The Macedonian ruler wanted troops to advance quickly into unsuspecting territories, giving opponents little time to establish defense strategies. As they moved into Asia and northeast Africa, Macedonian soldiers carried their own supplies. They were not supported by large contingents of personnel, pack animals, and carts. Instead, Alexander the Great coordinated multiple supply chains with multiple suppliers to ensure his military had all of the food, water, clothing, and arms it needed. He established supply chains with resupply warehouses and depots along campaign routes *before* the campaigns began. Alexander managed relationships with locals in new and conquered lands to ensure that supply depots were stocked. He also planned his movements with harvest cycles for optimum food supply levels and selected locations along rivers for easier transportation of heavy goods. Thanks to their effective establishment of complex and efficient supply chains, Alexander the Great made the ancient Greek kingdom of Macedon one of the largest empires in early history.

Armies throughout history have been successful thanks to effective supply chains, including the ancient Roman Empire and its extension across Europe, North Africa, and West Asia and the Mongol Empire and its extension across Asia and Eastern Europe. Armies have also failed because of logistics and supply chain management failures. French military leader and emperor Napoleon Bonaparte achieved great military successes for France when he created *military train regiments*, whose sole responsibility was to provide and transport military artillery and equipment. However, Napoleon encountered one of the world's biggest military disasters because of a lack of supply chain management.

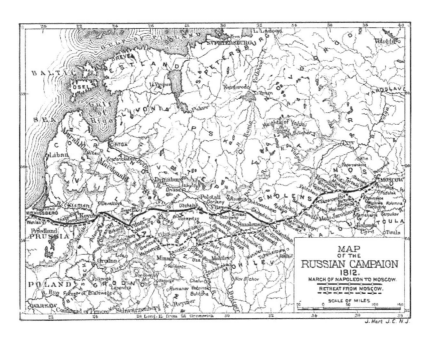

As Napoleon's soldiers advanced successfully across Europe, they lived off the land for their meals, with support regiments carrying an eight-day supply of provisions to be used only in case of emergency. When his troops advanced into Russia in June 1812, they followed the same practice of living off the land. As the French army advanced, the Russian army retreated and burned their own land, crops, and villages so that French troops could not eat or resupply. As the French army continued to advance, the Russian army continued to retreat and burn, even setting Moscow ablaze. The French troops grew hungrier and colder as the Russian winter set in. Waiting for a Russian surrender or peace offer that never came, Napoleon finally ordered his troops to retreat with the last leaving after six fruitless months. Napoleon assumed that goods would be available and did not coordinate and manage supply chains to feed his troops as Alexander the Great did over 2000 years earlier.

Chapter 3

Inbound Logistics: Purchasing

Purchasing touches almost every aspect of our daily work and home lives. Take a look around you right now. Make a mental list of all the items surrounding you: a desk, chairs, coffee mug, computer, pens, phone, shirt, clock, carpeting, and the list could go on and on. Did the items on your mental list magically appear one day? Did they grow up from the ground around your feet? Unless you happen to be a true Emersonian transcendentalist sitting in the middle of the woods with no clothes on, almost all the items on your list were once probably part of a supply chain and were purchased by someone. Even the walls around you were once sheetrock, plaster, and paint purchased by a builder.

Of all the activities within the world of logistics management, *purchasing* is one in which we may already be experts. Unless we happen to be lucky enough to have more money than sense, most of us are highly proficient purchasers. We take purchasing seriously because wise purchases leave us with more expendable cash for even more purchases. As you read this chapter, think about the last purchase *you* made and how similar or different your purchasing process was.

3.1 PURCHASING AND SUPPLY MANAGEMENT

When we think of purchasing, we think of buying something, typically at a store, online, or directly from another person. In the business world, **purchasing** is an activity under the larger umbrella of logistics management. It meets the materials and service needs of an organization by acquiring goods and services in the right quantity of the right quality, delivered to the right place at the right time while maximizing service to internal customers and minimizing the total cost to the organization. It is an inbound logistics activity and one of the two primary areas of materials management.

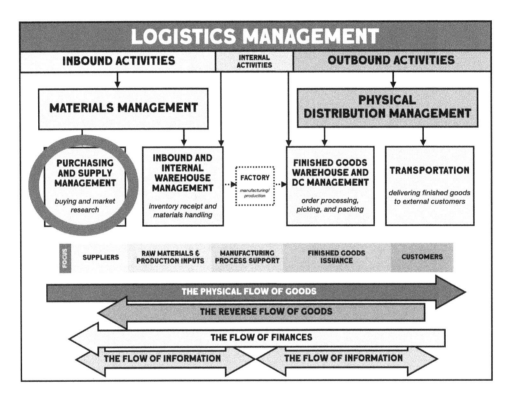

FIGURE 3.1 - PURCHASING & SUPPLY MANAGEMENT IN THE LOGISTICS MANAGEMENT MODEL

When referring to a department or function, many organizations use the term purchasing, while others use the terms **procurement** or **acquisition** to refer to the same thing. Some organizations even use all three words interchangeably! Generally, all three terms relate to the buying of goods and services for an organization.

The short-term goal of purchasing is the immediate acquisition of goods or services. The long-term goal of purchasing is a strategic one: working closely with suppliers of needed goods and services to ensure their long-term availability. For example, why place an order for 5000 gallons of screamin' streamin' yellow paint for your new line of sports cars if the paint manufacturer will be ceasing production of screamin' streamin' yellow in six months due to the rising cost of one of its ingredients? A longer-term strategic approach to purchasing and supplier relations is needed to ensure a continued supply at a known or relatively predictable price. This is where supply management comes in from our model of logistics management in Figure 3.1.

According to the Institute for Supply Management (ISM), **supply management** is "the identification, acquisition, access, positioning, management of resources and related capabilities the organization needs or potentially needs in the attainment of its strategic objectives." In short, it is the management of a company's inbound goods and services requirements to meet long term goals and objectives. Made even shorter, it's purchasing with a purpose! Do not confuse this term with supply chain management because they are two related but very different things. Supply management, which focuses on acquiring goods for the inbound supply chain of a company, is a subset of the larger realm of supply chain management, which focuses on all activities of the entire complex supply chain, both inbound and outbound across multiple companies. Some companies also refer to supply management as **supplier relationship management** or **strategic sourcing**.

As shrewd consumers in today's highly competitive marketplace, we want to make wise purchasing decisions. We try to buy high-quality products at lower prices to leave us with more money to spend on other things we need. Therefore, as individual consumers, we often view our suppliers and their salespeople through world-weary eyes. We think of them as competitors and adversaries, trying to get our business and increase their profits. With today's **supply management approach**, we don't view suppliers as competitors or adversaries. Instead, we view them as counterparts in a product's supply chain. Companies work with their suppliers to develop long-term relationships to ensure long-term supply availability and streamline the acquisition process to make faster and more effective inbound supply chains.

Using the supply management approach, a company's Purchasing Department works with its suppliers and its peers in the Production, Engineering, Finance, Marketing, and Quality Assurance Departments in a cross-functional team. This supply management team engages in many strategic, long-term activities related to purchasing or acquiring goods, including:

- *internal analysis,* in which companies look inward to examine their spending or purchasing processes to make them more efficient;

- *market research for future supply availability,* in which companies look not only at customer demand forecasts but also at long-term supply availability and cost increases to make long-term product design and production decisions;

- *strategic sourcing,* in which a company works to identify, develop, and manage key suppliers to build supply chain relationships that outperform those of its competitors;

- *contract negotiations,* in which an organization works with suppliers to agree on long-term supply contracts; and

- *supplier evaluation,* in which companies evaluate current suppliers regularly to ensure that they deliver the right quality and quantity of goods at the right time and place with invoices reflecting the right price and other negotiated conditions.

3.2 THE FIVE Ws OF PURCHASING: WHO AND WHAT

As we plunge ahead into the wild and exciting world of purchasing, let's begin by asking and answering the five Ws of purchasing: *who, what, where, when,* and *why.*

First, **who does the purchasing?** Most companies have a person in a position responsible for directly acquiring or approving purchases from suppliers. Different companies might have other names for this position, such as Purchasing Manager, Purchasing Officer, Materials Manager, Procurement Director, or Strategic Sourcing Director.

In small companies, the Purchasing Manager may be the sole Buyer or Purchasing Agent who alone conducts all purchasing-related activities for the company. In larger companies, however, this Purchasing Manager typically oversees a team of Buyers or Purchasing Agents who investigate suppliers, negotiate contracts, complete hands-on purchasing activities, and plan for product deliveries with the company's Warehouse Manager or warehouse team. Members of these purchasing teams can have a range of job titles, typically with words such as *purchasing, procurement, acquisition,* or *buyer* in the title. For example, before she married Prince William and became the Duchess of Cambridge, Kate Middleton's job title was *Accessories Buyer* for a luxury clothing line. Unlike "supply chain" or "logistics," purchasing has been in job titles since the Industrial Revolution when goods began to be made and sold en masse and transported quickly and in large quantities because of the expansion of railroads. Figure 3.2 shows a list of company officers from a railroad company in 1885, including a *Purchasing Agent.*

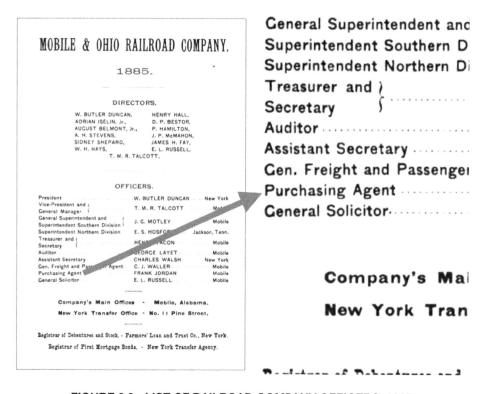

FIGURE 3.2 - LIST OF RAILROAD COMPANY OFFICERS, 1885

Second, **what is purchased?** A company purchases both *goods* and *services* needed to function that it does not already have or produce in-house. Remember that **goods** are tangible items that are owned and can be moved. These may include raw materials, semifinished goods, and finished goods used to produce a company's final product. **Raw materials**, sometimes called **commodities**, are unprocessed or minimally processed goods used to make other goods. Examples of raw materials include logs, iron ore, grain, and oranges. **Semifinished goods**, also known as **intermediate goods**, are goods produced to be used in the manufacture or production of other goods. Examples of semifinished goods include lumber, sheet metal, flour, and orange juice concentrate. **Finished goods** have completed a company's manufacturing, production, or assembly process and are ready to be sold to customers. Examples of finished goods include engineered hardwood flooring, replacement car fenders, Twinkies snack cakes, and cartons of orange juice.

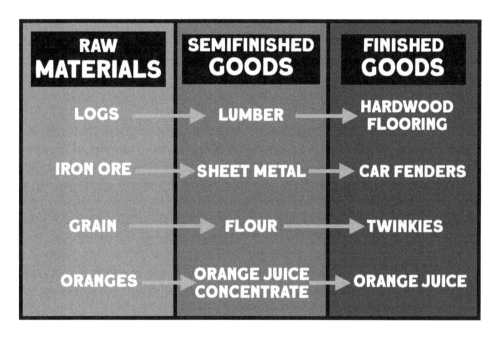

FIGURE 3.3 - RAW MATERIALS, SEMIFINISHED GOODS, AND FINISHED GOODS

Goods purchased also include *capital goods* and *MRO supplies*. **Capital goods** are durable (long-lasting), manufactured items used to produce other goods or services. Examples of capital goods include machinery, equipment, buildings, and vehicles. At Orange-U-Yummy, our orange juice manufacturer from previous chapters, the capital goods purchased might include juicing machines, pallet jacks, warehouse and office buildings, and a fleet of refrigerated delivery vans. **Maintenance, repair, and operating supplies**, or **MRO supplies**, are goods purchased that are essential to the operation of a company but that are not part of a finished product. For example, Orange-U-Yummy might purchase MRO supplies such as mops and cleaning liquids for the corporate offices, spare parts to repair factory machinery and delivery vehicles, and computer and safety equipment for day-to-day operations.

In addition to goods, companies also purchase services. Unlike tangible goods, **_services_** are intangible actions or activities that a company needs but cannot or does not do itself. For example, services purchased by Orange-U-Yummy could include a wide range of third-party services, from office janitorial service to rate negotiation assistance on cross-country refrigerated freight shipments.

3.3 THE FIVE Ws OF PURCHASING: WHERE

The third of the 5 Ws of purchasing is: **Where is purchasing done?** Much to the dismay of the neat-freaks within logistics management, purchasing does not occur within a neat, orderly, predictable environment. Instead, it is conducted within the growing, messy, chaotic world of the global market with multiple languages and currencies, coupled with the complications and security risks of online systems. Complications also occur at the company level. Large companies with operations spread across one or more countries must decide where their purchasing activities will take place: Will one office at corporate headquarters handle all purchasing? Or will a company's local offices handle purchasing activities for their regional operations themselves? Or will a combination of purchasing from both locations be required?

When purchasing decisions and activities are controlled from one central location or department within an organization, it is called **_centralized purchasing_**. When purchasing is centralized, a Purchasing Department takes all of the orders for a particular supplier across its company's operations and lumps them together into one order. Larger quantities of goods are purchased from a single supplier at one time, often leading to lower prices, volume discounts, and better payment terms for the purchaser. Think about the discount you get when you buy a package of four rolls of paper towels versus a package of 24 rolls. Centralized purchasing can also make a company's purchasing activities more efficient and lower its operational costs. Again, think of how much gas, time, and effort you are saving by making only one trip to the store in six months to buy 24 rolls of paper towels versus making six trips to the store over six months to buy four rolls of paper towels each time.

In 2009, Walmart's purchasing activities had been spread out across its locations in 15 countries worldwide. The company also purchased most of its goods through intermediaries and third parties. In 2010, the retail giant made a big move to centralize its purchasing activities to its Bentonville, Arkansas headquarters. This centralization allowed the company to have more efficient operations and spend less on purchasing activities and labor. The company also set a goal to acquire 80% of its goods directly from the manufacturers without intermediaries. Because Walmart's newly centralized sales orders were much larger than anything its suppliers had seen before, the company could attain lower prices and more favorable sales terms, such as on-time deliveries in shorter timeframes. The company's quarterly net income jumped from $3.4 billion in October 2010 to $6.1 billion in January 2011.

While reduced cost is a significant advantage of centralized purchasing, companies have to weigh this against the potential disadvantages of centralized purchasing. Decisions are made at the corporate level, removing power at the local level, and leaving the company less flexible to handle local emergencies when they arise. It also tends to eliminate local suppliers in favor of large, national, or global suppliers that can fill large orders. When implementing its centralized purchasing strategy, Walmart streamlined its products and eliminated many local vendors and products. Customers across many markets became unhappy because some of their favorite locally sourced items had been eliminated and would no longer be sold. Unhappy customers equaled a significant dip in Walmarts' sales numbers in mid-2011, which caused the company to reintroduce 8500 items back into their sales inventory.

When purchasing decisions and activities are controlled from different locations or divisional levels within an organization, it is called ***decentralized purchasing***. When purchasing is decentralized, multiple offices, locations, or facilities within a company handle their own purchasing functions and place orders for goods with suppliers themselves without routing orders through a central company department. When purchasing is decentralized, divisional and local managers have greater control over those elements of the purchasing process that directly impact their departments. They can plan for product deliveries that best suit their own time and place requirements instead of those of the organization as a whole — and they feel a greater sense of ownership of the process. Imagine if your extended family engaged in centralized purchasing, and your grandmother was the central purchasing officer. She would decide when, how much, and which brand of paper towels to purchase. Now imagine the sense of ownership, flexibility, and freedom you would feel if your family decentralized its purchasing, and you could decide when, how many, and which brand of paper towels to purchase. You could now purchase your favorite brand of select-a-size paper towels in small quantities to meet your family's needs instead of purchasing hundreds of rolls of super absorbency towels with a good looking lumberjack on its packaging to meet your grandmother's needs. You could also quickly purchase extra quantities of paper towels during emergencies, like when friends with toddler triplets visit and extend their stay for three weeks!

Sprouts Farmers Market, Inc., a growing natural and organic foods supermarket chain in the US, relies on a decentralized purchasing structure as part of its corporate identity. According to the company's *2018 Annual Report*, regional procurement teams purchase goods, which allows for greater flexibility in finding produce on local, regional, and national levels. The company reports that using this decentralized regional approach still allows for some cost savings because it orders produce in bulk, with the orders from multiple regional stores pooled together. The company also has the flexibility to honor its commitment to customers to source locally, defining "local" as goods from the same state or within a 500-mile radius of the store. Local sourcing results in fresher produce because it didn't have to travel far to get to the store. Local sourcing also results in locally made goods suited to regional preferences, such as Philadelphia-based Vesper Brothers Foods' pizza sauce in its Pennsylvania stores or the Arizona Spice Company's Black Scorpio Salsa in its Arizona stores.

Although the Sprouts approach to decentralized purchasing at the regional level instead of the store level provides some cost savings, it may present challenges in competing with the lower costs of larger grocery chains' centralized purchasing. In 2020, two natural grocery store chains similar to Sprouts, Lucky's Market and Earth Fare, filed for bankruptcy. Its biggest competitor, Whole Foods Market, shifted to an almost entirely centralized purchasing model and was acquired by Amazon in 2017, a deal that caused its biggest competitors to shake in their boots with temporary stock price plummets for Walmart, Target, and Costco.

Rather than rely on entirely centralized or entirely decentralized purchasing, some companies use a ***hybrid purchasing*** approach, combining both centralized and decentralized techniques. For example, Costco uses a centralized approach for low cost, bulk purchases of non-food items, with sourcing conducted through its Issaquah, Washington headquarters. Conversely, Costco uses a decentralized approach for greater regional flexibility in purchasing food items, with sourcing conducted regionally at the company's eight US regional divisions and ten international regional divisions.

Yum! Brands, Inc., the Fortune 500 company that operates the KFC, Pizza Hut, and Taco Bell with 50,000+ fast-food restaurants around the world, also uses hybrid purchasing. Unlike Costco's food versus non-food delineation, Yum! Brands bases its purchasing location decision on actual restaurant locations. According to its *2019 Annual Report*, Yum! Brands uses centralized purchasing for its US-based operations and franchisees to decrease costs and meet sustainability goals. However, for its international operations across 146 countries outside the US, the company uses decentralized purchasing with international franchisees selecting their suppliers, making it easier to comply with local laws and regulations.

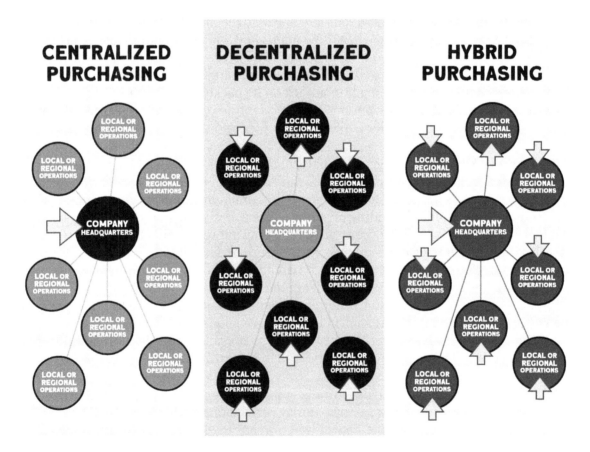

FIGURE 3.4 - WHERE PURCHASING TAKES PLACE

Finally, in addition to centralized, decentralized, and hybrid purchasing, another alternative is ***cooperative purchasing***, in which multiple companies or organizations join together to form a cooperative or consortium. The cooperative members combine their purchases to create larger orders from suppliers, allowing for greater leverage and reduced centralized purchasing cost. Offices in local, state, and national governments often form consortiums for cooperative purchasing, such as the Kansas City Regional Purchasing Cooperative for local government offices in Kansas City, Missouri, or the National Cooperative Purchasing Alliance for public agencies across the US.

3.4 THE FIVE Ws OF PURCHASING: WHEN

Fourth in our list of the 5 Ws of purchasing is: **When are purchasing activities conducted?** Purchasing is an ongoing activity and typically a continuous cycle of evaluating needs, evaluating potential suppliers, issuing purchase orders, evaluating supplier performance, and, again, evaluating new needs. When looking closely at how a company orders individual products from individual suppliers, purchase orders can be placed with varying amounts of time before the goods are needed.

FIGURE 3.5 - WHEN PURCHASING TAKES PLACE

Purchasing can occur as soon as the company notices it needs something. ***Spot buying***, also known as spot purchasing, occurs when a company buys goods or services to meet its immediate demands. Spot buying is commonly used when a company has an immediate need and no time to comparison shop and when a company does not have the space or desire to store these items in inventory for future use. For example, a furniture company is in the middle of a production run for bedroom sets in its most popular paint color, deep ebony. The paint supplier made a mistake in its shipment to the furniture manufacturer and sent 10,000 gallons of deep mahogany paint instead of deep ebony. The furniture manufacturer has all of its machines and workers ready to start a bedroom set assembly and painting run in five days and needs to find a paint as close to deep ebony as possible. The company is likely to engage in spot buying to acquire the required quantity of paint immediately from a supplier who offers a color close to the one they need. Spot buying can occur in emergencies, when companies are small or new and do not yet understand their future needs, and when special price or availability opportunities for items arise.

Companies often *forecast* their purchasing needs, which means they use previous purchasing data to predict in advance how much of an item they will need for a specific time period in the future, such as one week, three weeks, or two months. ***Buying to requirements*** is a type of purchasing for current and immediate future needs based on forecasting. For example, hospitals and hotels may use the buying to requirements approach for purchasing their linens. These facilities would have limited storage space and could not store more than a two-week inventory of sheets. They would look at historical purchasing and usage data from previous months and years to forecast how many sheets they will likely need for the next two weeks and place an order for that amount.

An automated form of buying to requirements is ***automatic inventory replacement***. A company automatically orders or re-orders goods using this purchasing technique when its quantity of an item reaches a predetermined amount. The goal of automatic inventory replacement is to maintain a set amount of an item without running out. For example, a manufacturer would have an automatic inventory replacement agreement with all of its critical parts' suppliers to ensure that it can continue its manufacturing operations without a Purchasing Manager having to take the time to determine a need and place an order with the supplier. You might also see examples of automatic inventory replacement at your local grocery store. For example, when the store's quantity of ice cream sandwiches reaches ten boxes, an order is automatically placed with the ice cream supplier for another 50 boxes.

Unlike the recurring purchases of automatic inventory replacement, a ***one-off purchase*** is a one-time purchase that will not be repeated in the foreseeable future. It is typically a purchase of a large, expensive item for a specific purpose, such as a hot tub purchase for your back deck or a government's acquisition of a replacement for the President's airplane. For a manufacturer, a one-off purchase might include machinery to produce and move goods. For a retailer, it might consist of trucks or cash register scanning systems, and for a hospital, it might be MRI or laser surgery equipment. These purchases could be for near-future to distant-future use depending on the amount of time the company wants to take to identify product needs, evaluate potential suppliers, and negotiate the purchasing terms.

Finally, ***forward buying*** is the practice of purchasing goods in advance of a company's requirements. It helps a company avoid supply shortages and ensures a constant supply of goods for manufacturing and other operations. When storage space is available, forward buying is also used to acquire goods at a lower fixed price when prices are likely to rise. During the COVID-19 pandemic in 2020, grocery stores and pharmacies used forward buying to ensure they could maintain inventories of cleaning supplies, soap, and toilet paper after an initial period of panic-buying depleted their stock.

3.5 THE FIVE Ws OF PURCHASING: WHY

The fifth and final question in our list of the 5 Ws of purchasing is: **Why is purchasing important?** For a company to function, it needs goods and services. In our competitive global environment, it is neither cost-effective nor efficient for a company to produce all the goods and services it needs itself. Imagine if an automobile company manufactured every single part found in each of its cars, from the rubber in the tires to the entire satellite radio system! Even the smallest cottage industries rely on purchasing some amount of raw materials and packaging. Along with being a necessary corporate function for companies of all sizes, effective purchasing can save these companies money and impact the corporate bottom line.

Let's look at an example of a honey producer called Honey-Bee-Good. This small, local company has to purchase goods and services to operate, from beekeeping equipment to glass jars and printed labels for finished honey, to advertising agency services for local radio and television ads with catchy jingles. As a new small business, Honey-Bee-Good did not initially have department managers. The company owner and various family members stepped in to do whatever company functions were necessary when necessary. The company had no Purchasing Department or Purchasing Manager. It purchased jars and labels from a packaging provider in small quantities as needed. As the company grew, it placed larger orders for jars and labels but continued to pay the original prices. After five years of steady growth, the Honey-Bee-Good owner and CEO decided that it was time to hire a Purchasing Manager because she was spending at least 60% of her time in purchasing-related activities.

On his first day of work, the new Purchasing Manager looked at Honey-Bee-Good's purchasing records and gasped in horror. He immediately sought bulk purchase bids from three different jar and label producers, including their current provider. The Purchasing Manager then negotiated a two-year contract with the company providing the best offer for Honey-Bee-Good, which, interestingly, happened to be the same company they had been using! However, under the new contract, the supplier gave Honey-Bee-Good a 15% discount on all orders over $500. So what effect would this have on Honey-Bee-Good's bottom line in the first year of this new purchasing contract?

As Figure 3.6 shows, the new 15% discount resulted in an increased profit of $0.30 per jar of honey sold for its annual sale of 100,000 jars. From simply renegotiating a high volume contract, Honey-Bee-Good is now $30,000 richer each year! This simple act of good purchasing, which took the Purchasing Manager only two days to complete, resulted in a 30% increase in the company's profits! Honey-Bee-Good's Purchasing Manager didn't stop here, however. He continued to look for other ways to increase company profits by improving the efficiency and cost of all corporate purchasing, from negotiating better purchasing contracts with beekeeping equipment providers to finding discount office supply wholesalers offering free delivery.

As we saw from our Honey-Bee-Good example, companies that use effective purchasing practices can reap the reward of *increased profits*. Another possible bonus of effective purchasing is *competitive advantage*. Purchasing practices such as *forward buying* and *reciprocity* can provide a competitive advantage to motivated companies like Honey-Bee-Good. A competing honey company lost a month of sales because its jar supplier's factory was ravaged by tornadoes and could not produce honey jars for one full month. To avoid a similar financial fiasco in the future, Honey-Bee-Good used *forward buying* to purchase a two-month supply of jars before the company needed them. For competitive advantage, Honey-Bee-Good also used **reciprocity**, a mutually beneficial practice between two companies in which they agree to buy each other's products or services. Honey-Bee-Good formed a reciprocal buying arrangement with its jar supplier, Jersey Jars. It purchased jars only from Jersey Jars, and its products were the sole "honey of choice" in the lunchrooms of all Jersey Jars manufacturing facilities worldwide.

	BEFORE DISCOUNT	AFTER 15% DISCOUNT
PRODUCTION LABOR COST PER JAR OF HONEY	$1.50	$1.50
PACKAGING COST PER JAR	$2.00	$1.70
CORPORATE OVERHEAD ALLOCATION PER JAR	$0.50	$0.50
TOTAL COST OF JAR PRODUCED	$4.00	$3.70
SELLING PRICE PER JAR	$5.00	$5.00
PROFIT PER JAR	$1.00	$1.30
PROFIT PER 100,000 JARS (ANNUAL PRODUCTION)	$100,000.00	$130,000.00

FIGURE 3.6 - IMPACT OF 15% DISCOUNT ON HONEY-BEE-GOOD PROFIT

Effective purchasing practices bring increased profits and competitive advantage. Companies can also have increased means to:

- provide better customer service; invest in marketing to attract new customers;

- construct new production and distribution facilities to expand the product's geographic reach;

- reinvest in product research and development to improve products and develop new product lines;

- attract and retain top-quality employees; and

- provide greater returns to shareholders.

3.6 THE FIVE Ws OF PURCHASING BONUS TRACK: HOW

Now that we explored the *who, what, where, when,* and *why* of questions in purchasing, let's add just one more: ***How are purchasing activities conducted?***

Think about how our purchasing activities have changed over the last twenty to thirty years. We used to purchase goods primarily by visiting stores or perusing catalogs and ordering items over the phone. While we still visit stores, we order many of our goods online. COVID-19 and social distancing tipped the balance. We began to purchase more of our personal goods online than through any other means because the business world has been using online and information technology-based purchasing for years.

Over the past two decades, purchasing in the business world has become increasingly fast, accurate, and precise thanks to rapid advances in information technology. The real-time transmission and receipt of information within purchasing and logistics management have resulted in extremely efficient organizations with streamlined supply chains. As web-based and cloud-based applications become faster and more powerful, it is far easier for an organization's Purchasing Manager to control and improve the purchasing process. Chapter 7 will explore information systems in the supply chain in greater detail, but let's briefly look at the role information technology and systems play in *how* purchasing happens.

Even before a purchase occurs, Purchasing Managers can immediately investigate potential suppliers online. Suppliers' websites, corporate analysis and information sites, trade-related sites with customer reviews, and the Better Business Bureau are invaluable sources of information that can be accessed immediately online. Purchasing Managers can also send immediate requests for information, proposals, and quotes to multiple potential suppliers via e-mail, corporate websites, and various third-party e-commerce platforms. Electronic bids are submitted, stored, and possibly evaluated all through a company's online information systems. Many of these activities are ***cloud-based***, a term used to describe applications or systems housed on providers' servers accessed via the internet by users' computers or mobile devices on an on-demand basis.

Not all information systems used in the purchasing process are web- or are cloud-based. Some of a company's purchasing activities are kept securely in-house, which means they are conducted entirely within an organization's facilities. In-house information systems can:

- determine and transmit information between a company's departments about goods needed to be purchased,

- create purchase orders and send copies to other departments,

- receive and check goods as they are received and transmit information about their quantity and condition to the Purchasing Department, and

- close out and file completed orders.

Purchasing information and systems within a company can be located on an ***intranet***, a private computer network for sharing systems, tools, information, and computing activities across multiple departments and locations of one organization, even when they may be thousands of miles apart.

When a company wishes to form a similar private information-sharing relationship with its suppliers or customers, it may develop an *extranet* or use *Electronic Data Interchange (EDI)*. An ***extranet*** is a web-based system of information sharing similar to the internet, but it is open only to the companies involved. An extranet can be used to transmit and receive a wide range of messages, documents, and other information. ***EDI*** is also used to share data between companies, but its focus is an immediate transmission of business information from computer to computer in a standard format. EDI transmissions contain only business data, with no accompanying files or messages.

Examples of cloud-based and EDI systems commonly used in purchasing are *MRP, VMI,* and *e-commerce*. ***MRP*** is a materials requirement planning software application used to analyze production and manufacturing data. It helps determine how much of a good or service a company needs to purchase and the timeframe necessary to complete production runs. MRP systems automatically generate purchase orders, which are sent immediately from buyers to suppliers through EDI and cloud-based systems. ***VMI*** is vendor managed inventory, which occurs when a buyer allows a supplier (or vendor) to monitor product demand to forecast demand patterns and set product shipment levels and schedules. Information between buyers and suppliers in a VMI system may be transmitted using either EDI or the internet.

e-Commerce, or *electronic commerce*, is the act of buying and selling goods on the internet and the associated flow of money and data. eCommerce can be either ***B2B*** (business to business) or ***B2C*** (business to consumer). Specific to the world of B2B and ***B2G*** (business to government) purchasing, ***e-procurement*** is an automated system of purchasing and payment between purchasers and suppliers. In e-procurement, all information surrounding the purchase and receipt of goods are captured and recorded electronically, and payment is automatically issued from the buyer.

Even when a company uses cloud-based, web-based, and intranet systems to share purchasing-related information and documents immediately, the humans involved sometimes need to speak face-to-face. To save the time and money it takes for participants to travel to meetings, companies rely on technology for face-to-face meetings. A ***virtual meeting***, also known as a ***video conference***, is a meeting of people in different locations. To meet, they use video, audio, or text communication through cloud-based video teleconference software such as Zoom, Skype, Google Hangouts, or Adobe Connect. These types of cloud-based software can record meetings for archival purposes or for others to view later. They also allow for document and screen sharing during virtual meetings, and individual participants can communicate privately in real time.

Now that we have explored the role of information technology and systems in *how* purchasing activities are conducted, let's dive into another aspect of how purchasing happens in the business world. Purchasing is not as simple as selecting a supplier and placing an order and making sure you have the right information systems. Companies strive for continuous improvement in their purchasing practices. No matter how great a new contract with a supplier may appear, it is of little use if the desired products are delivered at the wrong time or in incorrect quantities. Purchasing Managers monitor and manage the entire process of purchasing a good or service. The ***purchasing process*** begins when a company expresses a need for a product and ends when an order is closed after it is received.

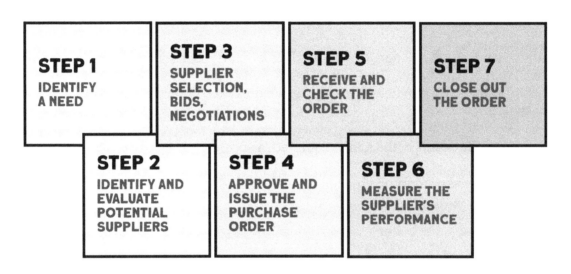

FIGURE 3.7 - THE PURCHASING PROCESS

The final sections of this chapter will explore the seven steps of the purchasing process. To help us better understand these steps, let's use a scenario that may be more familiar to many of us. Grandma's 85th birthday party is approaching in the next few weeks. Everyone in the family has decided to pool their resources to buy Grandma one magnificent, expensive, extravagant gift — an 85" ultra-high-definition television. Because you are studying purchasing, the family selects you to be its Purchasing Officer. Lucky you! Let's consider how *your* purchasing process is similar to the process of Purchasing Managers from large and small companies alike.

3.7 THE PURCHASING PROCESS: IDENTIFY A NEED

Step 1 in the purchasing process is to *identify a need*. Before Grandma's birthday, the family held a meeting to determine what Grandma needed most for her amazingly awesome birthday present. The family decided that an overly large television was what Grandma needed most. After the team of extended family members identified the need for the big birthday purchase, they informed the family Purchasing Officer (you) so that you could, in the words of Aunt Tillie, "Take care of it."

In most medium-sized to large-sized companies, when an employee or a department identifies a need for a good or service, they typically do not go out and acquire it themselves. If they did, there would be no reduced prices for larger orders, and employee labor time would be wasted placing orders, tracking orders, and receiving many small orders throughout the day. Orders for needed goods and services are instead placed through the company's Purchasing Manager or Purchasing Department, with employees in other departments communicating what is needed, in what quantity, of what quality, where, and at what time. A company's Purchasing Department depends on others' information to identify a need in the purchasing process.

Typically, an individual or a department needing specific goods sends a ***purchase requisition*** form to their company's Purchasing Manager. A purchase requisition is a request to the Purchasing Manager to purchase these goods, not an actual order for the goods. Most commonly contain:

- the specific details of the items requested, also known as ***specifications***;

- the preferred vendors or suppliers;

- the number of items needed;

- the date of the requisition;

- the desired date of receipt;

- the estimated unit cost of each item;

- the internal department or account to be charged; and

- the signature or details of a company official authorizing the purchase.

Purchase requisition forms differ from organization to organization. Some smaller companies typically use paper-based purchase requisition forms or fillable electronic forms completed by the requestor and hand-delivered, mailed, or faxed to the Purchasing Manager. As companies grow and purchasing becomes more complex, they use purchase order software applications with built-in purchase requisition forms, allowing for immediate transmission and storage of complex information. Larger organizations use ***enterprise software***, computer or cloud-based software to satisfy multiple information management needs across the entire company, such as purchase requisitions sent to the Purchasing Department from various departments and locations. Figure 3.8 is an example of a purchase requisition screen from SAP, a multinational enterprise software corporation.

When goods are requested, a purchase requisition form is used. When services are requested, however, a ***statement of work***, or ***SOW***, is used. The SOW describes the services needed, where and when they are required, and the type of vendor needed. It may also include specific personnel requirements, performance standards, assessment details, and payment terms and conditions. The Purchasing Manager then uses the SOW in soliciting bids from potential suppliers. After a supplier has been selected and a contract has been awarded, the statement of work becomes part of the contractual agreement. The SOW is the basis for evaluating whether or not the supplier is providing the contracted service when, where, and how needed.

FIGURE 3.8 - EXAMPLE OF PURCHASE REQUISITION SCREEN IN SAP SOFTWARE

Before we move on through the rest of the purchasing process, we must consider whether a company has existing contracts or other relationships with *preferred suppliers* for the goods or services requested. When suppliers and their products have been tried and tested, a company may feel comfortable with a specific supplier for a particular product or range of products, making that supplier a ***preferred supplier***. When this occurs, an organization does not need to complete Steps 2 and 3 of the purchasing process, which involves identifying potential suppliers, obtaining bids, selecting a supplier, and negotiating contracts. For example, Honey-Bee-Good negotiated a new two-year contract with its existing jar and label supplier Paxton Packaging. The Honey-Bee-Good Production Department then sent a purchasing requisition for jars to the Honey-Bee-Good Purchasing Manager (Step 1), who then sent a purchase order directly to Paxton Packaging (Step 4). Honey-Bee-Good completely bypassed the supplier identification, selection, and negotiation processes (Steps 2 and 3).

After Step 1, when a purchase requisition has been received for new goods or services, companies sometimes consider a ***make or buy decision***. In some situations, it may be more efficient and cost-effective to make the goods (or complete the services) themselves rather than buy the goods or services from suppliers. A company may elect to *make* a product or service itself if: it has the equipment and resources to produce the product or perform the service; it can make the product or service at a significantly lower cost than buying it; it cannot find a skilled supplier who meets the necessary product quantity, quality, and delivery time and place criteria; or staff and equipment are readily available in-house that might go unused otherwise.

Conversely, companies may elect to *buy* goods from outside suppliers or outsource desired services from a third party if they don't have the equipment or staff necessary. Even when a company has the needed equipment and resources, it may still make a buy decision if:

- producing the goods or performing the services itself is not cost-effective, as in the case of a one-off purchase;

- the company cannot match the quality of the supplier's goods or services internally;

- suppliers hold a patent or trademark that doesn't allow other companies to produce the goods; or

- the company wishes to have suppliers available as part of a global multi-sourcing strategy.

When companies decide to *buy*, the Purchasing Manager typically deals with only a small number of suppliers for each good or service — sometimes only one! When companies decide to *make* the required goods, the Purchasing Manager's job becomes considerably more complicated. For each good made, the Purchasing Manager will have to select suppliers and negotiate purchasing contracts for each part of the item to be produced. These contracts might include those for various raw materials, partially finished goods, and completed parts. For a single requisitioned item to be made, a Purchasing Manager may need to deal with many or even MANY, MANY suppliers.

3.8 THE PURCHASING PROCESS: IDENTIFY SUPPLIERS

Step 2 in the purchasing process is to *identify and evaluate potential suppliers*. Thinking back to Grandma and her big screen TV, would you, as your family's trusted Purchasing Officer, simply walk into a store and purchase the first 85" television you see? Unless you want the wrath of Aunt Tillie and Uncle Bingo plagued upon you, you are likely to want to spend the family money wisely. Therefore, you will probably investigate different televisions, performance ratings, prices, and service agreements at various retail stores.

Similarly, when Purchasing Managers receive a purchase requisition for a new good or service, they do not pounce on the first supplier who waves in their direction. Some may have the luxury of using **insourcing**, which occurs when a department, organization, branch, or subsidiary within a large company decides to acquire a desired good or service from a location within the company itself. However, most must use **outsourcing**, in which they instead search for and compare multiple suppliers that could provide the needed product or service.

With large or strategically important purchases, one way Purchasing Managers identify potential suppliers is through the **RFX process**. In this sourcing process, the buyer sends pre-purchase requests to potential suppliers in an *RFI*, *RFQ*, or *RFP*. The buyer sends an **RFI (request for information)** to a wide range of potential suppliers if they need more information about the goods or services to be purchased or more information about the suppliers themselves. In an RFI, the buyer asks for information about the desired product, the supplier, its locations, and its capabilities. After receiving responses to an RFI, a buyer may: (1) decide to issue a more detailed request, such as an RFQ or RFP, with the intent to buy from a selected supplier; (2) choose not to buy at this time; or, less commonly, (3) select a supplier immediately.

With the information obtained from the RFI, the buyer may send potential suppliers an RFQ or an RFP, depending on the type of information the buyer needs to make a supplier selection decision. An **RFQ (request for quotation)** is sent to potential suppliers when the buyer is ready to purchase specific goods or services and select a supplier based on cost or other quantifiable factors. The RFQ sent would outline the quantity, quality, time, and place the desired goods or services are needed. RFQs state deadlines for suppliers to respond, ask suppliers to outline the overall cost for the proposed purchase, and contain information about the buyer's expectations of the selected supplier, its performance, and the product or service. An RFQ is typically used to select suppliers for goods rather than services. It is also known as an **IFB (invitation for bid)** or an **ITB (invitation to bid)**.

Potential suppliers respond to an RFQ by sending the buyer a **quote**, also known as a **quotation** or a **bid**. The quote is a written response from a potential seller to a buyer outlining a list of the proposed prices for the desired goods or services. When a potential supplier sends a quote to a buyer, it is **binding**, which means that that seller must honor the proposed prices outlined for the timeframe outlined in the quote. Once the quote's deadline has lapsed, they are no longer obligated to sell the goods or services to the buyer for the prices outlined.

When a buyer needs more information from potential suppliers beyond proposed prices and basic quantifiable data, the buyer may send them an **RFP (request for proposal)**. Like RFQs, RFPs contain response deadlines, outlines of cost information needed, and information about supplier, performance, and product/service expectations. The RFP sent would describe the desired outcome related to the goods or services required but would leave room for the supplier to propose how to reach the desired result. For example, Honey-Bee-Good might send out an RFP to label suppliers stating that it needs 10,000 printed waterproof labels per month to adhere tightly to their jars and also easily be removed by customers who wanted to reuse the jars. In addition to cost information, Honey-Bee-Good would request that suppliers describe how their labels meet these criteria. Companies typically use RFPs to select suppliers for services. They also use RFPs to select goods when they need more information about how the supplier's goods can meet their needs or if the supplier will produce an entirely new item. An RFP is also known as an **RFO (request for offer)**.

Potential suppliers respond to an RFP by sending the buyer a **proposal**, a written response from a potential seller to a buyer divided into at least two parts: a **cost proposal**, which outlines the proposed price for the goods or services desired, and a **technical proposal**, which provides an in-depth description of the goods or services needed and how the seller will provide them. Buyers evaluate proposals on the merits of *both* the cost and technical proposals. As a result, the suppliers selected may not necessarily offer the lowest cost.

A buyer uses information gained from the RFX process to select the best potential supplier for the company's needs. RFX processes can be quite complex, and there is a lot of resulting data to be managed and evaluated after suppliers' information, quotes, and proposals are received. To help a company handle all of this information, they can use an **_eRFX system_**, a procurement software application that can collect, store, evaluate, and manage data surrounding all RFX processes. Some companies build eRFX systems into their enterprise software, which is the software used to satisfy multiple information management needs across an entire company. For example, the popular enterprise software SAP allows companies to create RFQs, send them out to potential suppliers, collect quotes from suppliers, and store their data for evaluation in the supplier selection process.

FIGURE 3.9 - ERFX SYSTEM WITHIN SAP ENTERPRISE SOFTWARE

It is highly unlikely that you would use an RFX system as your family's Purchasing Officer when buying Grandma's 85" television. However, suppose you were the manager of a chain of sports bars across the country and were replacing the televisions in them. In that case, you might use an RFI to gain information about television suppliers and the goods and services they offer relative to your need for 500 large-but-ultra-thin high definition televisions. If you identify the exact television model you wanted and would be basing your supplier decision purely upon cost, you might send potential suppliers an RFQ. If you weren't entirely sure which model you wanted yet and also wanted to see what potential suppliers might offer in a package with after-sales extended service, you might send potential suppliers an RFP.

The amount of energy and time a Purchasing Manager invests in preparing RFIs, RFPs, and RFQs in Step 2 typically depends on the strategic importance, availability, and value of the completed product for which the requested goods or services are needed. Relationships with existing suppliers will also influence the intensity of the supplier search. Below are four types of purchasing situations in order of increasing search intensity based on supplier relationships and strategic importance:

- **straight repurchase**, in which there is a contract for the good or service with an existing supplier at a set price. In this situation, no RFIs, RFPs, or RFQs are needed, and Step 2 is skipped entirely. For example, Honey-Bee-Good would have a straight repurchase of its honey jars and labels after signing a three-year contract with its supplier, Paxton Packaging.

- **straight purchase**, in which a new good or service of little strategic importance is needed. Because the product is less important, the time and energy required to write RFIs, RFPs, or RFQs to purchase goods cannot be justified. When Honey-Bee-Good buys toilet paper for its production facility restrooms, it does not take the time to send out an RFI to purchase products for its two bathrooms serving twenty employees. Instead, the Purchasing Manager makes bulk purchases from a local warehouse-style wholesaler.

- **modified purchase**, in which there is an existing supplier under contract and a change in the need, such as a larger number or different types of products. In this situation, the organization may ask the existing supplier to outline how it will meet the new or changing requirement. It may also solicit information from a few additional suppliers to compare against their current supplier. For example, if Honey-Bee-Good, Inc. bought out three other honey producers in neighboring states, it would triple its annual production output. The Purchasing Manager would need to ascertain its current supplier's ability to triple its jar and label production. If this packaging supplier could not meet the anticipated demand in the desired timeframe, Honey-Bee-Good would have to submit an RFI to additional potential suppliers.

- **new competitive purchase**, in which a new good or service is required, and the finished item is of high strategic importance or will be produced in very large quantities. In this situation, the Purchasing Manager will complete all or most of the activities covered throughout Step 2. For example, because of its threefold growth, Honey-Bee-Good needs to explore faster bottling machinery. The bottling machinery and corresponding conveyor mechanisms are costly items and are critical to the company's operations. Therefore, the Purchasing Manager will send an RFI to as many bottling machinery manufacturers as he can find. He will then spend many hours analyzing them before issuing a highly detailed RFP.

After a company has sent out an RFQ or an RFP and has received quotes or proposals from potential suppliers, it is ready to move on to Step 3, the bidding, selection, and negotiation process!

3.9 THE PURCHASING PROCESS: SUPPLIER SELECTION

Selecting the right supplier is often the most important decision a Purchasing Manager can make. When purchasing Grandma's 85" television, you are likely to study all the possible televisions' specifications and retailers' prices with great intensity. You are spending your family's hard-earned money, after all! You may even try to negotiate a lower price by playing one retailer against another. *"Well, Super Sam's is offering the same TV for a lower price. Maybe I should go there..."* In the end, thanks to your diligent work at this stage of the purchasing process, you manage to find a supplier that will install her television on the exact day you want and will provide Grandma three years of on-site technical support. You also spent $500 less than budgeted, allowing everyone to throw a big birthday bash for Grandma and her friends at a local family restaurant.

Just as you did with Grandma's television, after you have identified potential suppliers, it is time to select one and negotiate the deal. You are now on Step 3 in the purchasing process: *supplier selection*, *bids*, and *negotiations*. When selecting a supplier, a Purchasing Manager can use techniques such as *competitive bidding* or *negotiation*.

The technique of **competitive bidding** pits potential suppliers against each other for the organization's business. After sending out an RFP or an RFQ for a specific product, the buying company receives bids (i.e., proposals or quotes) from potential suppliers. In the purchasing process, a **bid** is an umbrella term for the proposal or quote sent from the seller to the buyer in response to an RFP or RFQ. The Purchasing Manager examines all bids received to find a qualified supplier who best meets the organization's needs, such as low cost or high service levels. This supplier selection technique of competitive bidding is typically used: in competitive markets with multiple suppliers offering the same item; when a large volume of the good or service is needed; if the organization does not yet have a preferred supplier for the product; and when there is enough time for the time-consuming competitive bidding process.

There are some situations in which the competitive bidding process is not a useful method of selecting a supplier, such as if:

- *After sending out an RFI, the Purchasing Manager finds that there are very few suppliers of the needed good or service;*

- *The purchasing process timeframe is short and does not allow for competitive bidding;*

- *Immediate supplier involvement is necessary for providing the product or service; or*

- *The item requested must be manufactured and its complexity does not allow for accurate cost estimates.*

In these situations, the Purchasing Manager may instead engage in the purchasing technique of *negotiation with one potential supplier*. In the world of purchasing, **negotiation** occurs when a buyer and a potential supplier engage in an open discussion to reach a mutually beneficial purchase agreement. The negotiation process may be as simple as a single telephone call or e-mail or as complex as a series of meetings, interviews, and site visits over a year. It can also help develop strong initial buyer-supplier relationships because both parties should openly discuss their abilities and expectations. Good negotiation takes finesse and is more of an art than a science. Suppose a Purchasing Manager is new to, uncomfortable with, or merely seeking support for an essential upcoming negotiation. In that case, they may elect to seek the services of a third-party broker or negotiation service provider.

Throughout competitive bidding and negotiation, the Purchasing Manager uses set evaluation criteria when considering potential suppliers. These criteria might include factors such as:

- *Does the supplier have the ability, experience, physical resources, and adequately trained workforce to provide the goods or services of the right quantity and quality at the right time and place?*

- *Is the supplier financially sound, and what do their current customers and employees think of them?*

- *How is their distribution handled? What is their track record for on-time deliveries?*

- *Is the supplier committed to this relationship? Are they ready to work with us now?*

The buyer must also consider selecting one supplier or multiple suppliers for the same goods during supplier selection. When there is only one supplier available for the goods or services, the buyer engages in a **sole source purchase**. There is no competitive bidding for this type of purchase because the seller has no competitors. With our Orange-You-Yummy example, let's say that orange juice manufacturer needs to purchase replacement parts for the juicing machinery that are only available from the machinery manufacturer. This supplier would be the only supplier available, requiring a sole source purchase.

Suppose there are two or more suppliers available for the goods or services needed, and the buyer decides to select only one supplier to provide these goods or services. In that case, the buyer engages in a **single source purchase**, which allows the supplier and buyer to develop a close relationship. The supplier gains quicker insight into the buyer's needs, often providing knowledge or technology to enhance the purchase. For example, the AMC movie theater chain has a single source purchase contract with Coca-Cola for its soft drinks. Because of single source relationships like this one, Coca-Cola understood its buyers' needs very well. The soft drink company saw that the movie theaters needed a more diverse range of flavors in sugar-free options and beverage dispensers that end users (moviegoers) could operate themselves, freeing up time for theater employees to handle more sales transactions. As a result, in 2009, Coca-Cola developed Coca-Cola Freestyle for its single source contracts with AMC theaters, shopping malls, and restaurant chains. Coca-Cola Freestyle is a freestanding, touch-screen soda dispenser in which end users can operate themselves and select from 165 possible drink products. The beverage seller's primary competitor, Pepsi, did not launch a similar machine for its single source buyers until five years later.

FIGURE 3.10 - COCA-COLA FREESTYLE FOR SINGLE SOURCE BUYERS

If there are two or more suppliers available for the goods or services needed and the buyer decides to use two or more suppliers to provide these goods or services, the buyer engages in a ***multiple source purchase***. These purchases are useful when flexibility is needed when events could disrupt the availability of products from suppliers. For example, an orange juice producer might source oranges from multiple suppliers in different world regions, such as Florida, Brazil, and China. This multiple source purchase maintains a steady supply of oranges. With different growing seasons in these three areas, the juice producer protects itself if a natural disaster hit one area of the world that reduced that year's orange crop.

When a sole source purchase or preferred suppliers are not used, and when a company must purchase a large quantity of a basic item or service, the buyer sometimes considers holding a reverse auction to select a supplier. In a ***reverse auction***, an organization announces the goods or services it needs to purchase. In-person, telephone, or online suppliers may bid their cost for the goods or services against other potential suppliers. The bids from suppliers go lower and lower, as opposed to traditional auctions with rising bids, until one supplier is left offering the lowest bid. Reverse auctions provide a much quicker purchasing process and sometimes a more cost-effective result than competitive bidding or negotiations. However, they can bring more significant risks of inferior quality goods and services from unvetted suppliers.

3.10 THE PURCHASING PROCESS: PURCHASE ORDERS

When it selects a supplier, the buyer is ready to move on to Step 4: *approve and issue the purchase order*. The terms of the purchase arrangement are established between the buyer and the supplier. These written arrangements are in a legally binding document called a **purchase order (PO)** or a **purchase agreement**. This document is signed or electronically signed by authorized officials representing both the buyer and the supplier and contains details outlining the purchase, such as:

- descriptions and specifications of the goods or services;

- the quantity to be delivered;

- the exact place, time, and method of delivery;

- the price of the overall purchase;

- descriptions of the quality required of the goods and related services; and

- the purchase order number and relevant due dates.

Smaller companies often create purchase orders using word processing or spreadsheet software. Medium to larger companies typically use intranet-based or cloud-based e-procurement systems or enterprise software to generate, send, and receive purchase orders, as shown in Figure 3.11.

FIGURE 3.11 - PURCHASE ORDER GENERATED BY SAP ENTERPRISE SOFTWARE

When goods or services are to be ordered multiple times from the same supplier, an organization may issue a **blanket purchase order (BPO)**, an open order for goods or services from a specific supplier within a specific timeframe, such as a year. When goods or services covered under a BPO are needed, a **routine order release** is issued, and the requested goods or services are delivered to the buyer. Blanket purchase orders are a frequently-used, efficient means of doing business for most large organizations, especially for regularly needed production and maintenance goods and services.

After a company has sent a purchase order or a BPO routine order release to a supplier, it is ready to move on to Step 5 of the purchasing process: *receive the goods and check the order*.

Thinking back to Grandma and her birthday surprise, you have selected the perfect 85" television at an amazingly low price. You placed your order with a local retailer, Ellie's Electronics, who will be delivering it to Grandma's house while she is out of town competing at the Poker World Championship in Las Vegas. When Ellie's Electronics arrives, do you simply let them leave the delivery on the front porch and drive off because you are just too comfortable in Grandma's shiatsu massage chair to get up? If you are the responsible Purchasing Officer that your family believes you are, you instead greet the Ellie's Electronics delivery people at the door, receive the order from them, check the order (making sure the television, remote, and instruction documents are all in the box and in good condition), and sign that you have received the order.

When suppliers deliver to a company, the Purchasing Department is not as physically involved in receiving the ordered goods as you were when receiving Grandma's TV. Instead, the Purchasing Manager relies on the Warehouse and Quality Control Departments to receive and inspect the order. The Purchasing Department does, however, monitor the entire order receipt process remotely. When the order is received and checked, the Purchasing Department is informed. This information is transmitted automatically in real time if the organization has an intranet- or cloud-based inventory management system linked to automatic identification technology. For example, the Purchasing Manager at Honey-Bee-Good immediately knows when and how many ordered jars are received into the company's warehouse because the boxes of jars are scanned using a bar code reader and entered into an inventory management cloud-based program. A short time later, after the Warehouse Manager has checked the order and entered additional information into the inventory management program, the Purchasing Manager knows the condition of the order received, such as if any jars were missing or broken.

Throughout the order receipt and checking process, the Purchasing Manager must stay informed. Ensuring that the order has been received in the right quantity, of the right quality, at the right time and place, and at the quoted price is a true measure of the purchase's success.

3.11 THE PURCHASING PROCESS: THE FINAL STEPS

From the end of Step 4 through to the end of Step 5 of the purchasing process, the Purchasing Manager must vigilantly monitor the supplier's actual performance, which brings us to Step 6 in the purchasing process: *measure the supplier's performance.* While it is great to find a supplier who offers amazingly low prices, the supplier must deliver what the buyer ordered in the right quantity, of the right quality, at the right time, and to the right place. It is also essential that the supplier be responsive to the buyer's request, even if it is just a request for additional information. The supplier must also be reliable, responsible, and respectful in all their before-sales, during-sales, and after-sales support. The supplier must be flexible to changes that may arise in the buyer's needs and schedule. All of these "must-haves" from a supplier can be the basis of ***performance metrics***, data used to measure a company's activities and behavior in meeting a particular goal. Thinking back to your example of buying the 85" UHC television for Grandma, you will likely receive a survey from the supplier full of questions asking you to evaluate their product and service in terms of performance metrics.

Another vital performance metric is the effectiveness of the supplier at expediting orders. A buyer typically orders goods or services from a supplier according to a predetermined schedule. In some cases, such as emergencies, the buyer may need goods or services sooner than agreed. A buyer views a supplier favorably if it can ***expedite*** the order, which means that it can deliver goods or services swifter and more efficiently than planned on a one-off or emergency basis.

The Purchasing Manager needs to evaluate supplier performance to enhance future purchasing operations and supply chain efficiency. When the Purchasing Manager finds that a supplier does not meet the performance criteria stated in the purchase order or other contractual agreement, they can contact the supplier to allow them the opportunity to improve. Being informed of poor performance can often result in subsequent higher-than-expected levels of supplier service. If the supplier's performance level does not improve, the buyer may cancel the purchase order and know to avoid that supplier in the future.

Although it is important to know when a supplier's performance is substandard, it is equally essential for a Purchasing Manager to know when a supplier's performance exceeds expectations, perhaps by consistently offering higher levels of service or lower prices. A company can add exceptional suppliers to its preferred suppliers' database, allowing for a more streamlined supplier selection process in the future. For example, buyers often solicit competitive bids from only a few preferred suppliers instead of the many suppliers available. They may also go straight to the negotiation process with one preferred supplier. For example, let's imagine that you were over-the-moon happy and satisfied with your television supplier's product and service for Grandma's 85" UHD TV. You and your extended family might file this supplier's name to their mental list of preferred suppliers and seek them out for all television purchase needs in the future.

After a buyer receives goods or services and evaluates the supplier's performance, the Purchasing Manager is ready to move to Step 7 in the purchasing process: *close out the order.* The Purchasing and Accounting Departments validate that the company received the goods ordered and that the supplier met the terms and conditions of the purchase agreement or contract. This validation is called a ***three-way match*** because the purchase order, receipt documents, and supplier invoice are compared. If all three match up, the supplier's invoice is approved for payment. The purchase order is closed out, marked as completed, and filed. When companies use procurement systems like the PurchaseControl cloud-based system, three-way matching is fully automated, speeding up the process and reducing the chance for human errors.

FIGURE 3.12 - THE THREE-WAY MATCH

A three-way match can also be checked after Grandma's birthday television purchase is complete when you (the family Purchasing Officer) and Aunt Tillie (the family Accountant) sit down to compare all purchase paperwork. Deciding that all amounts in the paperwork match up and seeing that Grandma is thrilled with the family purchase, you both close out the order and pat yourselves on the back for a job well done.

Grandma and her friends love the ultra high definition 85" TV! If only they could stop binge-watching *Hannibal*.

CHAPTER 3 REVIEW QUESTIONS

1. What is the difference between *purchasing* and *supply management*?

2. In a company, who does the purchasing? List job titles mentioned in this chapter and at least one additional title that you have heard before or that you find in an online search.

3. As shown in the examples in Figure 3.3, list at least two different *raw materials* with their related *semifinished goods* and *finished goods*.

4. What *MRO supplies* might a large bakery purchase? What *capital goods* might it purchase?

5. What are the advantages and disadvantages of *centralized purchasing*? What are the advantages and disadvantages of *decentralized purchasing*?

6. In your own words, define *one-off purchase* and *forward buying*. Provide an example of each from your own household purchasing experiences.

7. Jo-Jo's Jams manufactures and sells approximately 200,000 jars of its exclusive Champagne and Cherry Caviar Jam every year for $10 each and makes a profit of $5 from each jar sold. Jo-Jo's currently buys its empty jars with lids from So-So-Solids for $1.00 each. Jo-Jo's Purchasing Manager has negotiated a new purchase agreement with Goodfellas Glass, Inc. to purchase 200,000 jars with lids for $0.90 each. With either supplier, the production labor cost per jar of jam is $3.00, and the corporate allocation per jar is $1.00. Create a chart like the one in Figure 3.6 to answer the following:
   A. What was Jo-Jo's annual profit when So-So-Solids was its supplier?
   B. What will Jo-Jo's annual profit be after the switch to Goodfellas Glass?
   C. How much will Jo-Jo's Jams save each year by switching its suppliers? By what percentage will its annual profits increase?
   D. How many jars of jam would Jo-Jo's need to sell to match this increase in profit if it did not switch suppliers?

8. What is *enterprise software*? Why is it useful to an organization?

9. What is the difference between an *RFQ* and an *RFP*? When might each be used? Can both be used to procure the same product?

10. What is a *blanket purchase order*? What are the advantages of a BPO listed in this chapter? Although not listed in this chapter, what might at least one disadvantage of a BPO be?

CHAPTER 3 CASE STUDY

A LOOK AT ASCI'S SMARTTOOLS

In Alaska, oil, gas, and mining are all big business. However, unlike other locations across the US, exploration and extraction sites in Alaska are remote, but *remote* doesn't even begin to describe it. The North Slope, home of much of Alaska's oil and gas exploration and extraction, is located in the far northernmost reaches of the state bordering the Arctic Sea. No railways or reliable highways reach the area, and the Arctic sea is frozen over with solid ice packs for months at a time. Its location is thousands of miles away from any suppliers, making air transportation practical only for the lightest and most valuable items desired.

MELTING ICE ROAD, ALASKA DEPARTMENT OF TRANSPORTATION

At the onset of the long North Slope winters, ice roads are constructed across the frozen tundra. Some episodes of the harrowing and dangerous *Ice Road Truckers* have been filmed here! Although warm winter weather may sound like a blessing in Alaska, it is a curse for the North Slope because ice road construction can face lengthy delays. In the late spring, before the dirt roads are passable, the ice roads melt and make the tundra marshy and impassable. Compared to Texas, where most exploration, extraction, and refinery sites can be reached throughout the year by road or rail systems, Alaska's oil and gas industry faces unique supply challenges and enormous supply chain costs. One company that has devoted itself to reducing its Alaska customers' supply chain costs and risks is Advanced Supply Chain International, LLC (ASCI LLC).

ASCI LLC was founded in 1999 in Anchorage, Alaska, to provide supply chain services to the state's oil and gas industry. It is a high tech supply chain and asset management company for some of the major players in the oil and gas, petrochemical, refining, chemical, and mining industries across the world. One of the many services ASCI LLC offers to help customers cut costs is its web-based SmartTools. Reported to help reduce purchasing costs by up to as much as 37%, SmartTools are a type of ERP (enterprise resource planning) system that assists with supplier selection and integration, staging, order tracking, and strategic sourcing.

With the web-based SmartTools, ASCI LLC's customers can use its suite of online tools to manage all aspects of their inbound supply chain. One tool, the SmartCatalogue, helps purchasers quickly find the items they are looking for, from the commonplace to the obscure, all from a range of tried and tested reliable preferred suppliers. If purchasers want to find even lower prices, they can use the SmartAuction/Quote tool, which solicits, receives, and manages bids from multiple suppliers. If purchasers have large orders to place, they can use the SmartBundler tool to find the lowest costs for bulk orders. Before deciding to place an order with a particular supplier, purchasers can also use the SmartMeasures tool to peruse up-to-date supplier performance metrics, such as on-time delivery statistics. Once orders have been placed, purchasers can use the SmartTracker tool, which provides real-time information for tracking orders.

Although you might imagine that finding the lowest price is always at the forefront of a Purchasing Manager's mind, that is not necessarily the case on the North Slope. Here, receiving goods on time is essential. Most of the goods ordered are maintenance, repair, and operating (MRO) supplies, from highly complex widgets and thingamabobs for drilling to much-needed food and toiletries for the thousands of workers on the North Slope where the closest grocery or clothing store is hundreds of miles away. In this harsh and unforgiving environment, typical on-time arrival rates for goods can be as low as 30 to 40% for inexperienced companies and 50 to 60% for more experienced companies. This delay can lead to inventory shortages of spare parts needed for immediate repairs, resulting in temporary shutdowns. These shutdowns can cost oil and gas companies millions of dollars! With SmartTools and its SmartTracker and SmartMeasure functions, ASCI LLC's customers typically experience an on-time arrival rate of 80% for MRO supplies, resulting in fewer costly shutdowns and much happier workers with uninterrupted supplies of peanut butter and coffee.

References:
ASCI LLC website. (2020) Retrieved from http://www.ascillc.com/
Price, P. (2014) Personal interview with S. Hawkins, President ASCI, LLC.

Chapter 4

Inbound Logistics: Warehousing and Inventory Management

You have read Chapter 3, "Inbound Logistics: Purchasing," and are now a purchasing pro. You are well-versed in the five Ws of purchasing and know the purchasing process and its ins and outs. You might even be ready to try corporate purchasing using enterprise software or take a stab at strategic sourcing to save a company thousands of dollars. But now that you are prepared to buy truckloads and truckloads of goods, where will you put them all when they arrive?

Let's consider the case of Boston Bob. Bob is a couponer extraordinaire and knows how to find the best promo codes, usually ten pages deep in a Google search. He has text alerts for savings of regularly purchased items and keeps track of all his expenditures and savings on spreadsheets. Bob has never paid full price for any item in his life and follows the five Ws of purchasing for all of his purchases. However, because Boston Bob devotes the majority of his time to purchasing, he has little time to organize. When he brings groceries home, or his items from online orders arrive, he puts them wherever there is room, sometimes cramming cupboards and refrigerator shelves so tightly that spatulas are sometimes needed to pry things out.

When he needs something, Boston Bob can find nothing. He doesn't have a system for storing his purchased items, so he must pull everything out to find one item. After cutting his finger while chopping carrots, Bob spent so long searching for a bandaid that his blood had clotted, and the wound had almost fully healed before finding the big discount box of bandaids. Another time, he was a bit quicker when searching for a jar of mayonnaise for his bologna and peanut butter sandwich. Luckily, he happened to find a jar at the very, very back of the first refrigerator shelf he searched. Quite unluckily, the expiration date on the jar was May 2002. Although he was adept and purchasing, our dear friend Boston Bob has a thing or two to learn about warehousing and inventory management.

In Chapter 2, we saw that in manufacturing and production, inbound logistics management is called *materials management* and has two subsections. The first is **purchasing and supply management**, which is the financial side of selecting, ordering, and paying for goods. On this financial side, we would say: *Let's buy the goods!* The second subsection of **materials management**, which is also the focus of this chapter, is inbound and internal warehouse management. This physical side of materials management focuses on receiving items purchased into a warehouse and placing them on shelves. On this physical side, we might exclaim: *Let's receive and store the goods!*

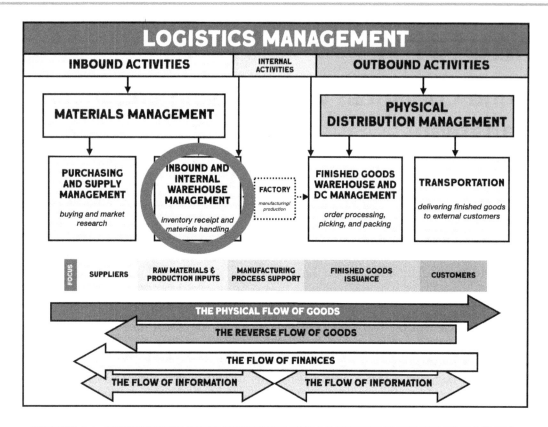

FIGURE 4.1 - WAREHOUSE MANAGEMENT IN THE LOGISTICS MANAGEMENT MODEL

4.1 WAREHOUSE MANAGEMENT

A manufacturing company has purchased goods. A week later, these goods arrive at the doorstep of the buyer's warehouse. These inbound goods are now ready to become part of the company's inbound and internal warehouse operations. Remember that in Chapter 1, we defined a *warehouse* as a building or area in which companies store goods. The act of storing goods in a building or area is called ***warehousing***.

When we think of a warehouse, many of us think of a big, old, dusty building with shelves piled high of even dustier boxes. Perhaps we imagine the dark warehouse of endless boxes and crates where the Ark of the Covenant ended up in *Raiders of the Lost Ark* or the empty and abandoned warehouse where most of *Reservoir Dogs* took place. Or perhaps we imagine the authors' favorite — the seemingly endlessly high, crammed, and dusty wand storage areas of Ollivanders in the Harry Potter films.

However, Warehouses are very dynamic facilities, with people, equipment, and materials in constant movement as goods rapidly flow in and out as need demands. While our antiquated visions conjure up only the notion of a storage facility, a warehouse is so much more!

The goods flowing into, within, and out of warehouses include raw materials for manufacturing; items to be distributed when sold; equipment, tools, spare parts, or supplies for manufacturing, distribution, or maintenance operations; and materials for finished goods packaging and distribution. Within a typical company warehouse, the following activities occur surrounding the flow of goods:

1. Goods come in and are inspected;

2. Goods are placed so they can be found when needed;

3. Goods are maintained and kept safe;

4. Goods are picked from their place when needed; and

5. Goods are prepared for outbound distribution to leave the warehouse for their next destination in the supply chain.

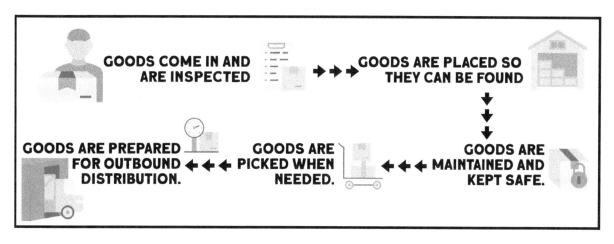

FIGURE 4.2 - ACTIVITIES WITHIN A WAREHOUSE

Companies manage these activities surrounding the flow of goods through the warehouse. *Warehouse management* is the planning, directing, and controlling of warehouse activities to achieve *efficiency* (don't let it cost too much) and *effectiveness* (get the goods where they need to be and don't let them get damaged). In this chapter, we will focus on *inbound* logistics and its corresponding inbound and internal warehouse management. Therefore, we will be looking only at numbers 1, 2, and 3 in the list of five warehouse activities above. We will look at numbers 4 and 5 in the next chapter when we move to *outbound* logistics activities.

Because warehouses are a bit more complicated than merely storing goods, let's build on our definition from Chapter 1. Let's now define a *warehouse* as a facility or area within a facility in which an organization receives, inspects, stores, picks, packs, and issues any of a variety of materials needed for an organization's operations or customers' orders.

Within a warehouse for a manufacturing or production company, a few additional activities occur surrounding the production of new finished goods. Below is a revised list of activities surrounding the flow of goods for a manufacturing or production company:

1. Raw materials and semifinished goods come in to the warehouse and are inspected;

2. Raw materials and semifinished goods are placed so they can be found when needed by manufacturing;

3. Raw materials and semifinished goods are maintained and kept safe;

4. Raw materials and semifinished goods are picked from their place when needed by manufacturing;

5. Newly finished goods come in from manufacturing, typically into a different warehouse or section of the warehouse, and are inspected;

6. Finished goods are picked according to customer orders and corporate distribution plans;

7. Finished goods are prepared for outbound distribution to leave the warehouse for their next destination in the supply chain, such as to a customer or a regional distribution center.

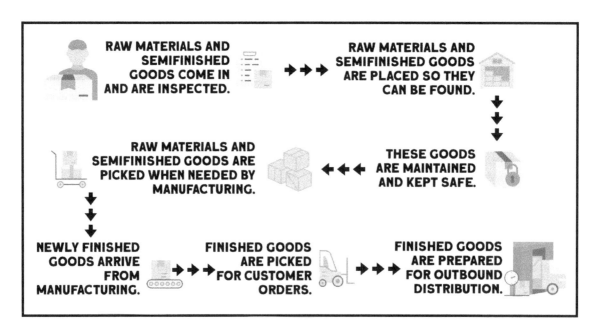

FIGURE 4.3 - ACTIVITIES WITHIN A MANUFACTURER'S WAREHOUSE

4.2 CASE EXAMPLE: WAREHOUSES IN A SUPPLY CHAIN

In any given supply chain, there are warehouses. There are multiple warehouses throughout a single product's supply chain for both inbound and outbound logistics activities. In the ice cream supply chain in Figure 4.4, warehouse facilities and warehousing activities are found in the product's official regional distribution warehouse and in warehouse facilities within the supplier's, manufacturer's, and retailer's locations.

FIGURE 4.4 - WAREHOUSES IN AN ICE CREAM SUPPLY CHAIN

Let's see what this looks like in a real-life example. If you are an ice cream lover, you may have heard of Ben & Jerry's, an American ice cream manufacturer founded in 1978 in Burlington, Vermont, and now a subsidiary of the British-Dutch company Unilever. Ben & Jerry's is known for its tightly packed pints, unique flavor combinations, and corporate philanthropy. According to the company's web site (www.benjerry.com), warehouses play an integral part of its ice cream supply chain. First, the warehouses within its ice cream manufacturing facilities in Vermont receive pasteurized and cooled milk from the St. Alban's Dairy Co-op. The warehouses keep the milk until the ice cream production process needs it.

FIGURE 4.5 - BEN & JERRY'S FACTORY IN VERMONT

After the delightfully delectable ice cream has been produced and individually packaged, it heads to the facility's freezer warehouse. As they head to the warehouse, all individual pints of ice cream undergo a visual inspection, and the Quality Assurance department tests randomly selected pints. Those with the enviable job of professional tasters get to take a bite from the center of each pint selected!

After meeting the Quality Assurance folks' stringent standards, Ben & Jerry's ice cream then undergoes a unique packaging process at each facility's freezer warehouse. As they flow along a conveyor belt, every other pint of ice cream is turned upside down by a device called the *inverter*. Next, a machine called the *bundler* places them in groups of eight and into a plastic *sleeve*, which is briefly heated to form tight, well-contained packages for shipping. Employees put the packages by hand onto pallets and again shrink-wrap the pallet when it's full of the yummy ice cream.

The shrink-wrapped ice cream pallets are then sent to the central Ben & Jerry's freezer warehouse and distribution center in Rockingham, Vermont. This central facility receives the ice cream in a temperature-controlled setting, stored it safely and securely, and then picks, issues, and perhaps re-palletizes it for distribution to retailers' warehouses and happy customers around the world!

4.3 TYPES OF WAREHOUSES

There can be many warehouses in a supply chain, but not all warehouses are alike. Many types of warehouses vary based on warehouse ownership and function. Depending on a company's needs, it might use any of the following types of warehouses:

- **Private warehouse:** a warehouse facility that is owned by a company to store its goods. Manufacturers, wholesalers, distributors, and retailers can own private warehouses. Although they are quite costly and involve a significant commitment, private warehouses allow companies complete control over their warehouse space. Ben & Jerry's freezer warehouse in Vermont and the giant amazon.com fulfillment centers worldwide are examples of private warehouses.

- **Public warehouse:** a warehouse facility that stores goods from multiple companies but is owned and operated by another company, such as a third-party logistics service provider, or by the government or a quasi-government agency. Although they don't allow companies as much control over space as private warehouse do, public warehouses offer the advantage of lower costs and flexibility, using and paying for only as much of a warehouse is needed at a given time. A small local self-storage facility used by pharmaceutical sales representatives to store medical samples and a large regional third-party refrigerated warehouse used by small grocery stores and gas stations would be examples of public warehouses.

- **Automated warehouse:** a warehouse facility that automates some or all of the movement, storage, and picking of goods so that machines handle more tasks and fewer rely on manual labor. The software systems and technology required to set up automated warehouses are costly. However, automated warehouses have more reliable order picking accuracy and may be less expensive to operate in the long term than warehouses without automation. As shown in Figure 4.6, an automated warehouse for large sheets of flat glass uses automated equipment such as robotic arms with suction cups to handle large sheets of dangerous and fragile glass when storing glass and picking orders.

FIGURE 4.6 - ROBOTIC ARMS IN FLAT GLASS AUTOMATED WAREHOUSE

- **Smart warehouse:** a fully automated warehouse that uses real-time data through artificial intelligence systems and automation technology to achieve optimum efficiency. In 2020, UPS made a big push to include smart warehouses in their distribution systems through their Warehouse Execution System (WES) that connected their global warehouse network and coordinated with each warehouse's Autonomous Mobile Robots (AMR).

- **Climate-controlled warehouse:** a warehouse facility that carefully controls the inside temperature and humidity based on the stored goods' needs. When we think of climate-controlled warehouses, we might first think of food and the refrigeration and freezer needs of many grocery store items. However, many companies need climate-controlled warehouses to avoid damage to their goods. For example, the warehouses for Martin Guitars in Nazareth, Pennsylvania and Sonora, Mexico must be kept precisely within the ranges of 72-77 degrees Fahrenheit and 45-55 percent humidity to avoid cracks and warping of the wood guitars.

- **Hazardous materials warehouse:** a warehouse facility that stores goods that require extra handling and storing safety precautions, such as poisonous materials, flammable gasses, and corrosive liquids. Hazardous materials warehouses have specific storage requirements for goods and protective equipment requirements for warehouse personnel handling the goods. A hazardous materials warehouse is also called a *hazmat warehouse* or a *dangerous goods warehouse*. After a bear spray incident at a New Jersey warehouse sending 24 workers to the hospital, amazon.com began to build a series of special hazmat warehouses in 2019 for the dangerous goods sold on its website.

- **Bonded warehouse:** a warehouse facility that stores imported goods until import duty has been paid. When moving goods internationally, most organizations consider the option of a bonded warehouse. When goods arrive from another country, the company receiving the goods must immediately pay excise taxes and customs duties. If a company secures a bond for potential taxes and duties of future incoming goods, it may temporarily store foreign inbound goods in a bonded warehouse. The company may then legally defer taxes or duties until the goods are removed from the bonded warehouse. Also, goods can be stored in a bonded warehouse, but they can also be assembled or partially assembled there. You typically can find bonded warehouses near international airports and cargo ports.

- **Distribution center:** a large warehouse facility that stores goods for a shorter time than other warehouses. Distribution centers (DCs) have the fast movement of goods from supplier to customer as their primary goal. Companies use information systems to control and automate operations at distribution centers to facilitate the quick movement of goods into and out of a facility. DCs are also located near transportation systems, such as highways or railroads, to facilitate the fast movement of goods to customers. Grocery store chains across the world have their own regional distribution centers where they receive groceries from suppliers and then distribute them to all of their retail grocery stores in a set region. These regional distribution centers are strategically located on highways and in between the stores they service. Strategic locations provide the quickest transportation time to each store.

- **Fulfillment center:** a warehouse facility storing products from one or more companies from which another company fulfills customers' orders, typically from online sales. This other company that owns and operates the fulfillment center is a third-party logistics service provider. Like distribution centers, fulfillment centers focus on the fast movement of goods into and out from the facility. The primary difference between the two types of warehouse facilities is that distribution centers typically distribute goods to retail stores and fulfillment centers send goods directly to end users based on online orders. A fulfillment center is also known as a *customer fulfillment center* or *CFC*. Known for its automated customer fulfillment centers, the British online supermarket Ocado partnered with The Kroger Company in the US in

2018 to bring automated customer fulfillment centers for online grocery shopping in multiple regions of the United States.

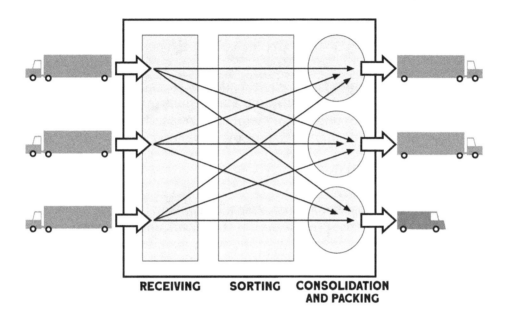

RECEIVING   SORTING   CONSOLIDATION AND PACKING

FIGURE 4.7 - HOW A CROSS-DOCKING FACILITY WORKS

- **Cross-docking facility:** a facility that receives finished goods from a variety of suppliers or locations at one end of the building; immediately breaks down goods, sorts them, and places them into trucks or containers at the other end of the facility; and ships them off to customers. The entire process at a cross-docking facility typically takes under 24 hours but can be as quick as one hour. A cross-docking facility allows finished goods to get to end users quicker and provides significant savings in warehouse costs because it eliminates the need for storage and order pickings. In a traditional warehouse, goods are held until a purchase order is received from a customer. At a cross-docking warehouse or distribution center, the customers for each item in the incoming shipment are known long before reaching the cross-docking facility. Typically, cross-docking occurs throughout the day as different vendors arrive with their various wares. When an outbound truck is full, it heads out to a retail store awaiting the products it contains, perhaps from scores of vendors! For example, the home improvement retailer Home Depot operates 18 enormous, mechanized cross-docking facilities called Rapid Deployment Centers (RDC) that take in goods from suppliers and rapidly place them into outgoing trucks to its stores across the country.

- **Consolidated warehouse:** a facility for multiple suppliers located in one area and used collectively to store and combine shipments of outbound goods to customers for larger, more cost-effective shipments. Consolidated warehouses, also called *consolidation warehouses*, can help suppliers save money on shipping costs and provide the flexibility of sending smaller, more frequent shipments. Alba Wine and Spirits Warehousing and Distribution LLC owns and operates a consolidated warehouse in Edison, New Jersey. Local wine and spirits producers store their beverages here in a secure, temperature-controlled setting, and Alba also provides order picking service and daily deliveries to the beverage companies' customers in New Jersey, New York, and Connecticut.

- **Cooperative warehouse:** a warehouse facility that is owned and operated by an industry-based cooperative organization. The primary goal of a cooperative and its warehouse is to help the cooperative members. Cooperatives are less focused on making a profit. For example, the Staplcotn cooperative warehouse in Mississippi is owned by the Staple Cotton Cooperative Association, whose members are cotton growers across the United States.

- **Government warehouse:** a warehouse facility owned and controlled by the government. These warehouses can be used by the government or private companies to store goods. When private companies use government warehouses, the costs are typically lower than other warehousing options, but there is considerably more paperwork involved.

- **External inventory yard:** an open, outside warehousing area used for storing various nonperishable goods. Also known as an ***outdoor storage area*** or a ***yard***, an external inventory yard can hold: lumber, stoneware, heavy iron or steel castings, heavy-duty electrical cable, outdoor machinery, scrap and waste materials, coal, other fuels, and garden materials and supplies.

FIGURE 4.8 - EXTERNAL INVENTORY YARD FOR TIMBER

Multiple warehouse types from the list above can describe a single warehouse. For example, you might have a private, automated, climate-controlled distribution center with a hazardous materials section. You might also encounter a bonded consolidated warehouse with an external inventory yard or an automated cooperative cross-docking facility. Some companies may also use labels to describe warehouse types that are different from those above, making it very important to know how your company and the companies in its supply chain label their warehouses.

When it comes to selecting a warehouse, companies must also weigh the following considerations:

- **Single-Story versus Multi-Story Buildings.** Single-story warehouse buildings are generally cheaper to construct, maintain, and operate. A single-story design also lends itself to a more efficient flow of goods through a warehouse. However, companies must sometimes consider multi-story warehouse buildings when land is scarce, and land costs are prohibitively high. In New York and Tokyo, a company may find that it is less expensive to install elevators and complex conveyor systems in a multi-story facility than to buy enough inner-city land to construct a single-story facility.

- **Purpose-Built versus Converted Buildings.** A purpose-built warehouse is a warehouse building that has been designed and constructed according to a company's individual needs and operational requirements. A converted warehouse is a structure originally designed for another purpose but later converted to a warehouse. With a purpose-built warehouse, companies can get the exact type and style of a building they want. When companies don't have the capital required for expensive new construction or another facility exists exactly where a warehouse is needed, converted warehouses can offer a beneficial option.

- **Own versus Rent Third-Party Facilities.** Situations arise when a company may not want to build, convert, or buy a warehouse building. For example, one company may lack the financial resources to build, convert, or buy a warehouse. Another company may experience frequent changes in demand, translating to frequent changes in warehouse space needed. A third company may be entering a new market and be unsure of future demand and warehousing needs. All three companies might consider renting space within a third-party warehouse facility or renting an entire warehouse building in these situations.

FIGURE 4.9 - REI PURPOSE-BUILT DISTRIBUTION CENTER IN GOODYEAR, ARIZONA

4.4 WAREHOUSE LAYOUT AND FLOW

Once companies select a warehouse type, they must focus on planning and organizing the warehouse interior for the efficiency and effectiveness of operations. The ultimate goal of warehouse layout design is to achieve efficient overall warehousing that contributes to successful and logistics operations by minimizing costs and maximizing customer service. A warehouse with poor design layout and flow can lead to increased costs and unsafe working conditions for employees. From 2015 to 2017 in the US, the number of warehouse fatalities doubled mainly due to the increasing automation of warehouses and poor layout design of areas in which humans and autonomous machinery interact.

When considering warehouse layout, we must first become acquainted with the **sections of a warehouse**. Most warehouses include:

- **Loading Bay:** Also called a ***loading dock***, this is the area of a warehouse with external docks where goods are (1) initially received into the warehouse from an inbound transpiration vehicle or (2) moved out from the warehouse onto an outbound vehicle, such as a truck or a train. These *inbound loading bays* and *outbound loading bays* may be located side-by-side in a warehouse or at opposite ends of the warehouse, depending on the warehouse's needs and the designed flow of goods.

FIGURE 4.10 - LOADING BAYS OF FISH PROCESSOR IN ICELAND

- **Receiving Area:** After they are unloaded from a vehicle into the loading bay, goods are temporarily held here while being checked against the order placed, inspected for quantity and quality, and coded and labeled for subsequent storage. This area is also called a *reception area*.

4.11 - RECEIVING AREA OF LOGISTICS SERVICE PROVIDER'S WAREHOUSE IN ALASKA

- **Storage Area:** This is the area in the warehouse where goods are held until they must be shipped out. Goods may be stored in this area on shelving units or directly on the ground, especially for larger or palletized goods.

- **Order Picking Area:** Goods are selected from this area after a company receives an order. The order picking and storage areas may be: 1) the same areas; 2) opposite aisles flanking the same row of goods; or 3) separate areas of the warehouse, especially in automated or live storage systems.

- **Value Added Area:** In some warehouses, companies provide value-added services to outbound goods in this area. Value-added services include monogramming for clothing, memory or graphics card add-ons for computers, kitting small appliances with the correct regional plugs, bundling combinations of goods to be sold together such as *Frozen 2* bicycle and Elsa or Olaf helmet bundles for children, and customized packaging based on regions, holidays, or sales promotions.

- **Packing and Unitization Area:** In this area of the warehouse, outbound goods are packed, packaged, and consolidated into unit loads, such as within pallet loads or into containers. This area is also called the *packing and consolidation area*.

- **Staging Area:** This is where packaged or unitized goods are labeled for issuance to the next destination in the supply chain and held until transportation arrives. It is also called a ***dispatch area***. In some warehouses, the *packing and unitization area* and the *staging area* are combined into one.

4.12 - STAGING AREA FOR AIR CARGO PALLETS AT CHARLESTON AFB IN SOUTH CAROLINA

- **Service Area:** This is the section or multiple sections of a warehouse where support activities occur, such as management offices, employee break rooms, warehouse changing rooms, bathrooms, and electrical recharging areas for vehicles, robots, and handheld equipment.

When designing a safe, efficient, and effective warehouse layout, organizations select the location of these sections to achieve a logical, sequential flow of goods. A warehouse's layout should (1) minimize the manual, mechanical, or automated work needed to put away and retrieve goods and (2) maximize warehouse floorspace for quick and safe movement for all warehouse operations. Depending on the warehouse building, its interior configuration, and the company's warehousing needs, the inbound and outbound loading bays may be located at the same end or, as shown in Figure 4.13, at opposite ends of the warehouse building.

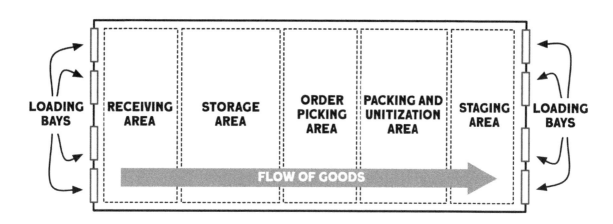

FIGURE 4.13 - WAREHOUSE LAYOUT AND FLOW

Besides the location of the warehouse sections, an organization must also consider the goods flowing into and out of the warehouse to design an effective and efficient layout. The size, weight, and handling requirements of goods have a significant impact on warehouse layout. For example, large and heavy goods will need to be stored in areas with wide aisles that allow plenty of maneuvering room for special handling equipment. The next time you go to a big box home improvement store or a large hardware store, compare the paint section's aisle width to the kitchen cabinetry section's aisle width. Far less space is needed to store and retrieve one-gallon tins of paint than is necessary for bulky kitchen cabinets.

The goods issuance frequency has a significant impact on warehouse layout and the location of goods. In smaller warehouses, inbound and outbound loading bays may need to be placed on the same side of the warehouse building if only one side of the building has road access. In such cases, as shown in Figure 4.14, goods are placed in shelves closer to the loading bay side of the building when they are needed more frequently.

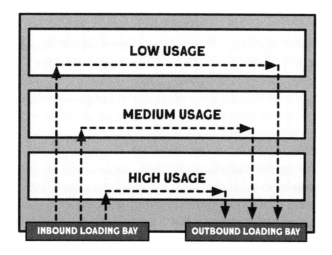

FIGURE 4.14 - WAREHOUSE LAYOUT AND GOODS PLACEMENT BY ISSUE FREQUENCY

4.5 MATERIALS HANDLING

Now that you understand warehouse types and warehouse layout, the next important part of warehouse management is materials handling. In its simplest terms, ***materials handling*** is how *materials* (physical goods in raw, semifinished, and finished states) are *handled* (moved short distances and stored). As areas of study, both *materials handling* and *transportation* examine the movement of goods. However, materials handling focuses on the short-distance movement of goods within a warehouse or other facility, while transportation focuses on the long-distance movement of goods between facilities. In some settings, materials handling drops the *s* and is called *material handling*.

Well, even to those of us most unacquainted with supply chain management, it's quite evident that materials must be handled as they flow along the supply chain. Those pints of ice cream don't grow little legs and walk themselves from the factory warehouse to the grocery store! Why, then, is it important to study or focus on this handling of goods? In three words: **space**, **labor**, and **service**!

Effective materials handling maximizes space available to store more goods in the same space. Materials handling can also reduce the space needed to store and handle goods, creating more efficient warehouse layout and design. Materials handling can reduce the amount of labor involved in handling goods and make a safer working environment for those handling them. Finally, materials handling can enhance service provided to internal customers and external end users by minimizing product damage and improving distribution speed.

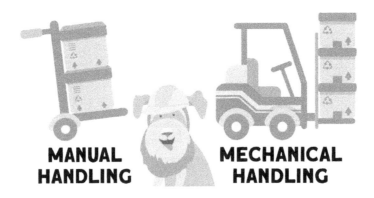

MANUAL HANDLING   **MECHANICAL HANDLING**

FIGURE 4.15 MANUAL VERSUS MECHANICAL HANDLING

Warehouse and supply chain managers can achieve the benefits of space, labor, and service by practicing two key principles of materials handling: **product flow** and the **unit load**. First, to attain supply chain efficiency, materials handling experts examine the flow of products or materials through an organization. For example, they analyze whether it is more efficient to handle goods *manually* or *mechanically* at different points within a warehouse. With ***manual handling***, goods are moved and lifted by hand or by using hand-operated devices. With ***mechanical handling***, goods are moved and lifted using a mechanized device. To understand the difference between the two, when boxes of everyone's favorite chewable mouthwash for their canine companions, Greenies Breath Buster Bites, are more easily carried by a person or moved from place to place in a warehouse by hand truck, this is *manual* handling. When those same boxes of Greenies Breath Buster Bites are carried around the warehouse by forklift, it is now *mechanical* handling.

Materials handling experts often determine that it is more efficient to handle the same goods manually or mechanically in different warehouse areas. At the Ben & Jerry's ice cream factory, ice cream pints are handled *mechanically* as they travel by automated conveyor to the freezer warehouse and into multiple-pint sleeves for shrink-wrapping. The shrink-wrapped pints within the sleeves are then stacked *manually* (by hand) onto pallets for additional shrink-wrapping in preparation for shipping. In this process, it is much quicker and more efficient for the many ice cream pints coming from the factory to be handled mechanically by conveyor. After shrink-wrapping the pints into eight units, manual handling becomes more effective than mechanical handling. Units of packaged ice cream must be stacked firmly and evenly onto pallets before they undergo a final visual inspection to ensure zero product defects.

FIGURE 4.16 - EXAMPLE OF A UNIT LOAD

Now that you understand product flow, the second key principle of materials handling is the unit load. A ***unit load*** is any quantity of a material assembled and restrained to be handled, moved, stored, and stacked as a single object. In our Ben & Jerry's example, eight individual pint containers of ice cream were placed into a plastic sleeve and shrink-wrapped to be handled as a single unit or a *unit load*. Eight shrink-wrapped pints of ice cream could be handled eight times quicker than eight individual pint containers of ice cream. Figure 4.16 shows an example of a unit load of eighteen shrink-wrapped wooden briquettes.

The two core structures of the unit load within materials management are the *pallet* and the *container*. A ***pallet*** is a flat, unit load structure used to support materials for stable transportation and storage. Goods are shrink-wrapped, stretch wrapped, or strapped onto a pallet to form a secure load. The pallet's primary function at the base of the load is to maintain a gap between the floor and the load so that a lifting device, such as a forklift or a pallet jack, can place its forks under it without affecting the load's stability or security. Most pallets are wood, but alternatives include plastic pallets for messy or perishable items, metal pallets for heavy goods, and paper pallets for lightweight and disposable applications. Figure 4.17 shows the formation of a unit load on a wooden pallet at the port of San Antonio, Chile. Boxed fresh vegetables are being stacked onto the pallet and then stretch wrapped for stability and security. Forklifts can now move the stacked boxes of vegetables onto ships as a single unit.

4.17 - STRETCH WRAPPING A UNIT LOAD ON A WOODEN PALLET IN CHILE

The second core structure of the unit load is the ***container***, typically a large, rectangular, metal box that is 8 feet wide by 8 feet 6 inches high by 20 or 40 feet long. Containers may also be 10, 48, or 53 feet long and 9 feet 6 inches high. These quite ordinary-looking large boxes have accomplished the extraordinary feat of revolutionizing the shipping industry. The standard size and style of the container allow international and intermodal transport of goods. ***Intermodal transport*** is the transportation of goods using more than one form of conveyance, such as road *and* rail or air *and* water. Figure 4.18 shows intermodal transport with containers moved by trucks in position to be moved to a cargo ship at southern the tip of South America in Ushuaia, Argentina.

FIGURE 4.18 - INTERMODAL TRANSPORT IN ARGENTINA

A factory in Shanghai, China producing toys for an upcoming family film about wizards, hobbits, or superheroes can fill an entire container with thousands of action figures. This container can then travel by rail from the factory to the Port of Shanghai. The container can then journey across the Pacific Ocean to the Port of Los Angeles by ship, where it can be unloaded and then travel by rail to Pittsburg, Pennsylvania. At this point, the container of much-awaited action figures can be unloaded from the rail tracks and loaded immediately onto a tractor-trailer frame. It can now travel by truck 20 miles to a popular retail chain's distribution center, where someone will open the container to distribute its precious contents to multiple stores in the area.

Using a container has allowed thousands and thousands of highly desired new action figures to be handled as a single unit throughout this process, increasing the speed and ease of handling. It also reduced the risk of damage and theft because the container was sealed the entire time. Finally, because of its standard size, the container could be stacked when it was awaiting further transportation at the cargo and rail ports, maximizing the storage space at multiple container ports in this outbound chain from the factory to the retailer.

Unless you are part-superhero, items formed into pallet or container unit loads become too heavy or too large to handle by hand. It's now time to bring in the big guns: ***materials handling equipment***. Materials handling equipment are the manual or mechanical devices used to move, store, or lift unit loads or individual items during any supply chain segment. Using such equipment can speed up operations, reduce costs, and even reduce the risk of back injuries to warehouse personnel. While there are probably almost as many types of materials handling equipment as there are materials to be handled, there are five distinct categories of materials handling equipment:

- **Transport equipment** moves goods and unit loads from one place to another, typically within a warehouse or external inventory yard facility. This category of materials handling equipment includes: *industrial trucks*, such as forklift trucks; *cranes*, such as the large cranes found at cargo ports used to move containers from ships to rail or truck frames; and *conveyors*, such as those used to move pints of Ben & Jerry's ice cream from the factory to the freezer warehouse.

- **Positioning equipment** repositions goods into place for subsequent handling. At the Ben & Jerry's factory warehouse, an *inverter* is used to turn every other ice cream pint upside down for subsequent handling and packaging.

- **Unit load formation equipment** restrains goods and forms them into a single unit load. *Shrinkwrapping*, *stretch wrapping*, and *strapping equipment* used to secure goods onto pallets are all examples of unit load formation equipment.

- **Storage equipment** hold materials in warehouse and external inventory yard facilities for both short and long-term timeframes. Examples include the *shelving and racking systems* standard in most warehouses and storerooms.

- **Automatic identification and communication equipment** identifies goods to assist with inventory control and materials flow. *RFID* tags and readers, *bar code* printers and readers, and other *optical reading systems* are examples of automatic identification and communication equipment.

FIGURE 4.19 - IDENTIFICATION, TRANSPORT, AND STORAGE EQUIPMENT IN A WAREHOUSE

4.6 INVENTORY MANAGEMENT

This chapter has explored types of warehouses, the flow of goods in a warehouse, and how goods are moved around within a warehouse. The collection of goods, materials, and physical resources held by an organization in warehouse facilities, manufacturing locations, distribution centers, external inventory yards, in transit, or anywhere else in its internal supply chain is called *inventory*. If it is a tangible item and a company holds it for any length of time, from minutes to months, it is likely to be classified as inventory.

Inventory is critical to a company's operations. It takes many forms in many places throughout the supply chain. Inventory within a typical manufacturing company includes:

- *raw materials*, goods unprocessed or minimally processed from their natural state and to be used to assemble or produce a finished product;

- *work-in-process*, partially finished goods which are likely to be finished at a later point in the supply chain;

- *finished goods*, fully assembled, produced, or manufactured goods to be delivered to the customer; and

- *maintenance, repair, and operating (MRO) supplies*, goods essential to a company's operations, but not used to become part of the finished product.

These four types of inventory can be found throughout a product's entire supply chain, from the suppliers of the raw materials to the finished goods delivered to the final customer. Companies keep track of how much inventory there is at any location at any given time. They also track how much of what to order to maintain pre-established inventory levels. The goal is to ensure that the right inventory of the right quantity and quality is available at the right time and place within the company. To achieve this goal, companies use both *inventory management* and *inventory control*.

Inventory management occurs when a company keeps track of and organizes inventory to use it or distribute it when and where needed so that it can be reordered and replenished when and where needed. Inventory management helps companies in strategic decision making regarding inventory that can impact the company's bottom line.

Because of the amount of inventory and complexity of locations to be tracked and forecasted for order replenishment, companies often use *inventory management systems*. These systems combine network-based or cloud-based software and corresponding inventory-related hardware and company-specific inventory management processes. For example, a company could use an inventory management system specifically for inventory forecasting for future demand based on bar code tracking of how much inventory it orders and issues. This inventory management system would include handheld and conveyor barcode scanners, barcode label printers, software to manage the information about inventory based on inventory scanned, and company-specific processes programmed into the software regarding how inventory codes are assigned based on product type and supplier. Other inventory management systems include those based on:

- *materials requirement planning (MRP)*, a decision-making methodology used to determine the timing and quantities of materials to purchase;

- *manufacturing resource planning (MRP II)*, a decision-making methodology which integrates systemwide manufacturing, inventory, and finance operations to achieve optimum financial results in inventory and manufacturing resource control; and

- *distribution resource planning (DRP II)*, a system focused on receiving, warehousing, and holding goods at the lowest possible cost within the distribution system while still meeting customers' inventory needs through efficient distribution activities.

The essential objective of inventory management is ensuring that the right inventory of the right quantity and quality is available at the right time and place. The practice of **inventory control** monitors and regulates inventory and inventory levels to achieve a company's inventory management objectives. In a nutshell, inventory control is about how much inventory to hold and where to hold it. Some of the inventory control techniques used in warehouses include:

- *economic order quantity (EOQ)*, an inventory model that determines how much inventory to order by determining the inventory holding level or the amount that will meet customer service levels while minimizing ordering and holding costs;

- *just-in-time (JIT)*, an inventory control methodology that typically involves holding very little inventory developed by the Japanese auto industry that controls material flow into assembly and manufacturing plants by coordinating demand and supply to the point where desired materials arrive just in time for use;

- *ABC analysis*, a classification system used to help companies place their range of inventory into categories based on which items are used and issued most frequently;

- *safety stock inventory*, the practice of holding extra quantities of items in inventory beyond typical demand in case something unusual happens and additional inventory is needed; and

- *vendor managed inventory (VMI)*, the practice of allowing the supplier to take full responsibility for the goods held in the customer's warehouse, especially in terms of managing inventory availability.

Inventory represents a substantial financial asset on an organization's balance sheet. An essential part of inventory control is ensuring that the inventory held corresponds to the inventory represented within the company's computer-based or cloud-based inventory control records, which typically inform its inventory management systems. A full *physical inventory check* must be conducted for most organizations to provide validated inventory quantities for the company's annual financial accounts. A ***physical inventory check***, also called a ***physical inventory*** or ***physical count***, occurs when a company manually counts its items held in inventory. Common forms of physical inventory checking include:

- ***periodic inventory checking***, in which a complete physical inventory check is performed at timed intervals. Typically, these intervals occur quarterly or at the end of the fiscal year. A periodic inventory check is sometimes carried out on a non-working day or during off-hours because the warehouse is closed and allows inventory checkers the time and space to count carefully and check discrepancies.

- ***continuous inventory checking***, in which a section of items within a warehouse is checked every week throughout a twelve-month period. This form of inventory checking allows a warehouse to continue operating 365 days a year.

- ***spot checking***, which is designed to verify portions of the inventory held without prior notification to warehouse staff. Spot checking is used primarily as a security and antitheft measure and not for final annual inventory calculations. It is usually used in combination with other forms of physical inventory checking.

FIGURE 4.20 - EVIDENCE OF A PHYSICAL INVENTORY CHECK AT A LOCAL RETAILER

Holding inventory can be very expensive for an organization. Whether a company maintains inventory in a warehouse for two days or two weeks or two years, there is a corresponding cost. The cost of keeping inventory, called the ***inventory holding cost*** or the ***carrying cost***, is made up of the cost of the warehouse space, the cost to heat or cool the space, warehouse electricity and insurance costs, taxes, the cost of handling the items while they move into and out from the warehouse, the cost of items breaking or being stolen, the administrative cost to manage the inventory, and the cost of the company's money being tied up in inventory when it could be invested elsewhere.

Despite this long list of expenses, it can be advantageous for a warehouse to hold inventory, especially when inventory deliveries are unreliable or when a company wants to take advantage of seasonal and bulk discounts from its suppliers. Companies also hold inventory to provide good customer service by ensuring they have enough inventory on hand to accommodate their customers' fluctuating demands. Manufacturing companies also hold inventory to reduce the chance of costly manufacturing stoppages if raw materials were to run out and to have flexibility in the size of production runs to adjust for new customers and changes in existing customers' orders.

Efficiency-minded companies manage and reduce this cost of inventory holding by determining the most efficient and effective inventory levels needed for individual items. To manage and control these inventory levels, companies must determine two key factors: **how much** to order or reorder and **when** to order or reorder. This information helps organizations supply a constant flow of inventory to their internal operations and external customers. Inventory management systems and inventory control techniques help get the information needed to establish optimum inventory levels and manage inventory flow.

CHAPTER 4 REVIEW QUESTIONS

1. What is the difference between *warehousing* and *warehouse management*?

2. What is a *fulfillment center*? How is it different from a *distribution center*?

3. Why might a *cross-docking* facility be useful for a company like Walmart?

4. In your first year of owning a small, new dog biscuit production company, would you be more likely to own or rent warehouse space? Why?

5. In your own words, describe the sections of a warehouse. Describe what might happen in each section of your dog biscuit warehouse.

6. In a warehouse, where would you be more likely to place goods that are issued frequently? Why?

7. What is a *unit load*? Why is it beneficial in warehouse operations? What is an example of a unit load that you have seen in a store?

8. What are two of the core structures of the unit load? Describe the size and function of each.

9. What is the difference between *transport equipment* and *positioning equipment* in materials handling?

10. What is *inventory control*? How is it related to *inventory management*? What benefits might both bring to a company?

CHAPTER 4 CASE STUDY

ACCUBAR AND BEVERAGE INVENTORY MANAGEMENT

When we think of inventory management, we tend to think of massive warehouses or even acres of external inventory yards. Although there is nary a warehouse building nor an external inventory yard in sight, restaurants carry a significant amount of inventory that must be processed and managed. There are food ingredients to manage, and there are also plates, glasses, menus, bathroom supplies, and thousands of gallons of beverages that customers consume every day. Restaurants that offer even a standard variety of alcoholic beverages bring more complexity to the inventory that must be maintained. There are many types of alcoholic beverages with a dazzling degree of variation within each type, including variation by brand, age, and price. Restaurants and bars that offer a range of wines must maintain an even more complicated degree of variety within their alcohol inventory because they may stock hundreds of different wines, varying in price, rating, type, winery, and region and year of production.

You might think that maintaining an alcohol inventory would be as simple as placing a bottle on a shelf and pouring from it as needed. However, with hundreds of bottles to maintain, how can a bartender know where to find each bottle needed? How can a restaurant manager know when stock is running low on specific wines or liquors or if certain alcohols are just not selling? Worse yet, how can a restaurant owner know when money is being lost because bartenders are offering free drinks to friends or bottles of champagne are finding their way into employees' rucksacks?

Restaurant and bar managers can manage a complex inventory of hundreds of wines, liquors, and beers using a beverage management system. One such system popular with many American restaurants and bars is AccuBar, a cloud-based beverage inventory system that utilizes handheld scanning devices, smartphones, and tablets. The system can manage inventory, process incoming orders from suppliers, establish automatic reorder points, and identify slow-moving stock.

Used in Wolfgang Puck's restaurants and Jimmy Buffett's Margaritaville chain, AccuBar is based on a simple bar code scanning system. For example, when receiving wine orders from suppliers, a restaurant scans the bar code on each wine bottle using the handheld scanner. Scanning into the AccuBar system allows the incoming inventory to be checked for discrepancies or breakage before the supplier's driver even thinks about hopping back into the truck and driving away. For bottles that do not have barcodes, AccuBar can assign bar codes and create labels to print and affix to these items as they arrive.

To make inventory management even simpler, AccuBar creates barcoded neck tags that can be affixed to bottles with or without bar codes to make scanning easier so that bartenders don't have to search for elusive bar codes in dimly lit bars. With bar code labels or neck tags firmly in place, restaurant employees use handheld devices to scan bottles when checking inventory or when taking them from inventory, such as when you have decided at long last to buy that bottle of Dom Perignon. When checking inventory, a drawing function on the handheld device allows the checker to draw a line on a picture of the beverage bottle to show the quantity remaining in the actual bottle.

Smartphones and tablets can also be used and run through the AccuBar app for both iPhone and Android when initially scanning incoming inventory. As bar codes are scanned, the handheld device, phone, or table sends information to a cloud-based beverage management system. The AccuBar system can generate instant reports on inventory held, beverage cost percentages, which beverages are slow movers, if any inventory is missing, or if there is too much of an item.

The AccuBar system interfaces with restaurant POS (point of sale) systems. Establishments using the AccuBar system have found that they have increased their inventory management efficiency and accuracy, reduced their long-term information technology costs, and improved loss prevention. It's much harder to steal or misuse alcohol when someone can easily find out if it's missing!

AccuBar also has an iWineList app for tablets and smartphones. The app provides an accurate and complete wine list based on the restaurant or bar's AccuBar system data. Customers can use a tablet to search through hundreds of wines using criteria such as winery, type, region, price, ratings, and year. Some restaurants and bars have reported a 10 to 20% increase in wine sales after switching to iWineList, perhaps because people are more apt to experiment or go outside their price range when they have more information. As one wine steward explained, people seem more likely to trust the device than the waiters.

Reference:
Accubar website. (2020) Retrieved from http://www.accubar.com/

Chapter 5

Outbound Logistics: The Order Cycle and Outbound Goods

You have read the past couple of chapters. You know all about the inbound activities of logistic management, especially those related to buying goods and storing goods — or purchasing and warehouse management, to be more exact! Let's imagine that you are Sue the Superior Supply Chain Manager. You manage the warehouse for Faux Vintage Fashion, a regional clothing chain that sells clothing, shoes, and jewelry that brand new but appear vintage, catering to the busy hipster on a budget. You order a wide variety of goods for the 25 Faux Vintage Fashion stores across the Pacific Northwest of the United States and Canada. These goods come from different suppliers across Asia, Mexico, and Eastern Europe. Black beaded flapper dresses, faun colored fedoras, pink poodle skirts, Mad Men menswear, bell-bottom bluejeans, mint-colored moon boots, and shoulder pad suit jackets all find their way to your warehouse.

As fabulous fashions come into the warehouse, you know exactly how to receive, store, and handle them. And because you read Chapter 4, you even perform regular physical inventory checks to ensure all your inventory is accounted for and still in good condition. You've got a full warehouse, but now what? You don't want to be all dressed up with nowhere to go, so you decide to read Chapter 5 to learn about the first stages of outbound logistics: responding to orders and getting goods out the door and on the way to customers!

FIGURE 5.1 - OUTBOUND LOGISTICS ACTIVITIES FROM A CLOTHING WAREHOUSE

5.1 PHYSICAL DISTRIBUTION MANAGEMENT

A few chapters ago, we mentioned that the management of outbound logistics activities is called ***physical distribution management***, particularly in the world of manufacturing and production. Physical distribution management aims to manage outbound logistics activities to ensure that external customers receive the right finished goods of the right quantity and quality and at the right time and place while minimizing related costs and maximizing customer service. Physical distribution managers can minimize costs, for example, by picking orders quickly and accurately, and they can maximize customer service by ensuring that packing materials are matched to the right size for the product and will keep the product safe during shipping. Have you ever received an item the size of a grapefruit rolling around in a box the size of a small child? And then had to deal with disposing of the gargantuan box that won't fit in your trash can?

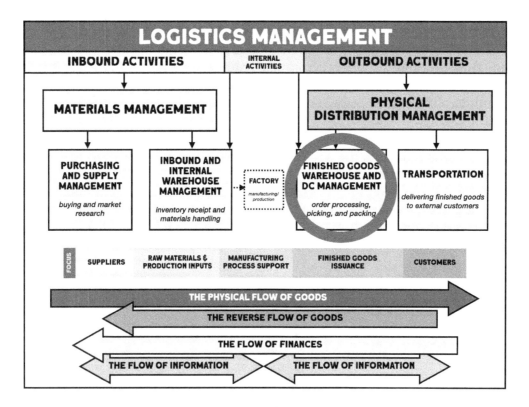

FIGURE 5.2 - OUTBOUND FROM THE WAREHOUSE IN THE LOGISTICS MANAGEMENT MODEL

Physical distribution management is concerned with the outbound movement of a company's finished products to the next location in the supply chain, whether it's to an external customer or another warehouse or location in the same company. Extractors of raw materials, producers of component parts or semifinished goods, and manufacturers of finished goods are all engaged in physical distribution management.

Each type of organization has its own finished product, even though it may bear little resemblance to the final product seen by the end user. A bauxite ore extractor is engaged in physical distribution management after extracting ore from the ground and sending it to its direct customer, an aluminum processing plant. The aluminum processing plant is likewise engaged in physical distribution management after producing large aluminum sheets from the bauxite ore received and sending the aluminum sheets to its customer, a bicycle manufacturer. Finally, the bicycle manufacturer is also engaged in physical distribution management after producing bicycles with frames made from the aluminum sheets and sending finished bikes to their national retail chain customers' regional distribution centers. The original finished product, bauxite ore, bears little resemblance to the final finished product, a children's bicycle. Despite the differences in the products involved, the same practices and principles of physical distribution management occur throughout the entire supply chain.

FINISHED PRODUCT ➡ FINISHED PRODUCT ➡ FINISHED PRODUCT
BAUXITE ORE   ALUMINUM SHEETS   CHILDREN'S BICYCLES

FIGURE 5.3 - DIFFERENT FINISHED PRODUCTS IN THE SAME SUPPLY CHAIN

Furthermore, many of the practices and principles found in physical distribution management and the outbound flow of goods also apply to supply management and the inbound flow of goods. For example, after our bicycle manufacturer assembles its finished product, the Raging Roadster Dirt Bike, it must store and move finished bicycles to get them to regional distribution centers for its customer, Safe-T-Toys. When it receives the finished Raging Roadsters, Safe-T-Toys must also move and store the finished bicycles as part of its inbound logistics management. The finished bikes are stored at warehouses and moved around by forklift at both the manufacturer's facility and the Safe-T-Toys facility. However, the first is an outbound logistics activity, and the second is an inbound logistics activity. Because Chapter 4 covered the basics of goods movement and storage, this chapter will focus on those activities and principles unique to *outbound* logistics processes.

Since the start of the industrial age, companies became focused on the manufacturing function, such as the cost of acquiring raw materials and producing the finished product. The activities covered within the realm of physical distribution management were given little consideration and merely regarding as necessary delivery functions. The oil crisis of the 1970s changed all that as oil prices skyrocketed, making those critical delivery functions very expensive. The entire supply chain was now under scrutiny as a possible means of reducing a company's operating costs. This holistic focus gave birth to three functional areas in manufacturing companies: procurement, materials management, and physical distribution.

Like its procurement and materials management counterparts, physical distribution management is an important area within logistics management. When practiced efficiently and effectively, physical distribution management can:

- **minimize cost.** With efficient physical distribution management, especially at the global level, a company can significantly reduce logistics costs. One core outbound logistics activity is physically taking items from warehouse shelves based on customers' orders, also known as order picking. Let's imagine that a multinational candy manufacturer called Ewwey Gooey, Inc. implemented improvements to its order picking process worldwide. This improvement shaved 3 minutes from each large order picked from warehouse shelves. With 200 orders picked every day at each of its 200 warehouses worldwide, Ewwey Gooey has now reduced its global order picking time by 2000 hours daily with its simple 3-minute order picking improvement. With a $20 per hour average worldwide salary for its order pickers, Ewwey Gooey has saved itself $40,000 per day! Reductions in order picking time and similar physical distribution practices can significantly decrease an organization's overall logistics costs. With the company operating five days a week for 52 weeks a year, this order picking improvement has saved the company a whopping $10,400,000 in one year!

- **increase customer service.** Effective physical distribution management can have an enormous impact on the customer service an organization provides. With the popularity of e-commerce and just-in-time deliveries, customers expect to receive goods shortly after ordering them. Just think about the last time you ordered something online and how frustrating it felt when you had to wait five whole days for it. Gasp! The more effective its physical distribution management practices, the closer a company can come to on-time deliveries to customers. In some locations, customers can choose to have amazon.com deliver goods in under an hour or choose to have them delivered at a later date for credit toward digital book and music purchases.

- **work to fulfill marketing's promises.** A company's Marketing Department promises its customers that they will receive the right quantity and quality of goods at the time and place desired. Without efficient and effective physical distribution management, it would be impossible for an organization to fulfill these promises, leading to future sales declines. Have you ever seen a super-fantastic sale advertised, only to show up at the store, and they don't have the advertised item in stock? Most of us don't have the time to wait around until the item in stock. Instead, we tend to check out a few other stores to see if they have a similar sale or even ask them to price-match the original store's sale.

For the remainder of this chapter, we will examine the initial stages of physical distribution management and the role it plays in: responding to an organization's order cycle, handling and preparing outbound goods through effective picking and packing, servicing the Marketing Department's distribution channels, and engaging in reverse logistics.

5.2 RESPONDING TO THE ORDER CYCLE

A critical part of outbound logistics management and effective physical distribution management in a company is the *order cycle* and its ability to respond. The **order cycle** is the process and time involved for a company to process an order from a customer, from the moment the company receives a customer's order until the moment the customer receives the goods ordered. The order cycle is also known as **order-to-cash**, **OTC**, and **O2C**. In Chapter 3, we looked at the *purchasing process*, which we defined as the entire process of purchasing a good or service from the moment the company expresses a need for a particular product to the moment the product is received and the purchasing order is closed out. The purchasing process focuses on the activities involved in ordering goods from the *buyer's* perspective. The *order cycle* focuses on the activities involved in receiving an order for goods and filling the order, all from the *supplier's* perspective.

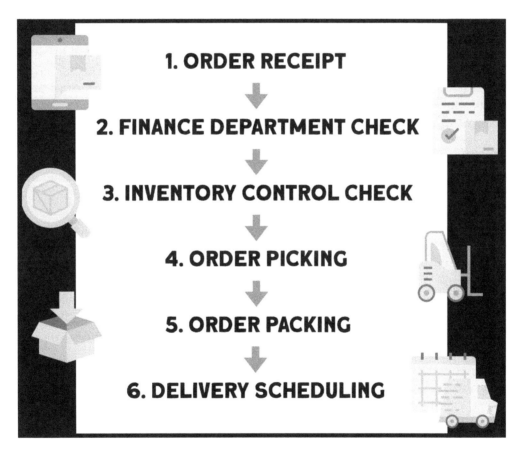

FIGURE 5.4 - ORDER CYCLE FROM THE SUPPLIER'S PERSPECTIVE

For efficient and effective physical distribution management, a supplier must respond to the six steps of the order cycle. One of the goals of physical distribution management is for a company to achieve competitive advantage. Companies can do this by reducing the **order** *cycle time*, the amount of time it takes to complete the entire order cycle through its six steps. These six steps and how they have an impact on overall order cycle time are:

1. **Order Receipt.** During the purchasing process, the buyer desires specific items from a supplier and places an order for them, typically through a purchase order or purchase agreement. During *order receipt*, the first stage of the order cycle, the supplier receives a buyer's purchase order. The degree to which a company's order receipt procedures are automated and digitized has a substantial impact on overall order cycle time. For example, during the order receipt stage for a small yarn company called Yabba Dabba Yarns, purchase orders are received by email and by phone. Yes, by phone. You are probably thinking, "How 2010!" The Yabba Dabba Yarns employee receiving the order by phone or email manually enters the order into its computer ordering system. Then, the employee prints and hand-delivers the order to the company warehouse for order picking. Yabba Dabba's competitor, Serious Strings and Things, has streamlined its order receipt process by receiving buyers' purchase orders through its website and smartphone app. These cloud-based orders are then sent directly to the warehouse for pre-approved buyers. Order receipt at Yabba Dabba Yarns may take up to one or two hours, but it takes less than a second at Serious Strings and Things! Yabba Dabba Yarns is not unique in its order receipt procedures. Many small to medium companies cannot afford to invest in the information technology infrastructure for fully automated, digitized, and cloud-based order receipt.

2. **Finance Department Check.** After the buyer's order is received, if the order is not pre-paid or from a pre-approved buyer, it is sent to the supplier's Finance Department to verify the customer's status. This check determines if the customer is a pre-existing one, is in good credit standing with the company, and has preexisting sales and service terms, such as if orders are sent before payment. With a digitized and automated system, the Finance Department check may take only seconds. Suppose a supplier does not have well-kept records about its previous transactions with buyers. In that case, the Finance Department may spend ridiculously large amounts of time checking up on past buyers and extra resources in unnecessary credit checks. It may even mistakenly approve buyers who have defaulted in the past! Finally, companies often skip this step when customers pre-pay for orders or are pre-approved.

3. **Inventory Control Check.** After the Finance Department approves the buyer's order, it sends the order to the Inventory Control Department or system, which then checks on the availability of the finished goods requested in the order. If the goods are available, Inventory Control then *allocates the requirements* or, for those of us not yet fully proficient in logistics jargon, assigns the desired goods located in inventory to the specific order. At the risk of sounding like a very broken record, this stage of the order cycle, too, can be made an instantaneous one with order processing automation and digitization, often with customers being able to see quantities of available items in inventory before even placing an order!

4. **Order Picking.** Now that the company has verified the customer's financial status and the items' availability, it can begin to get the items and fill the order. The items requested are *picked*, which means they are physically taken from inventory in the

warehouse. Later in this chapter, we will explore some of the techniques used for more efficient order picking.

5. **Order Packing.** After a company picks the items in the order, it prepares them for shipment. An order is ***packed*** (items are placed into packaging), ***unitized*** (items are placed into unit loads such as onto pallets or into containers), and physically prepared for shipping. Later in this chapter, we will explore order packing's influence on a company's bottom line.

6. **Delivery Scheduling.** Finally, after the inventory is picked and packed, the company schedules a delivery time and place with the customer through its transportation system. The delivery occurs through a ***distribution channel***, the route and means by which an organization distributes its finished goods. As with all six order cycle steps, companies can achieve greater scheduling efficiency and effectiveness when the process is automated, digitized, and wireless or cloud-based. Imagine a Walmart regional distribution center with 40 loading bays and a steady stream of container trucks, bringing goods in from suppliers and taking them away to retail stores. If the scheduling of the bays alone wasn't precise down to the minute, chaos might reign, with container trucks backed up for hours waiting for available bays.

Much of the first three steps of the order cycle are automated or conducted through digital systems. These are typically quick steps based on company-specific technology and procedures. Steps 4 through 6 may have technological support, but they are much more physical. These steps focus on the handling and movement of goods.

After an order has been received and checked as outlined in Steps 1 through 3, a company's finished goods are picked and packed from a warehouse, such as a separate warehouse building, a massive distribution center, a cross-docking facility, or a storage area near a manufacturing floor. Chapter 4 covered the concepts of warehousing and materials management, but the focus was on inbound activities. However, warehousing and materials handling occurs during both inbound and outbound logistics processes. The same principles and practices of warehousing and materials handling from inbound logistics apply to outbound logistics and physical distribution management, including the importance of product flow, unitization, and equipment utilization. For example, companies often use the same warehouse equipment for both inbound and outbound materials management. Imagine a small furniture retailer's warehouse. Goods have been waiting an extra two hours on a container truck at the inbound loading bay because the forklift for inbound materials was still charging its batteries, even though the forklift designated for outbound goods was currently not in use. Therefore, rather than covering old ground with the repetition of warehousing and materials handling concepts, let us charge ahead to explore a couple of new issues relevant to handling outbound goods.

5.3 ORDER PICKING

After Steps 1 through 3 have been accomplished and a company receives and checks an incoming order from a customer, the company is ready for ***order picking***, which is the physical distribution management activity of selecting a required quantity of specific goods from storage in response to an order received. Order picking also includes documenting when a company moves a needed amount of particular goods from a storage location to the packing or shipping area. The order picking stage can have a significant impact on a company's revenue saved or lost.

When companies pick items quickly, they can quickly fill and deliver orders, users are happy, and buyers pay the company sooner. When companies pick items slowly, orders take longer to fill, customers become annoyed, and customers do not pay the company until the order is filled. Within the world of order picking and physical distribution, there are various order picking techniques, the most common of which are: *single order picking*, *wave picking*, *batch picking*, *cluster picking*, and *zone picking*.

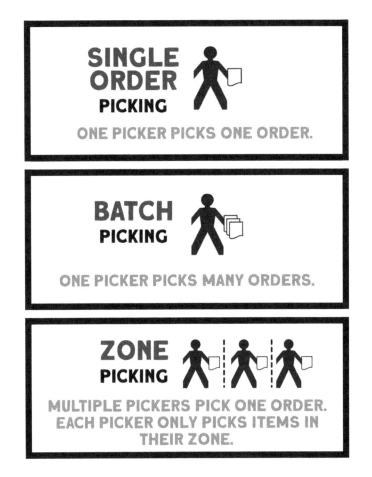

FIGURE 5.5 - THREE ORDER PICKING TECHNIQUES

In ***single order picking***, also known as ***discrete picking***, each order is picked by one person working from a single picking document for that order. Orders may be picked at any time within the picker's schedule, as long as the company meets the delivery deadline. Compared to other order picking styles, single order picking increases accountability and reduces errors, but it is slow and at the mercy of human limitations. One variation of single order picking is **wave picking**, in which orders are picked one item at a time by one picker, but the company schedules orders to be picked within specific timeframes.

In **batch picking**, one person picks multiple orders, or a *batch* of orders, following multiple picking documents simultaneously and typically picking the same item for multiple orders. Batch picking reduces the picker's traveling labor time by picking multiple orders at once but can increase the risk of incorrect selection and sorting. These risks are significantly reduced, however, in automated picking systems. A variation of batch picking is **cluster picking**. One person picks multiple orders simultaneously and places them into separate containers for each order immediately when selected. Like batch picking, cluster picking reduces the picker's traveling labor time, but unlike batch picking, the items picked may not necessarily be the same items across orders. In most large grocery stores, you are likely to see cluster picking when an employee travels around the store, picking items from various locations and placing them into different containers on a wheeled cart, each representing a delivery or curbside order for different customers.

FIGURE 5.6 - CART FOR CLUSTER PICKING AT A TESCO GROCERY STORE

In **zone picking**, a warehouse is divided into sections or *zones*. A different employee is assigned to each zone and is responsible for picking items within that zone. Pickers bring the items picked to the central order consolidation and issue section to *consolidate* the entire order. The items picked from different zones by different pickers are put together to fill one order in one shipment. Zone picking does not reduce the labor used, but it can speed up the order picking process in large or high volume warehouses.

In more extensive warehouse operations, automated and robotic order picking systems are used to assist order picking. Although these systems and their related equipment are costly to purchase and set up, they can save a significant amount in labor costs, dramatically reduce picking time, and increase order picking accuracy. Three forms of automated picking systems are:

- **handheld scanner picking,** in which the picker uses handheld equipment with a list of items to be picked or to scan barcodes from a printed list of items to be picked. The handheld equipment also allows the picker to view an optimal walking route for picking the order based on a warehouse map and scan the barcodes of items as they are picked. This handheld equipment may be a picking-specific mobile device or a smartphone with an inventory and picking system app, allowing smaller businesses to benefit from an automated picking system without being too expensive.

- **pick to light,** in which the person picking the order, the **picker**, uses handheld equipment to scan the barcode for the item to be selected, which makes a light illuminate immediately below the bin or shelf of the item. This system saves pickers considerable time and increased pick accuracy because they don't have to search for small numbers on shelves, especially with the chance of making mistakes at the end of a long day.

FIGURE 5.7 - PICK TO LIGHT ORDER PICKING SYSTEM

- **voice picking,** in which pickers wear a headset which tells them which item to pick next and exactly where the picker should go to find the item. After picking the item, the picker speaks into the headset to confirm that they have picked the item and are ready to get instructions for the next item. This system has a bonus of allowing the picker to operate entirely hands-free without holding a handheld scanning device, a tablet, or even a clipboard.

5.4 ORDER PACKING

After completing Step 4 of the order cycle, items for a customer's order have been picked from the warehouse and must undergo order *packing* in preparation for subsequent shipment. **Order packing** is the physical distribution management activity of placing goods securely into packages to be ready for outbound transportation. Goods are placed into physical materials for end-use, sale, storage, distribution, or transportation. These materials are called **packaging**. Additional materials to secure items internally are also called packaging, such as straps or styrofoam package filler. When goods are being picked in a warehouse before order packing occurs, there may already be multiple packaging layers. Imagine an order for 3000 boxes of lightbulbs. The company may store the lightbulbs on warehouse shelves in large boxes of 150 bulbs each. Within each of these large boxes are 50 smaller boxes of three lightbulbs per box. These smaller boxes are the ones the customer will see on store shelves. Within these smaller boxes are additional materials to keep the lightbulbs from breaking during storage and transport. These materials are all examples of packaging, from the larger boxes to the smaller boxes to the materials in the smaller boxes. And this is before the warehouse has packed the order for shipping!

Items from the picked order are packed to ensure they are safe and secure in transit to the next location in the supply chain, which means that a new layer of packaging is added during the order packing process. This process of order packing has an enormous impact on the efficiency and effectiveness of the supply chain. Poor order packing can lead to stolen or broken products, less efficient use of transportation and subsequent storage space, and materials handling equipment malfunction. Efficient and effective order packing and the packaging used, however, should:

- *Keep items safe and secure.* Insufficient or inadequate packaging can damage items in transit. When packaging can be opened too easily, items can be stolen by opportunity thieves at any point along the supply chain.

- *Be easily labeled, transported, and stored.* Packaging must be easily labeled so that the customer's inventory receipt department can identify its contents. Packaging must also meet a supplier's and customers' requirements for transportation and storage. For example, companies may have to design packaging to be placed and stacked easily onto pallets or into containers during the order packing process. It may also have to be placed onto storage racks of specific dimensions.

- *Be handled properly by materials handling equipment.* Packed goods will inevitably be handled at both the producer's and customer's facilities. Packaging must be easily handled by both the supplier's and the customer's materials handling equipment, which are not necessarily the same. For example, packaging may have to be handled by a forklift truck at one location and a conveyor at another.

For physical distribution management, packaging provides necessary safety and security for valuable goods. Without it, goods can lose all of their value in transit. Just imagine the mess, spoilage, and smell of a truckload of raw eggs being transported loosely in 3'x 3' boxes! Within the world of physical distribution management, packaging presents a bit of a conundrum. For items to be the safest and most secure, extra layers of thick packaging are required. However, both the materials used and the extra space consumed for this safe and secure packaging are quite costly. Therefore, many companies are now looking at cost-efficient yet effective packaging. For example, organizations are looking for "greener," reusable packaging, and packaging that allows for more space utilization.

FIGURE 5.8 - STACKING AND UNITIZATION INSTRUCTIONS ON PACKAGING

5.5 SERVICING MARKETING'S DISTRIBUTION CHANNELS

After a customer's order has been picked and packed, the next step is to schedule the order delivery. Different companies have different delivery scheduling systems and procedures. Still, the uniform concept is that deliveries are scheduled and subsequently conducted through the *distribution channel* to the customer. So what is a distribution channel?

A ***distribution channel*** is a marketing term for the series, or *channel*, of companies that goods pass through after leaving the seller, and the same goods reach the eventual end user. The companies involved in this physical flow of goods include distributors, logistics service providers, brick-and-mortar wholesalers and retailers, online wholesalers and retailers, and internet marketplaces.

Although there is overlap between a company's supply chain and its distribution channel, they are different concepts relevant to different disciplines. Way back in Chapter 1, we defined the supply chain as a company's network of goods, systems, information, and people that connects and moves goods between the company, its suppliers, and its final customers. The supply chain covers both the *inbound and outbound* flow of goods to a company that manufactures or produces a product. The distribution channel, however, is concerned solely with the *outbound* flow of goods. Also, the terms are from two different disciplines. *Supply chain* is a term from the world of logistics, while *distribution channel* is from marketing.

The Marketing Department of a company determines the nature and structure of its product's distribution channel and the level of service the company will provide. Selecting and following through on the most appropriate distribution channel structure will ensure that the customer receives the right quantity and quality of the right product at the right time and place. While the Marketing Department selects and designs the distribution channel, the Logistics Department carries out the Marketing Department's plans and strategy by physically moving goods through the distribution channel established. Therefore, it is the responsibility of physical distribution management to ensure that the company meets all of Marketing's distribution channel goals and promises to customers. Physical distribution management plays a significant role in servicing the Marketing Department's distribution channels.

Distribution channels are structured according to customers' needs, the nature of the product, and the supplier's location and nature. There are various distribution channels, with as few as two members or as many as five or more members. As the distribution channels become more complex, so must the corresponding physical distribution management system used to meet the Marketing Department's distribution channel delivery goals and the promises it has made to its customers. Let's now explore the three categories of distribution channels from simplest to most complex: *direct channel*, *indirect channel*, and *multichannel*.

Direct channel distribution is the simplest and shortest channel with only two members: the manufacturer and the end user. Channels of distribution are also named according to the number of levels of intermediary companies involved. A direct channel is the ***zero level channel*** because there are no intermediaries involved in the flow of goods between the manufacturer and the end user. Direct channel distribution occurs **between organizations** for large or expensive orders, often to save money with bulk discounts and without intermediaries' added expense. An example of this would be a home builder company that buys windows and doors in large quantities directly from a manufacturer like Andersen Corporation or The Pella Corporation. Direct channel distribution between two businesses can also occur when the manufacturer produces very expensive or one-off items, such as when Boeing makes aircraft for Ryanair, Turkish Airlines, and the United States federal government.

Direct channels of distribution also occur **between a manufacturer and individual end user**, often called a **_D2C_** or **_direct to consumer relationship_**. These D2C direct channels are often found:

1. *When the goods are perishable items in regional proximity,* such as when customers go directly to a nearby farm to buy produce or a local Starbucks coffee shop to buy a pound of freshly ground coffee.

2. When *a company provides additional services and product training for complex products,* such as Apple stores do for their computers, servers, smartphones, tablets, and wearable tech devices with Apple Genius Bars to provide customer support.

3. When *companies produce unique products for a niche market and sell directly* through their retail and online stores, such as LL Bean does for outdoor clothing or sixthreezero cruiser does for electric bicycles.

Things get a bit more complicated with **_indirect channel distribution_**, which occurs when goods pass through more than two channel members, including the manufacturer, the end user, and one of more intermediaries. These intermediaries can include distributors, logistics service providers, wholesalers, internet marketplaces, and retailers. These retail locations that are intermediaries do not belong to the original manufacturer, however. For example, when you go to a Krispy Kreme doughnut store to buy a dozen original glazed doughnuts, you are the end user in direct channel distribution. When you buy the same dozen of Krispy Kreme original glazed doughnuts, you are the end user in indirect channel distribution because Walmart is the intermediary retailer.

As previously mentioned, channels of distribution are also known by names according to the number of levels of intermediary companies involved. For indirect channel distribution, each intermediary company added to the channel increases the number of the channel name. For example, in a **_one level channel_**, goods would flow through one additional company in the path from manufacturer to end user. Let's pretend it's 2017, and you bought a pound of Starbucks coffee at a big box store or large retail chain, such as Target. You are the end user in a one level channel because Target is the retail intermediary between you and the manufacturer, Starbucks.

In a **_two level channel_**, goods would flow through two additional companies in the path from manufacturer to end user. Still pretending it's 2017, you buy a pound of Starbucks coffee this time at Zippy's, your local gas station convenience store. You are now the end user in a two level channel because Starbucks sells the coffee to a coffee distributor called Coffee Wholesalers, Inc., who sells the coffee to Zippy's Convenience Store, who sells the coffee to you as the end user.

Finally, in a **_three level channel_**, goods would flow through three additional companies in the path from manufacturer to end user. In three level channels, the additional company is typically an agent or distributor. This time, let's stop pretending and picture yourself in the present day. You are now again buying a pound of Starbucks coffee from Zippy's Convenience Store, but this time you are the end user in a three level channel. How can that be?

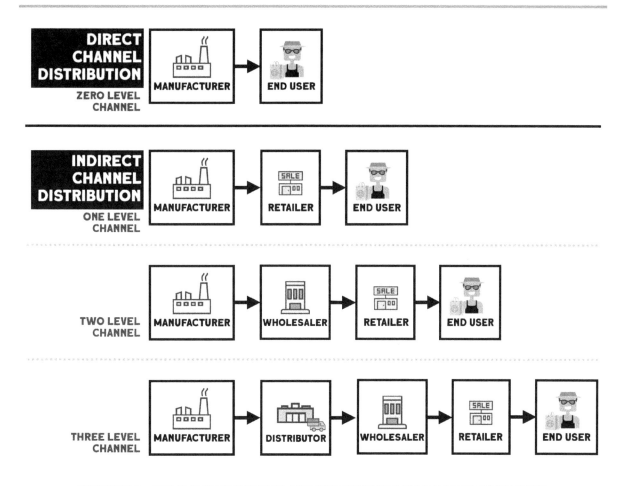

FIGURE 5.9 - EXAMPLES OF DIRECT AND INDIRECT CHANNELS OF DISTRIBUTION

Where did you pick up an extra intermediary? In 2018, Starbucks and Swiss food and drink giant Nestle signed a deal where Starbucks supplies the coffee beans and product name, but Nestle controls the retail operations for Starbucks bags of coffee and K-cups sold in retail stores. Starbucks provides the coffee to Nestle, who sells the coffee to a coffee distributor called Coffee Wholesalers, Inc., who sells the coffee to Zippy's Convenience Store, who sells the coffee to you, the end user.

Interestingly, in its relationship with Nestle and a similar relationship with PepsiCo for its bottled beverages, Starbucks lengthened its distribution channels while many industries in recent history are doing the reverse. In the 1980s and 1990s, you could only buy individual computers through a computer store or similar retailer that bought them either from a wholesaler or manufacturer. Today, many of us buy our laptop and desktop computers directly from the manufacturer's website or retail showroom with no intermediary companies involved. For decades in the United States, laws have required car manufacturers to sell new cars through dealer intermediaries, preventing direct-to-consumer sales. Tesla has been pushing the boundaries of this one level channel with its direct to consumer sales model.

There have been lawsuits and law changes allowing Tesla to shorten the car industry's distribution channel in many states.

Even the simple can of tuna has shortened its distribution channel over the past 50 years. In the 1970s, you would purchase a can of StarKist tuna at a small, locally-owned grocery store, who purchased it from a grocery supply coop, who bought it from a canned fish wholesaler, who purchased it from the manufacturer. In the 1980s and 1990s, the tuna distribution channel shortened by one level with the growing popularity of larger regional grocery store chains, who purchased directly from the wholesalers, thus eliminating the grocery store coop level. In the 2000s and 2010s, warehouse stores and big-box grocery stores like Costco and Walmart bought their tuna directly from the manufacturer, further shortening the distribution channel to one level channel when you purchased your cans of StarKist. In the 2020s, with the popularity of e-commerce and the move to online grocery shopping due to COVID-19 social distancing, end users could now buy their cans of StarFish tuna directly from the manufacturer via the amazon.com online marketplace. End users could even buy cans of their competitor's tuna, Wild Planet Albacore, straight from the manufacturer on their website, even for a discount of almost 50% for those willing to buy 48 cans.

The length of distribution channels for some industries has been shortening to save money on transportation and mark-ups costs. Imagine that every member of a channel added 25% to the end user price to cover the transportation, marketing, and administrative overhead costs that channel number *plus* their required profit. Therefore, a shirt that costs $20 to manufacture would cost the end user:

A. $25 if the manufacturer sold it to the end user directly;

B. $31.25 if the manufacturer sold it to a retailer who sold it to the end user;

C. $39.06 if the manufacturer sold it to a wholesaler who sold it to a retailer who sold it to the end user; or

D. $48.83 if the manufacturer sold it to a distributor who sold it to a wholesaler who sold it to a retailer who sold it to the end user.

There's a whopping 144% increase from the $20 cost to manufacture the shirt with the three level channel of distribution.

FIGURE 5.10 - DISTRIBUTION CHANNEL LENGTH AND END USER PRICE INCREASES

Some situations require longer distribution channels, mainly when multiple distribution channel members help manufacturers reach more markets through distributors, wholesalers, and online marketplaces. Multiple distribution channel members can also help companies focus on their core capabilities. For example, Starbucks focused on making coffee instead of putting it in bags or refrigerated beverage bottles and then getting it to grocery store shelves. In these situations, logistics managers work with the marketing department and other supply chain management team members to reduce supply chain costs, such as transportation and inventory holding costs. They must also rely on warehousing and transportation software systems to efficiently and effectively handle and transport goods through these longer channels and provide inventory visibility. With these systems, all distribution channel members know where the goods are and ensure no delays occur.

Some manufacturers reach their end-users most effectively through more than one distribution channel, known as *multichannel distribution*. Many of the companies mentioned in our earlier examples of direct and indirect channels use multichannel distribution, also known as *hybrid distribution channels*. For example, Apple uses a zero level channel when it sells computers directly to end users through its website and showroom stores. Still, it uses a one level channel when it sells computers through large retailers like BestBuy and Costco. Wild Planet uses a zero level channel when it sells tuna directly to end users through its website. The company takes it even further by using one, two, and three level distribution to reach end users when it sells through retailers, from big box stores to small local organic cooperatives.

Finally, although it's not a distribution channel, *omnichannels* is a related marketing concept that often gets mistaken for multichannel distribution. *Omnichannels* are the multiple marketing and sales channels (not distribution channels) that a company uses to reach its end users. With an *omnichannel retail strategy*, a company creates a seamless experience for customers between the multiple media used to reach them, such as websites, apps, print advertising, and the physical retail space. For example, a Starbucks customer has the same Starbucks experience whether they are

- using the Starbucks app to pre-order a coffee,

- browsing its website to find the closest retailer that sells its coffee beans,

- listening to music on its Spotify playlist,

- admiring beautiful cups of coffee from around the world on its Instagram page, or

- merely sitting in one of its local coffee shops and drinking a cup of coffee.

Through cross-over of products, sales, aesthetics, and even music between these multiple sales and marketing channels, Starbucks creates a seamless customer experience that is quintessentially Starbucks.

5.6 WHAT HAPPENS WHEN GOODS ARE OUT THE DOOR?

After completing the order cycle and goods have been picked, packed, and scheduled to be on their way through the distribution channel, what's next? Physical distribution management has a few more responsibilities after the ordered goods have left the warehouse and are on the way to the buyer. Three of these out-the-door activities at the tail end of physical distribution management are: *coordinating transportation, controlling inventory in the distribution system,* and *reverse logistics.*

Transportation forms the critical bridge between those who *have* the goods, such as manufacturing or warehouse facilities, and those who *want* the goods, such as retailers or customers. One role of the Physical Distribution Manager is **coordinating and controlling outbound transportation** of a company's finished goods, including transportation scheduling and management. When relevant, it also includes the management of third-party transportation suppliers. Chapter 6 will explore the topic of transportation in greater depth, including modes of transport and current transportation industry terminology, practices, and regulations.

FIGURE 5.11 - INVENTORY VISIBILITY WITH DELIVERY TRACKING APPS

Chapter 4 showed that inventory control systems help organizations determine the most efficient and effective inventory holding levels for individual items. Companies use **inventory control systems within physical distribution management** to stay informed about its inventory, including how much of an item is available and its exact location. Physical distribution managers should know where inventory is within the company's manufacturing or warehouse facility *and* within the supply chain or distribution channel. Different locations and companies within the supply chain use information technology to share accurate and real-time information about inventory location. This technology creates *inventory visibility*, real-time knowledge of the location and quantities of inventory, even when it is no longer under the supplier's control, such as in the truck of a third-party logistics service provider or waiting in the loading bay of a customer. Inventory visibility allows organizations to plan more effectively for manufacturing, warehousing, and transportation operations. It also helps reduce costs by allowing an organization to move more to just-in-time operations and hold less just-in-case inventory.

Inventory visibility also enhances customer service because it helps a company control how to get the right quantity and quality of finished goods to the exact time and place customers desire. Inventory visibility is possible through technology systems and hardware, such as computerized inventory information systems, bar code printing and scanning, radio frequency identification technology, Global Positioning System technology, and wireless connectivity. Don't worry. We'll explain all of these concepts later in Chapter 7 when we uncover the exciting world of information technology in the supply chain!

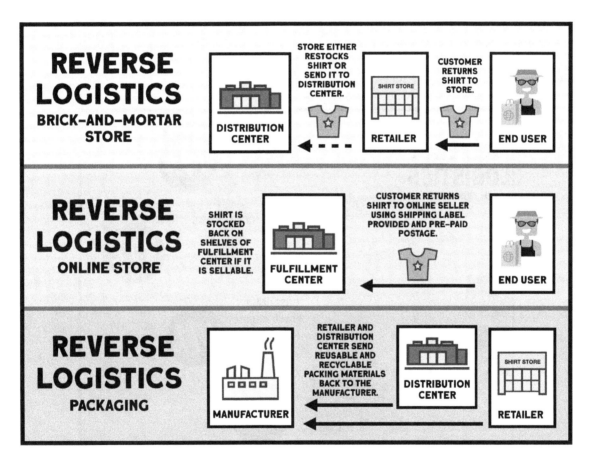

FIGURE 5.12 - REVERSE LOGISTICS FOR PRODUCTS AND PACKAGING

After the supplier delivers goods to the buyer, there is sometimes a corresponding backward flow of related goods from the buyer to the supplier. As covered in Chapter 1, this ***reverse supply chain*** is the flow of goods and related resources from the customer back to the supplier in a network of supporting systems, information, and people. After a product has been sold and delivered to a customer, reverse supply chains begin when goods or related resources flow back to the supplier as product returns, damaged goods to be repaired, and items to be recycled or reused. The area of supply chain management that focuses on reverse supply chains is called *reverse logistics*.

Reverse logistics occurs if there are product and packaging returns. With online purchases continuing to rise year after year, product returns also continue to grow. According to invespcro.com, customers return almost 9% of products purchased from brick-and-mortar stores while returning approximately 30% from online purchases. Effective and well planned reverse logistics is an essential part of product returns. An overwhelming majority of buyers report they would be repeat shoppers for an online retailer if their returns process is easy and if return shipping is free. Packaging returns is also an essential part of reverse logistics as consumers and companies are increasingly environmentally conscious. Some customers prefer to buy from suppliers who can recycle or reuse order packaging when returned. Companies must consider incorporating reverse logistics and inventory visibility into its supply chain to meet customers' needs. Physical distribution managers must be ready for the influx of products and packaging returning backwards up the supply chain,

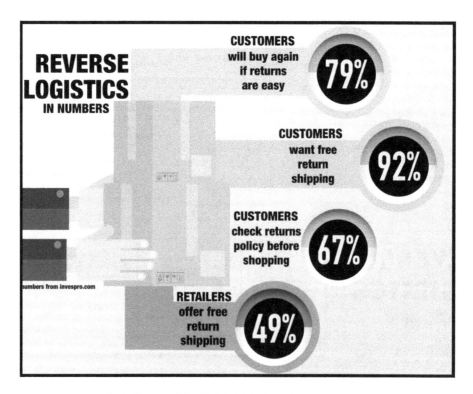

FIGURE 5.13 - REVERSE LOGISTICS BY NUMBERS

CHAPTER 5 REVIEW QUESTIONS

1. What is *physical distribution management*? What benefits can effective physical distribution management bring to a company?

2. How are the *purchasing process* and the *order cycle* similar? How are they different?

3. After a company receives an order from a customer, what checks does the supplier perform? How and why are these checks conducted?

4. If you were setting up *order picking* function in a small furniture warehouse, which type of order picking would you be least likely to use from the choice of single, batch, and zone picking? Why?

5. What are the benefits of *voice picking systems*? What are the benefits of *pick to light systems*? In what situations might a company choose to use one system over the other?

6. Why is *packaging* important in preparing goods for transportation?

7. What are *distribution channels*? How are they similar and different from supply chains?

8. What is the shortest distribution channel? Why might a company choose this channel type?

9. How did Starbucks' relationships with Nestle and PepsiCo change its distribution channels?

10. What is *inventory visibility*? Describe an example of when you have ordered something online and had either good or bad inventory visibility from the supplier.

CHAPTER 5 CASE STUDY

PHYSICAL DISTRIBUTION: THE WALMART ADVANTAGE

If you live anywhere in the United States, you have most likely been to a Walmart store. These enormous stores sell everything from clothing to electronics to furniture to groceries, all with Walmart's promise of "Everyday Low Prices." Since 1962, this Arkansas-based discount store has grown to a gargantuan worldwide retail chain with 2.2 million employees and annual sales of over $524 billion. Walmart's popularity and explosive growth have been attributed to its ability to offer a wide range of goods at prices consistently lower than its competitors. The company's undying ability to offer low prices lies in its ability to control its physical distribution management structure and costs. Ah, the power of logistics!

The roots of the retail giant lie in rural America. In its nascency, Walmart located its stores in small country towns not served by reliable distributors. To get affordable and dependable shipments of discount goods, the company decided to purchase a fleet of trucks and establish its own distribution network. Over the years, Walmart's fleet has grown to 6,100 trucks, 61,000 trailers, and 7,800 truck drivers. Complete control of its trucking network allows the company to control its distribution channels and schedule. Peak seasonal deliveries, nighttime deliveries, and expedited shipments when rush orders are needed are all easily accommodated, allowing the company to replenish its shelves four times faster than comparable discount chains. For example, if your local Walmart suddenly ran out of an unexpected must-have Christmas toy, you are very likely to find it restocked on Walmart shelves in a short day or two.

In addition to owning a significantly sized fleet of trucks, Walmart also owns and operates an extensive network of 162 distribution centers. Each distribution center is larger than one million square feet and operated by highly advanced information technology systems, RFID and barcoding systems, and automated materials handling equipment. You are also likely to find people and hand trucks there, too! At least one distribution center (DC) provides service for every store owned by Walmart, and each DC accommodates approximately 100 retail stores surrounding it in a 150-mile radius. In 2020, 79% of Walmart's in-store merchandise came through one of its distribution centers. Some of the distribution centers are specialized, with six disaster distribution centers located across the country for rapid response to natural disasters.

Another critical component of Walmart's physical distribution system is the practice of cross-docking, which speeds goods rapidly through the supply chain and decreases the need to store goods in its distribution centers. Suppliers' trucks pull up to a Walmart distribution center, and goods are immediately pulled from these trucks and placed onto a series of Walmart trucks bound for different retail stores. The amount placed on each Walmart truck is precisely the amount of goods that a store needs. This practice allows for goods to be delivered quickly without having to be inventoried and stored. With the extensive use of cross-docking and distribution centers, Walmart stores can receive goods and get them on the shelves in under 48 hours from the time goods are requested.

One of the company's standard physical distribution practices is real-time connectivity between its distribution centers and the Electronic Point of Sale (EPOS) system in each of its retail stores. When a customer buys an item, it is scanned at the cash register into the store's EPOS system. This information is sent directly to the distribution center servicing the store so that it knows to send one more of the item the customer just purchased. This IT connection between the store and its distribution center allows for immediate order placement and fulfillment and is connected to inventory management systems, allowing for constant inventory visibility.

Walmart has also been growing a network of 40 e-commerce fulfillment centers across the country to respond to its online and app sales. Its primary website gets 100 million visitors per month. They can shop through Walmart's programs such as NexDay Shipping, Online Grocery Pickup, Grocery Delivery, and Express Delivery. In their omnichannel strategy, customers can shop or find product information in stores, on the Walmart website, or through the Walmart app, all of which offer a uniquely "Walmart" experience. Walmart saw its newly expanded e-commerce and fulfillment centers tested during the Covid-19 pandemic because its e-commerce sales grew a whopping 74% in just one fiscal quarter from February through April in 2020.

Thanks to its leading practices in physical distribution management and its flexibility to adapt to online customers' needs, Walmart holds on to its place as one of the world's largest companies and the number one largest in sales for the 2020 fiscal year.

References:
Walmart website. (2020) Retrieved from http://www.walmart.com/
Walmart. (2020) Walmart Inc. 2020 Annual Report. Retrieved from http://www.walmart.com/

Chapter 6

Outbound Logistics: Transportation

At the beginning of Chapter 3, we asked you to look around and notice all the items purchased by someone. Look around again and note all the items near you that have been purchased by someone at some time. Now consider each of these items on your *purchased* list. Where was each of them made? If you're not sure, pick the items up, turn them over, and look for a "Made in" label. Were they all made in your hometown? Better still, were any of them even made within 500 miles of where you are standing or sitting right now?

Chances are, few of the purchased items in your surroundings were made within 500 miles of you, and most were probably manufactured in another country. But how did these items find their way to your surroundings? Did they suddenly sprout up from the ground one day, or did Scottie beam them down from the Starship Enterprise overhead? Unless you have a far more exciting life than most of us or know something about *Star Trek* that the rest of us don't know, neither of these options is possible, so the items must have arrived at your location by way of **transportation**.

6.1 INTRODUCING TRANSPORTATION

The focus of logistics and supply chain management is the physical flow of goods. What provides, supports, and propels this flow? Transportation! The essential activity of transportation forms the backbone of logistics and supply chain management. Without it, these disciplines would not exist.

Transportation is the act of moving goods or people from one place to another using a vehicle, infrastructure, or both. In logistics and supply chain management, transportation focuses primarily on the movement of *goods* to a desired location. Transportation of goods forms the critical bridge between where goods are located and where goods are desired, such as between manufacturing or warehousing facilities and immediate customers' locations.

In our model of logistics management activities, transportation is one of the main categories of outbound logistics activities within the area of physical distribution management. One of the roles of a company's Physical Distribution Manager is to coordinate and control their company's finished goods' outbound transportation.

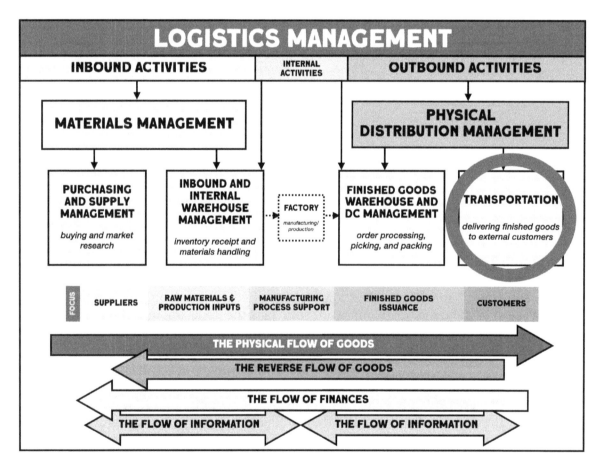

FIGURE 6.1 - TRANSPORTATION IN THE LOGISTICS MANAGEMENT MODEL

Transportation is critical not only to physical distribution, logistics, and supply chain management but also to the entire global economy. As most of the world has moved away from localized, hunter-gatherer, and farming economies during the past few thousand years, transportation has become an increasingly essential element to human comfort and survival. It plays a critical role in providing us with the food we eat, the clothes on our backs, the medicine we take, and the homes where we live. As a result, transportation plays a significant role in the economy of markets around the world. The GDP for the transportation industry for 2019 alone was a staggering $561.2 billion, and the US Bureau of Transportation Statistics' *2020 Pocket Guide to Transportation* reports that overall transportation-related expenditures formed 9% of the US gross domestic product in 2019.

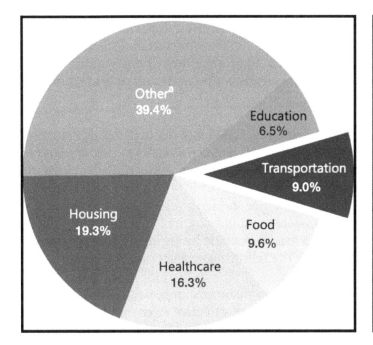
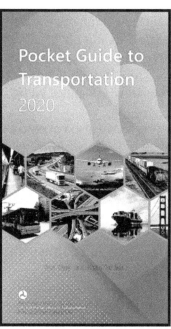

FIGURE 6.2 - US GROSS DOMESTIC PRODUCT BY MAJOR SPENDING CATEGORY

Transportation also allows countries to engage in global trade and build strong relationships with other countries worldwide. As we will explore later in this chapter, changes in transportation legislation and regulation in the 1970s and 1980s have led to dramatic global trade growth over the past fifty years. For example, the value of global trade exports grew from $318.02 billion in 1970 to $19.45 trillion in 2018.

6.2 TRANSPORTATION UTILITY AND TRADEOFFS

In Chapter 2, we introduced the concept of utility. Remember that, along with minimizing cost and maximizing customer service, logistics and supply chain management create value for the members of a supply chain. This value is also called **utility**, a term from economics that refers to customer satisfaction when they consume a company's goods or services. The four types of utility are *form*, *time*, *place*, and *possession*, but only two fall squarely within the realm of transportation.

Place utility is the value added to goods when they are at the right place within the supply chain, exactly where a company's internal and external customers want them. Place utility is created by effective transportation and physical distribution management, which helps a company send their outbound finished goods to customers' desired locations and receive inbound goods from geographically distant or widely dispersed suppliers whose products may be cheaper or better quality.

Time utility is the value added to goods when they are available exactly when both internal and external customers want them. Like place utility, time utility results from effective transportation and physical distribution management. Transportation decisions and optimization allow a company's Logistics Department to provide time and place value to its customers. This chapter will explore various transportation decisions and optimization methods that offer time and place value.

In Chapter 2, we also covered the tradeoff principle. When making logistics decisions and balancing the competing objectives of *reducing costs* versus *increasing customer service*, logistics managers use the ***tradeoff principle***. Under this principle, the advantages and disadvantages of decisions are weighed based on the degree to which they provide: maximization of cost savings, resource use, and customer service level increases. Transportation decisions play a significant strategic role in determining a company's total supply chain costs and service levels. Transportation decisions are often made by striking a balance between the advantages and disadvantages offered by the following six criteria:

- **Cost.** Transportation costs increase as delivery distances increase, making cost a central factor in determining the geographic limits for cost-effective sales or purchases. While you may prefer the taste of strawberries grown in Egypt and Spain, unless you are a millionaire, you may have to consider the prohibitive cost of transportation and settle for California-grown strawberries if you live in California.

- **Speed.** For many products or situations, speedy delivery times may be more important than the delivery cost. For example, quick delivery is essential for perishable goods, such as Maine lobster and Alaska King crab, both of which must be flown to their hungry customers. Goods immediately necessary to a large manufacturing operation also need a speedy delivery, such as a spare part required to repair an ice cream producer's freezer, which will be flown in as quickly as possible before too much ice cream melts!

- **Safety and Security.** A company's goods are often its most substantial financial assets. To protect the value of these assets, a company must ensure that the transportation system handling its goods keeps them safe from damage and secure from theft at all times. Safety and security are especially essential criteria for transportation decisions involving high-cost or hazardous goods. Imagine the difference in the importance of safety and security for a cross-country shipment of birthday piñatas versus a cross-country shipment of Dom Pérignon vintage champagne. The piñatas are low-value items that are not likely to spoil or become damaged. At the same time, the vintage champagne is high value, breakable, desirable to opportunity thieves, and in need of temperature-controlled transportation.

- **Convenience.** For a transportation plan or system to be the successful backbone of any logistics or supply chain, it must be convenient for all supply chain members. Transportation decisions must consider how easy it is for customers, retailers, wholesalers, distribution centers, warehouses, and manufacturers to interface with those transporting goods. Consider a furniture retail store in Hawaii that needs to ship goods from Los Angeles to Honolulu. A third-party transportation provider that the furniture store is considering is slightly cheaper than other providers. Still, it does not offer en route communication about the approximate time of shipment delivery. The furniture store might be less likely to consider selecting this slightly fastest transportation provider but instead consider one with inventory visibility or a one who can guarantee and communicate delivery times.

FIGURE 6.3 - INCREASED RELIABILITY WITH BICYCLE MEAL DELIVERY IN ROME, ITALY

- **Reliability.** Even when costs are low, when deliveries are fast and convenient, and when goods are kept safe and secure, a transportation system or third-party transportation provider is no use to a company when it is not reliable. If transportation can't consistently and reliably get goods where they need to be when they need to be, a company loses the time and place utility that reliable transportation provides. The next time you are in the center of a big city, order a meal to be delivered. Big cities typically have traffic delays and streets with restricted access, so a bicycle courier or motorized scooter will more likely deliver your meal.

- **Flexibility.** For companies that need to transport a wide range of goods of different sizes, weights, and handling needs, a flexible transportation system is essential. For example, the transportation system of warehouse-style retailers carrying goods from regional distribution centers to individual stores would need to be flexible enough to handle a wide range of goods within one shipment, from dish detergent to televisions to king-size mattresses.

6.3 TRANSPORTATION BASICS

We have just defined *transportation* within the world of logistics as the act of using a *vehicle* or *infrastructure* to move goods or people. But what are vehicles and infrastructure?

FIGURE 6.4 - EXAMPLES OF VEHICLES

A ***vehicle*** is a machine used to carry and move goods or people from one point to another. When we use the term vehicle, we generally think of land and air travel. Vehicles include machines that move goods or people on land, in the air, on water, or along tracks. A vehicle used on land, such as on roads, is called a **motor vehicle**. Examples of motor vehicles include trucks, buses, cars, motorcycles, snow machines, and all-terrain vehicles. Vehicles used in the air are called **aircraft**. Examples include airplanes, helicopters, hot air balloons, and blimps. Vehicles used on the water are called **vessels** or **watercraft**. Anything carrying goods or people on the water is a vessel, from massive cargo ships to the tiniest rowboats and kayaks. A vehicle used on tracks is called a **railed vehicle**. Examples include trains, trams, monorails, and funiculars.

In transportation, **infrastructure** is an organized set of facilities and systems in fixed locations that allow goods and people to be moved. A transportation infrastructure typically provides the underlying framework supporting vehicle movement. For example, a rail infrastructure of railroad tracks, stations, and terminals supports the movement of trains carrying goods or people. However, in some cases, the infrastructure may be the only means for moving goods, such as a pipeline infrastructure, which moves oil and gas without using a vehicle.

FIGURE 6.5 - EXAMPLES OF TRANSPORTATION INFRASTRUCTURE

When representing or describing transportation across infrastructures and between two or more locations, language from the mathematical concept of spatial networks is often used. This language is used in many other fields, such as computer networking, artificial neural networks, social science, telecommunications, biology, and even supply chain design optimization. Let's define some of the terms from this language of spatial networks related to transportation, beginning with *networks*, *nodes*, and *links*. We will also outline how the same words are used slightly differently in supply chain network design.

A ***transportation network*** is a visual representation of the flow and structure of transportation. It includes all the locations where a vehicle starts, stops, or engages in any action related to the vehicle or the goods or people being transported. In essence, a transportation network is an outline of transportation infrastructure spanning a specific location or a particular flow of goods or people. In supply chain management, there is also a field of study called ***supply chain network optimization***, which involves studying, designing, and making changes to a supply chain structure to improve efficiency and effectiveness. In this context, a ***supply chain network*** is essentially a visual representation of either an internal or external supply chain.

All transportation networks and supply chain networks include a structure of *nodes* and *links*. In transportation, a ***node*** is a location in a transportation network that is a beginning, ending, or connection point where the flow of goods or people starts, stops, or changes. Nodes can be airports, warehouses, highway exits, cargo ports, street intersections, and railroad stations, to name a few. Depending on the depth of detail you need to represent in your transportation network, nodes can be major or minor points in a flow of goods or people. For example, the Australian island state of Tasmania provides a highly detailed online map of land and property in Tasmania called the Land Information System Tasmania (LIST). The List website defines its road-based nodes as any of the following: "the end of a road, a junction of two or more road segments, a graded separated intersection, a place where the value of an attribute changes, a small roundabout, or a barrier." It even describes the situations in which cul-de-sacs, bus stops, traffic lights, and gates would be considered nodes.

In the world of supply chain optimization, nodes are typically any place where goods start or stop along a supply chain in the voyage from supplier to customer. A supply chain network's nodes could include the supplier's factory, a warehouse, a distribution center, a fulfillment center, a cross-docking facility, a retail store, and the customer's location.

In both transportation and supply chain networks, a ***link*** is a single connection between two nodes. In transportation networks, links are segments of the transportation infrastructure that allows goods or people to be moved from one point to another, such as roads, railways, and waterways. In supply chain networks, there is a broader view of links. They are the transportation used between links and include both infrastructure and vehicles. Links are *how* goods get from point A to point B.

Remember that both transportation networks and supply chain networks are visual representations of networks of nodes and links. As shown in Figure 6.6, circles and lines are often a standard way of representing nodes and links in network diagrams, even in other disciplines, from telecommunications to social science. Circles represent nodes. Lines represent links. The Israel Railways map on the left in Figure 6.6 is an example of a transportation network diagram, and the illustration on the right is a supply chain network diagram. Sometimes arrows are used to represent the flow of goods or people along a link in network diagrams. Supply chain managers often look at transportation networks and supply chain networks to see the big picture of how and where goods are flowing. This information can help them analyze the supply chain's efficiency and effectiveness. It can also help analyze the efficiency and effectiveness of existing and proposed transportation systems for moving their company's goods.

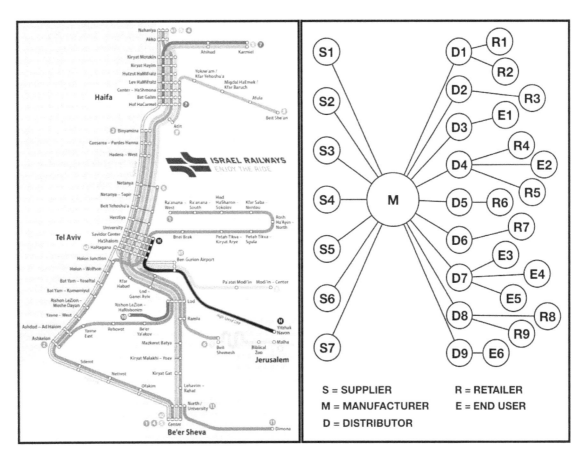

FIGURE 6.6 - TRANSPORTATION AND SUPPLY CHAIN NETWORK DIAGRAMS

In transportation, a series of one or more links connecting two nodes is called a **route**. For example, the route from your house to the nearest coffee shop may involve multiple links (different streets), and it may involve several nodes such (street intersections). Still, you drive a single route within your town's transportation network to get from one node (your home) to another (the coffee shop). A route can be a physical, human-made construction between two nodes, such as railways, highways, and pipelines. However, a route can also be a planned, pre-established path through water or air between two nodes, such as established sea corridors for cargo ships or scheduled flight paths for airplanes. The starting and ending points along a transportation route are called **terminals**. These are locations where goods can be unloaded and reloaded onto different vehicles using different modes of transportation, such as sea to air. Terminals are also locations for vehicle maintenance, routing and dispatch, weighing shipments, and conducting administrative work. If you've ever been to an airport, a train station, or a cruise ship terminal, you've been to a terminal!

In addition to terminals, another type of significant node is a **hub**, which is a node with many inbound and outbound links. At these hubs, goods or people can be transferred from one link to another and even from one mode of transportation to another. Large airports are often called transportation hubs. For example, Frankfurt Airport is called a hub for Lufthansa passengers, and a FedEx cargo airport in Tennessee is called the FedEx Memphis Hub.

6.4 MODES OF TRANSPORTATION

When companies are making decisions about transporting goods, they must decide how they will move their goods, and they must consider modes of transportation. In logistics and physical distribution management, a **mode of transportation** is the physical structure by which the goods are carried. The five modes of transportation are *road*, *rail*, *water*, *air*, and *pipeline*.

FIGURE 6.7 - GOODS TRANSPORTED BY ROAD

At the risk of stating the extremely obvious, a **road** is a surfaced route used by vehicles for moving goods or people. Within most countries around the world, road is by far the most commonly used mode of transportation. When measured by both value and weight, road is the mode of transportation used for most goods transported within the United States. Figure 6.7 shows a few things transported by road, from beer in Germany to DHL packages in Italy and recycled cardboard in Brazil to a cycling bar in Canada.

The primary advantage offered by road as a mode of transportation is that, within most countries, more locations are accessible by road than any other mode of transportation. For example, in the United States, the National Highway System measures approximately 223,668 miles! Imagine going anywhere from your home. Which mode of transportation will you use first? Unless you live on a riverbank or next door to an airstrip, you would most likely walk out your door and hop into a car or bus to travel along the road system.

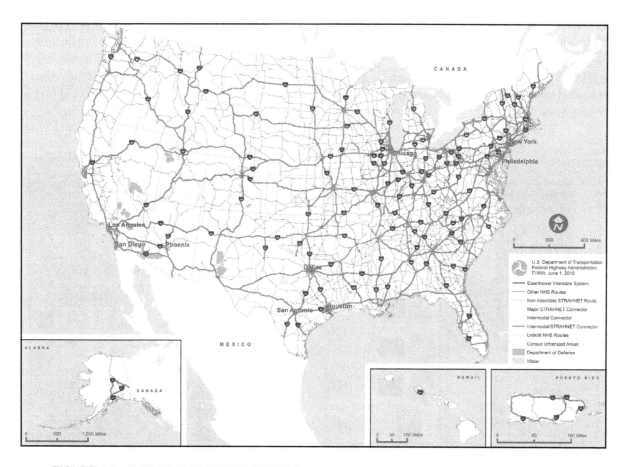

FIGURE 6.8 - NATIONAL HIGHWAY SYSTEM, US FEDERAL HIGHWAY ADMINISTRATION, 2018

Compared to other modes of transportation, road offers a more cost-effective movement for smaller deliveries and shorter distances, such as those up to 500 to 800 miles. It is also highly flexible and allows for last-minute changes and adjustments. For example, suppose there are production delays at a factory. In that case, it is far easier to change the delivery schedule for a container of goods traveling by road than one traveling by prescheduled barge, train, or airplane.

Although flexible and highly accessible, road also presents disadvantages as a mode of transportation. Traffic jams, congestion, and adverse weather can all affect road delivery times. Labor costs are also higher because the number of drivers or operators required per amount carried is much higher than for other modes of transportation. For example, one truck driver can transport one or two container loads of goods while a crew of five people can transport over 1000 forty-foot containers using a cargo ship. Over the past decade, there has also been a growing shortage of qualified truck drivers. In a 2019 analysis, the America Trucking Associations found that a truck driver shortage has grown steadily since 2011. The US trucking industry was short 60,800 drivers in 2018, up more than 10,000 since the previous year.

Weight also plays a factor in road transport. The per ton-mile cost of road transport is higher than that of rail or water. Therefore, it is cheaper to ship a cargo container full of Nintendo Switch consoles and Animal Crossing merchandise from Seattle, Washington to Anchorage, Alaska by water than by road, even though both modes of transportation are available. Also, size and weight limitations on national road networks limit carrying weighty items and large machinery.

6.9 - VEHICLE WEIGHT AND SIZE LIMIT SIGNS IN ENGLAND, POLAND, AND JAPAN

The transportation mode of **rail** is typically used to transport large, heavy, and bulky items and large quantities for long distances. Although rail offers the advantage of transporting large and heavy goods that can't be moved by road, it is used less frequently. Data from the

US Bureau of Transportation Statistics in 2017 showed that only 15.35% of the value of the goods moved between the US and Canada or Mexico used rail transportation. A significant majority of 63.3% used truck transportation.

FIGURE 6.10 - CARGO AND PASSENGER RAILROADS AROUND THE WORLD

Most of the US freight railroads are privately owned and operated. The rail companies also own most of the track. These privately owned freight railroads fall into four classifications: *Class I railroads*, *regional railroads*, *local line-haul carriers*, and *switching and terminal carriers*.

Class I railroads in the United States have an operating revenue of at least $433.2 million. Although small in number, Class I railroads carry most of the goods moved by rail. The seven Class I railroads currently operating in the US provide 221,000 jobs and 140,000 miles of rail tracks. **Regional railroads** are not Class I but have at least 350 route-miles or an operating revenue of at least $40 million. There are currently twenty-one in the US. **Shortline railroads**, also called **local line-haul railroads**, are local freight railroads covering less than 350 miles of track and have an annual operating budget of less than $40 million. Most operate within one state and connect two industries that need to move goods

133

between them, serve as a conduit between two larger railroads, or provide tourist passenger service. Finally, while there are no revenue or size restrictions to define them, **switching and terminal (S&T) carriers** are local freight railroads that provide switching services, terminal services, or both instead of long-distance rail movement. S&T carriers are often found in ports and industrial areas and can funnel traffic between larger railroads.

The primary advantage of rail is that rail cars can accommodate very large, heavy items, like the large and unusually shaped playground equipment at the Port of Alaska in Anchorage, shown in Figure 6.11. It is also a less expensive mode of transportation for larger volumes over longer distances than road. Rail offers greater reliability than many other transportation modes because it is less likely to experience traffic delays or adverse weather. Furthermore, most maritime cargo ports are connected to rail networks, making rail a vital element of global supply chains.

6.11 - PLAYGROUND EQUIPMENT TRANSPORTED BY RAIL IN ALASKA

The primary disadvantages of rail are its geographic and time limitations. Rail networks are limited and in fixed locations. Rail carriers also typically operate only at specific times, making them less flexible than motor carriers. Rail is also not a suitable transportation mode for fragile goods, nor is it cost-effective for small quantities moving short distances. Finally, there are sometimes very long transit times compared to road and air.

Water is a mode of transportation used to transport large quantities of nonperishable and bulk goods domestically and internationally. In domestic trade, goods travel by water within the country and along the coast through inland and intracoastal waterways. There are approximately 25,000 miles of navigable inland, intracoastal, and coastal waterways in the US. Twelve thousand of these miles are part of a commercially active waterway system maintained by the US Army Corps of Engineers, with eleven thousand fuel-taxed for commercial operators. This inland and intracoastal waterway system serves 38 of the 50 United States.

In international trade, the majority of goods travel by ocean. These goods enter and leave through cargo ports. A ***cargo port*** is a facility that receives and docks cargo ships. It uses specialized equipment to transfer goods to and from ships. At ports around the world, cargo ships get loaded or unloaded 10,000 times every week. The cargo ships at these ports are various specialized vessels adapted to the type and amount of goods being transported. The most common categories of vessels used to transport goods are:

- **container ships,** which carry containerized goods. There are more than 5,000 container ships around the world. Many carry more than the equivalent of 12,000 twenty-foot containers, which is written as 12,000 ***TEU (twenty-foot equivalent unit)***. Some can even carry 23,000 TEU!

FIGURE 6.12 - CONTAINER SHIP BEFORE AND DURING LOADING IN USHUAIA, ARGENTINA

- **bulk carriers,** which carry bulk cargo such as cement, grain, ore, or coal. Some can hold as much as 400,000 metric tons deadweight, or DWT, which is the cargo's weight and everything else the ship carries, such as fuel, water, and people.

- **tankers,** which carry bulk fluids and gases, such as crude oil, gas, chemicals, and even molasses. More than 4,000 tankers worldwide can carry 10,000 DWT.

- **roll-on/roll-off ships,** also called ***RoRo ships***, which carry cargo on wheels, such as trucks, trailers, cars, and railway carriages. They can also carry cargo too big or heavy for standard container ships.

- **barges,** which are flat-bottomed vessels used to transport heavy goods along rivers and canals. Barges are typically used for bulk goods or large items that might not be easily transported by road or rail.

6.13 - MORE VESSELS USED TO TRANSPORT GOODS

One of the primary advantages of using water transport is that large quantities of goods and bulky items are moved at one time. It is also reliable and does not suffer the traffic-related delays in road transportation. Water can also be less costly because it is far less expensive than air for international trade, and there are no costs for using ocean waterways.

Water is, however, perhaps the slowest mode of transportation, making it unrealistic for shipping perishable or time-sensitive goods. These long transit times also increase the insurance costs of goods. Scheduling is also limited in water transport. Ships sail on fixed schedules, limiting delivery scheduling flexibility, and fog or severe weather can easily cause sailing cancellations.

Air is the mode of transportation more commonly used for perishable and time-sensitive goods. In the air industry, some airlines are exclusively for cargo. Examples of all-cargo airlines include FedEx, UPS, and Volga-Dnepr Airlines, pictured on top in Figure 6.14 delivering a Mars rocket for NASA. Other cargo airlines are subsidiaries of passenger airlines, such as British Airways World Cargo, Alaska Airlines Cargo, and Cathay Pacific, as shown in Figure 6.14 on the bottom.

FIGURE 6.14 - CARGO AIRLINES

Air's primary advantage is that it is the fastest transportation mode, allowing it to reduce delivery times dramatically. Air's shorter delivery time is suitable for perishable goods. It also reduces the risk of damage, and it requires less packaging of goods. As long as airports are available, air transport can move goods to anywhere in the world.

Even with these significant advantages, air moves far fewer goods than road, rail, and water. With air, all of its benefits come at a price. Air transport is very costly, especially compared to other modes of transportation. Like water, air also allows for less scheduling flexibility. Flights are generally at fixed times, and adverse weather can delay flights and cause transportation delays. Furthermore, airplanes are strictly limited in the weights and item dimensions they can carry.

Pipeline is the mode of transportation used to carrying goods from point to point through a steel or plastic pipe. While oil and natural gas are the goods most commonly transported by pipeline, any form of liquid, such as drinking water, hot water for heating, sewage, and even milk and beer, can be carried by pipeline. Although expensive to construct, pipelines yield extremely low transportation costs. Figure 6.15 shows a gas pipeline near Dubendorf, Switzerland (top) and a water and wastewater pipeline in Nanortalik, Greenland (bottom).

FIGURE 6.15 - PIPELINES IN SWITZERLAND AND GREENLAND

6.5 CARRIERS AND THIRD-PARTY PROVIDERS

When a company has goods to be moved from one location to another, it must decide *who* will physically move these goods: the organization itself or a *carrier*. A **carrier** is a company that provides a third-party transportation service to other companies to move their goods. Companies typically use carriers to move goods great distances or if they require specialized transportation modes, such as rail or ocean cargo ships. Most companies that sell goods don't have their own rail lines or cargo ships. As of this writing, there isn't an amazon.com train line or cargo ship... yet!

A single carrier may use any combination of one or more of the five modes of transportation, road, rail, water, air, and pipeline. Carriers also may own or lease the vehicles and vessels they use. Terminals, too, are typically privately owned or leased by carriers. Carriers, along with government entities and other private parties, may also own the paths over which transportation carriers operate, such as railway tracks, roads, and seaways. Here are a few examples of carriers you may have seen or heard of before:

- CSX Transportation, which operates the largest railroad in the eastern United States

- Matson Navigation Company, a subsidiary of Matson, Inc., which provides Pacific shipping services between the US, Asia, and the South Pacific

- Swift Transportation, which is a large motor shipping carrier based in Phoenix, Arizona, with over 23,000 trucks in its fleet

- FedEx Express, which is one of the world's largest air cargo carriers based in Memphis, Tennessee, with a fleet of planes that fly to destinations across six continents every day

FIGURE 6.16 - MATSON CONTAINER SHIP HEADING TO KODIAK, ALASKA

Carriers are further classified into *common carriers* and *private carriers*. A ***common carrier*** is a company or organization that transports goods or people customarily across specified routes and offers its transportation services to the general public. A ***private carrier*** is a company used by another company under a special arrangement to transport its goods, such as chartered ships and cargo planes. Unlike a common carrier required by law to treat all customers equally, a private carrier may refuse to provide service to a potential customer for any reason. Let's say that you have two dogs, Fernando and Jaimie Lee, who have landed roles in a new Netflix series called *Hot Dawgs*. You need to immediately transport both pups from Anchorage, Alaska to Los Angeles, California. You can send Jaimie Lee, an adorable but irascible beagle, in the cargo hold of Anchorage's next flight to Seattle on Alaska Airlines. In this situation, you are using a *common carrier*. Unfortunately, Alaska Airlines cannot take Fernando. The lovable pooch is a Chow Chow, a breed restricted from flying in the cargo hold because of potential breathing problems. Fernando is too big to fly in the plane's passenger cabin, so you need to find another way to get him to Los Angeles. Luckily for Fernando and his future life of fame as a Netflix canine star, you find a charter air service called Pampered Pooch Planes. The service will fly Fernando from Anchorage to Los Angeles in a private jet by himself with a vet to monitor his breathing and feed him treats in flight. In this situation, you are using a *private carrier*.

Two other types of transportation service providers that work closely with carriers are *freight consolidators* and *freight forwarders*. A ***freight consolidator*** collects and combines small, separate shipments from different companies into larger shipments to achieve lower transportation rates. For most carriers, the cost of delivering a container of goods is just about the same no matter how empty or full the container is. Therefore, it is less than ideal to have a situation of less-than-truckload (LTL) shipments. A consolidator works to combine small shipments to create full container-load or truckload shipments, thus achieving significant cost savings for the companies shipping smaller quantities of goods. Some freight consolidators are companies that are not carriers but offer consolidation service between shippers and carriers. Other freight consolidators are carriers themselves that provide consolidation service with their shipments.

FIGURE 6.17 - LTL SHIPMENTS AND CONSOLIDATORS

A *freight forwarder* is a company that is not a carrier that arranges for the shipment of another company's goods. Although the freight forwarder doesn't move the goods, it is involved in the shipment from start to finish, finding the best modes and carriers to use for a shipment. Freight forwarders are especially useful because they use their knowledge of carriers, rates, and carrier quality to lower transportation costs while finding the desired transportation service level. Freight forwarders also work across multiple transportation modes to help companies find the best solutions for getting goods to their customers.

Transportation involves more than a company itself or a carrier simply picking up and moving goods from one location to another. Transportation also includes the complex world of transportation management, or the planning, directing, and controlling of how goods are moved and handled throughout the transportation process. Most raw materials and consumer goods today are not only moved across countries but across oceans. To navigate the murky and complicated waters of transportation management, companies often turn to *third-party logistics service providers*, also known as *3PLs* or *3PLPs* or *TPLs*, to provide some or all transportation, transportation management, and warehousing services a company might need. 3PLs typically bundle a range of these services under one cost structure. Transportation management activities covered by a 3PL might include:

- planning shipments and selecting transport carriers;

- keeping track of shipments in transit;

- determining freight costs before shipping;

- checking and paying carriers' freight bills;

- filing claims with carriers for damaged goods;

- transportation budget planning and management;

- transportation administration and human resource management;

- monitoring and maintaining service quality;

- conducting carrier rate negotiations;

- keeping up with local, state, federal, and international transport regulations;

- planning and handling transport information systems; and

- conducting transport systems analysis.

6.6 INTERMODAL AND MULTIMODAL TRANSPORTATION

For goods to reach us, they may travel by a single mode of transportation or multiple modes of transportation. ***Intramodal transportation*** occurs when goods are moved in one shipment using only one mode of transportation. Multiple vehicles can carry the goods, but the mode does not change. For example, let's say you live in Aspen, Colorado, and buy a pint of Ben & Jerry's ice cream at your local boutique grocery store. The yummy pint travels from the Ben & Jerry's factory in Vermont in a refrigerated container truck to a cross-docking facility in Denver, Colorado. The ice cream is transferred from the truck to a refrigerated van bound for your grocery store in Aspen. In the pint of ice cream's voyage from Vermont to Denver to Aspen, two vehicles are used, but only one mode of transportation, road, is used.

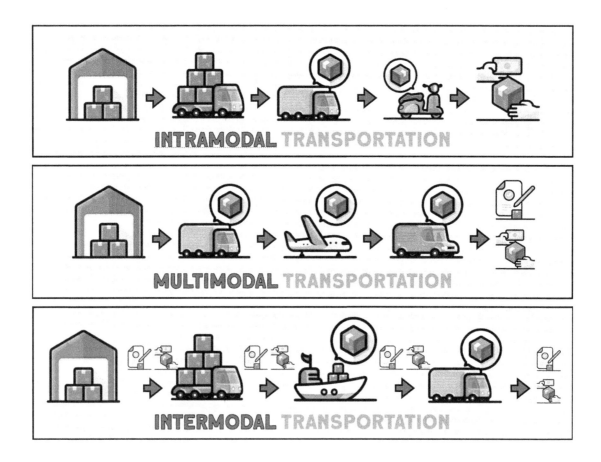

FIGURE 6.18 - INTRAMODAL, MULTIMODAL, AND INTERMODAL TRANSPORTATION

However, when moving goods, companies are not restricted to a single mode of transportation. Both *intermodal transportation* and *multimodal transportation* occur when different transportation modes carry goods in the same shipment from the shipper to the destined receiver. The difference between intermodal and multimodal transportation involves *who* is responsible for the shipment. ***Intermodal transportation*** occurs when goods are moved in one shipment using two or more modes of transportation with different contracts and parties responsible for each mode. In this situation, either the sender or receiver of the goods arranges for multiple companies to ship the goods across various modes of transportation.

FIGURE 6.19 - INTERMODAL TRANSPORTATION FROM SHIP TO TRUCK

Multimodal transportation similarly occurs when goods are moved in one shipment using two or more modes of transportation, but there is just one contract, and one party is responsible for the entire shipment. Multimodal transportation offers the advantage of dealing with only one carrier and one contract for the shipment's journey. In contrast, intermodal transportation provides the flexibility to make changes and select carriers for different stages of the shipment journey based on price or service.

To make things a little confusing, you may hear the term *intermodal transportation* more frequently because it is often used as a blanket definition for any time goods are moved in one journey using multiple modes of transportation. The critical thing to remember is to know how the companies you work for and interact with use this terminology so you can use it correctly. Although the language of logistics may change from company to company and country to country, the concepts remain the same.

6.6 THE LEGAL SIDE OF TRANSPORTATION

As a final note for our look at transportation, transportation managers and decision-makers need to be aware of the laws and regulations of the regions in which they are moving goods. The history of transportation in the United States is essentially one of *regulation* and *deregulation*. **Regulation** occurs when a government establishes rules or restrictions to control human or societal behavior. **Deregulation** occurs when government rules or regulations that constrain the market forces are simplified or removed entirely.

Toward the end of the nineteenth century, a small handful of railroads became very powerful in the United States. Unchecked competition abounded, bankrupting some railroads while making monopolies of others. In 1887, the federal government enacted the Interstate Commerce Act to tackle the tough job of regulating American railroads. In the early 1900s, Congress gave a broad range of powers to the Interstate Commerce Commission or ICC, which included control of entry and exit into the industry, setting shipping rates, allocating routes, and overseeing services. Although initially established to control the railroad industry, Congress expanded the ICC's powers in the 1930s to cover the emerging motor and air carrier industries. Regulation provided a valuable stabilizing force to transportation industries for many years, but its resulting lack of competition led to inefficiencies, higher prices, and railroad bankruptcies by the 1970s. The federal government then began to reverse its regulatory policies and deregulate the transportation industry. The Surface Transportation Board, or STB, later replaced the ICC under the Termination Act of 1995.

Not to leave American transportation completely deregulated, on October 15, 1966, Congress established the **Department of Transportation**, or **DOT**, to coordinate and plan federal transportation and to set safety regulations. This cabinet-level department currently has the following nine individual Operating Administrations that involve regulating transportation:

- the **Federal Aviation Administration**, or **FAA**, which regulates civil aviation, handles air traffic control, construct and operate airports, certifies aircraft and aircraft personnel, and protects US assets during the launch and reentry of commercial space vehicles;

- the **Federal Highway Administration**, or **FHWA**, which manages highway design and construction and conducts highway transportation research;

- the **Federal Motor Carrier Safety Administration**, or **FMCSA**, which regulates the trucking industry in the US with a focus on safety and reducing crashes and fatalities involving trucks and other large motor vehicles;

- the **Federal Railroad Administration**, or **FRA**, which regulates railroad safety, conductors rail policy and safety research, and administers and supports railroad assistance;

- the **Federal Transit Administration**, or **FTA**, which provides technical and financial support to public transportation systems in the US, such as buses, passenger ferries, subways, light rail systems, commuter rail systems, and people movers;

- the *US Maritime Administration*, or *MARAD*, which assists the development and operation of the US Maritime Service and the US Merchant Marine, regulates the transfer of US vessels to other countries, and establishes sea routes and service on these routes;

- the *National Highway Traffic Safety Administration*, or *NHTSA*, which writes and enforces the US Federal Motor Vehicle Safety Standards, regulates fuel economy and theft resistance measures in motor vehicles, and conducts research and analysis on highways traffic fatalities and safety;

- the *Pipeline and Hazardous Materials Safety Administration*, or *PHMSA*, which develops and enforces pipeline regulations; and

- the *Saint Lawrence Seaway Development Corporation*, or *SLSDC*, which operates and maintains the US portions of the joint US-Canada Saint Lawrence Seaway facilities.

These DOT Operating Administrations set and enforce regulations that impact transportation and supply chain management within the United States. Figure 6.20 shows an example from the US General Accountability Office of multiple federal laws and regulations that govern school bus safety. Notice that two different Operating Administration within the Department of Transportation, both NHTSA and FMCSA, have regulations that govern school bus operations for safety.

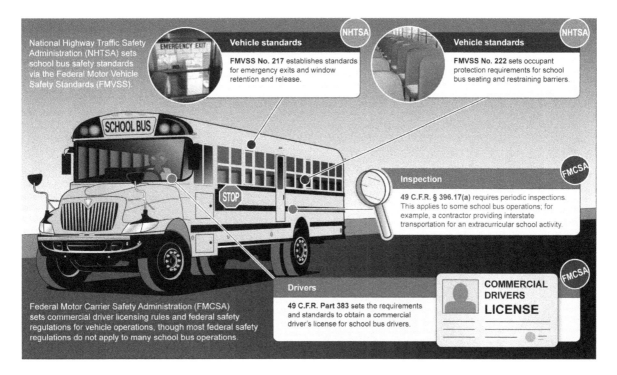

FIGURE 6.20 - EXAMPLES OF TRANSPORTATION FEDERAL LAWS AND REGULATIONS

As a recent commercial transportation example, the FMCSA, or in case you've forgotten —
the Federal Motor Carrier Safety Administration, established a regulation in 2012 known as
the ELD Mandate. The mandate required all commercial vehicles had to have an electronic
logging device, or ELD, installed by December 2019. ELDs record a vehicle's operations and
the driver's activities, which can help ensure that drivers do not drive fatigued or longer than
they are supposed to according to the FMCSA Hours of Service regulation.

Whether in the US or any other location in the world, it is vital to become familiar with the
federal, regional, and local transportation agencies, laws, and regulations for safe and effective transportation operations in a supply chain.

CHAPTER 6 REVIEW QUESTIONS

1. What is *transportation*? What is its role in supply chain management?

2. What are the six criteria that should be considered and balanced in transportation decisions? Describe a time when you have made a transportation or delivery decision weighing the advantages and disadvantages of at least two of these criteria.

3. In your own words, what is a *vehicle*? List four types of vehicles and provide a specific example of each.

4. What is a *transportation infrastructure*? What is a *transportation network*? How are these concepts related?

5. What is the difference between a *supply chain network* and a *transportation network*?

6. Define *node* and provide three specific examples of nodes in a transportation network and three specific examples of nodes in a supply chain network.

7. What are the five *modes of transportation*? Which mode is used most often for transporting goods in the United States? Provide an example of another location in which one of the other modes might be used more.

8. When is it more advantageous to use *rail* over other modes of transportation?

9. Why might a manufacturing company use a *carrier*? Why might the same company use a *freight forwarder*?

10. Define each *intermodal transportation* and *multimodal transportation*. How are they similar? How are they different?

CHAPTER 6 CASE STUDY

THE BIRTH OF INTERMODAL TRANSPORTATION

Imagine that it's the early 1950s. You are an American businessman who grew up in a farming family during the Great Depression. Having an entrepreneurial spirit and wanting to help your family, you start a trucking business for farmers. By 1940, your business has expanded to an impressive 30 trucks. By now, in the early 1950s, it is up to 1,776 trucks and 37 transport terminals along the East Coast. You often take your trucks to shipping docks where they are unloaded onto ships. You would observe scores of longshoremen transferring goods by hand and by cargo net from your trucks to boats, seeming to take forever as you waited on the dock. You often thought it would be much simpler if you could transfer your truck's entire trailer to the ship instead of carrying goods one by one.

"I had to wait most of the day to deliver the bales, sitting there in my truck, watching stevedores load other cargo. It struck me that I was looking at a lot of wasted time and money. I watched them take each crate off the truck and slip it into a sling, which would then lift the crate into the hold of the ship."

In your trucking business, states are now increasingly placing weight restrictions on trucks and imposing fees on overweight ones. Your trucks cross many states up and down the Atlantic seaboard with different weight and fee structures. Every shipment is a balancing act to see how much weight is worth hauling per truck. You know that things would be much simpler if you could move your truckloads by sea to avoid all the costs of multiple state fees, fuel, truck maintenance, and truck drivers' wages. You consider the idea of driving trucks onto trailer ships and transporting entire trucks, goods and all, but you realize that there is too much wasted space and not enough can be transported at once because of the area the trucks take up. You know that real savings will come in being able to stack trailers of goods.

In 1956, you manage to get a bank loan to buy two World War II T-2 tankers and refit them to carry containers both above and below deck. You redesign your trucks as a flat truck bed with wheels with a removable container set on top. You create a new design for this container that is steel, strong, stackable, and able to protect goods in rough seas. This is not an entirely new concept, however. Military and passenger train lines use containers, but they are in different shapes and sizes. Full trucks and train cars have been loaded onto ships for an onward voyage for more than three decades. The groundbreaking innovation is standardized containerization on a large scale with a standardized means of handling containers. What is even more groundbreaking and future-changing is the advent of intermodal transportation, with quick and easy transition of large amounts of goods between multiple modes of transportation.

On April 26, 1956, your first containership, the Ideal X, loads a container every seven minutes, and the entire ship is loaded in under eight hours. On the same day, the ship sets sail on its maiden voyage from New Jersey to Texas. When longshoremen load ships by hand, the cost is $5.86 per ton. With your new containers, containerships, and handling equipment, the cost is now an unbelievable $0.16 per ton. Upon seeing the Ideal X, a top official of the International Longshoremen's Association said, "I'd like to sink that son of a bitch."

Your inventions forever changed the world of supply chain management and made large scale trade possible. By the end of the 20th century, about 90% of the world's goods traveled in a shipping container. In 2001, you died an unsung hero as one of the most important innovators in logistics, transportation, and globalization. Everyone has heard of and seen your inventions, but almost no-one in the world has heard of you. You are Malcom McLean.

References:
Mayo, A. and Nohria, N. (2005) The Truck Driver Who Reinvented Shipping. Harvard Business School Working Knowledge. Retrieved from: https://hbswk.hbs.edu/item/the-truck-driver-who-reinvented-shipping
PBS. (2004) They Made America: Malcom McLean. Retrieved from: https://www.pbs.org/wgbh/theymadeamerica/whomade/mclean_hi.html/

Chapter 7
Logistics Information Systems and Technology

One of the earliest global supply chains was the Silk Road, linking Europe's farthest western reaches to Asia's farthest eastern reaches. The transcontinental Silk Road encompassed a more-than 5000-mile stretch of trade routes from China's Han Dynasty to Europe's Roman Empire. When an emperor in Rome wanted to place an order for specific colors of fine silks from Luoyang, his order could travel to silk merchants only as fast as humans or horses or camels could carry it. The emperor would also have little to no idea of where his silks were en route and when they might arrive.

Had our emperor lived in today's age of advanced information systems and technology, he would be able to transmit his order to China in the blink of an eye, such as a Walmart in Arkansas does when it orders flip flop sandals from Beijing manufacturers. With today's technology, the emperor would also have been able to know precisely where his order was as it traversed vast geographic distances on its way to Rome. He would even know when the order would be delivered and be alerted to transportation delays, such as heavy rains or highway robberies by bandits in the Central Asian steppes.

Information technology and information systems have become an integral and critical part of logistics and supply chain management, woven deeply and entirely into and throughout every supply chain. Although it would take many pages to cover the broad spectrum of information technology and information systems used in global and local supply chains, this chapter provides a basic introduction to information systems and technology and their role in logistics and supply chain management.

7.1 DEFINING INFORMATION

Before exploring information systems and technology in the world of logistics, we'll first take a moment to discuss what we mean by information and the role it plays in decision-making. But we will begin where it all starts with *data*.

The terms *data* and *information* are often used interchangeably, but they are quite different. **Data** are facts gathered by research or observation and then represented by groupings of nonrandom symbols, such as letters, words, numbers, and values. For example, an inventory checker in a hardware store counting the number of power tools finds that there are eight Nervous Neil's No-Nonsense Nail Guns in stock. The data regarding the number of nail guns observed is eight.

The inventory checker then needs to enter this data, eight Nervous Neil's No-Nonsense Nail Guns, into a handheld device or onto a piece of paper on a clipboard so that others may subsequently receive the message that there are currently eight nail guns in stock. By recording and transmitting this data that others receive, the inventory checker is transforming *data* into **information**, which is data that has been received and understood by the recipient of a message. In our example, the recipient might be a logistics manager or a cloud-based inventory control system.

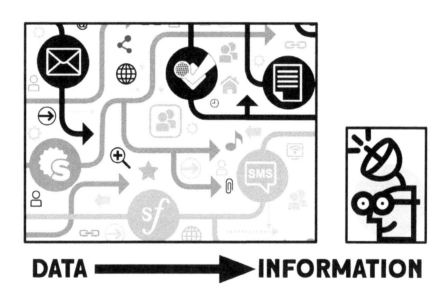

FIGURE 7.1 FROM DATA TO INFORMATION

Information is a critical component of decision-making. Without information, there is no basis upon which to make effective decisions. Imagine selecting a new car to buy without basic information such as gas mileage, safety ratings, and purchase price! In the world of logistics management, companies use information to make a wide range of decisions on an ongoing basis. At every point within a supply chain, supply chain members must make important decisions. Clear, accurate, and timely information is critical to this process. Ultimately, decisions can only be as good as the information used to make them.

To ensure that information is clear, accurate, and timely, businesses have turned to the many tools and techniques offered by information technology and information systems. Before the days of computers, information transmitted was a fraction of what it is today. The speed, accuracy, and volume of information transmissions were dependent on human beings' limitations. How quickly someone could run or ride a horse to hand-deliver information, how neatly and thoroughly someone could write the information, and how much information someone could write onto a parchment or sheet of paper all limited information transmission.

In the early days of humans, information was conveyed by word of mouth, from one person to the next. Then, in approximately 3000 BCE, one of the earliest forms of written communication, cuneiform, was developed by the Sumerians in Mesopotamia. Written communication helped to convey information more accurately and consistently. Cuneiform was a system of pictograms hand-carved into clay tokens and tablets using reeds, making it a slow form of communication. The volume of information transmitted through the written word increased over time, beginning with scrolls in ancient Egypt and Greece, manuscript and block print books hundreds of years later, and the invention of Johannes Gutenberg's moveable type in the 1450s. While books allowed large volumes of information to be transmitted accurately, it was a slow process, dependent on how quickly books could be printed and distributed by man or horse.

FIGURE 7.2 CUNIEFORM CLAY TABLETS (LEFT) AND EARLY PRINTING PRESS (RIGHT)

However, the speed of information transmission took a dramatic leap in the mid-1800s, with Samuel Morse's development of the telegraph transmitter and receiver. With the telegraph, information was transmitted instantaneously from one person to another by cable and later, wirelessly. Instantaneous communication took a further leap forward with Alexander Graham Bell's telephone in 1877, which allowed immediate verbal communication between two people separated by great distances.

Although the telephone and telegraph increased information transmission speed, they did not provide the accuracy and higher volumes of information transmission provided by books and other written communication forms. Telephones and telegraphs were limited by how quickly someone could speak or produce taps, how well the recipient could hear and interpret the information, and how much information could be conveyed within a limited timeframe.

FIGURE 7.3 SENDING AND RECEIVING MESSAGES BY TELEGRAPH

The development of the computer and information technology throughout the second half of the twentieth century provided the perfect marriage of speed, accuracy, and capacity for information transmissions. With computer technology and communication systems such as the internet, thousands of pages of information can be transmitted immediately from one end of the world to another. The information recipient can then use computer-based or cloud-based software to instantaneously sift through the thousands of pages received, resulting in a single page or — even a single sentence — of needed information. Wow!

As we mentioned earlier, information is an essential component of decision-making. Information systems and technology have made this process easier, faster, and more reliable, from data collection to final decision. **Raw data**, which are the facts and figures surrounding an actual thing or event, are now instantly collected, compiled, and transmitted using technology tools such as computer-linked RFID readers and bar code scanners. A recipient then receives this raw data through the internet or intranet. The recipient may then use software programs to help sort, count, and categorize the data for interpretation and transformation into *information*. This new information may then be compared to additional information, perhaps stored within computer systems, to transform it into decision-making *knowledge* in the recipient's mind.

FIGURE 7.4 - FROM DATA TO DECISION

Our ability to generate and store data through internet-based and cloud-based information systems has increased dramatically in the last decade. As a result, we have begun to produce such large volumes of structured and unstructured data that our current software systems and databases can't easily store them to turn them into useful information. Sometimes there's so much data coming at us so quickly that it's like trying to fill a water bottle with a firehose. These seemingly impossibly large data sets are called **big data**, which describes data sets with the three Vs: *volume, velocity,* and *variety*. The data sets are too large to be stored and processed by traditional information systems, too fast to be collected effectively and accurately, and too varied in their formats to be gathered and stored. Big data is stored in specially designed databases, transforming it into information. The big data information is analyzed using specially designed big data software to turn it into knowledge for making decisions. The act of going through these large sets of data to identify patterns and relationships used in decision-making is called **data mining**.

7.2 INFORMATION IN LOGISTICS

Companies use information to make decisions throughout all logistics management processes. Physical goods flow downstream along a supply chain, but information must permeate every aspect of the chain and flow between members in both downstream and upstream directions. This permeation of information sharing throughout all logistics management processes makes for highly effective and efficient supply chains.

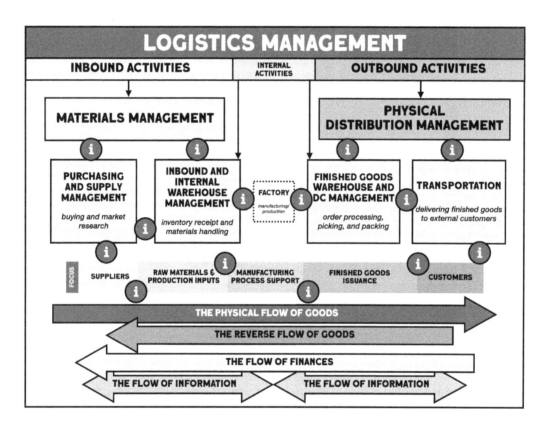

FIGURE 7.5 - INFORMATION IN THE LOGISTICS MANAGEMENT MODEL

A few examples of information flowing to and from members of the supply chain include:

- the **customer**, who provides information about product needs and requires information about product availability, quality, price, and delivery times;

- the **Marketing Department**, which provides information to the customer and requires information from Production and finished goods Warehousing about product availability;

- the **Manufacturing** or **Production Department**, which provides information about production lead-times and production capabilities and requires information about supply deliveries;

- the **Purchasing Department**, which provides information to suppliers about goods needed and requires information from other departments about needs and timeframes;

- the **supplier**, who provides information about goods and transportation availability and requires information about quantities and timeframes when purchasing and delivering goods; and

- the **warehouse**, which provides information about inbound orders and loading schedules for outbound transport and requires information from purchase orders.

At the risk of sounding like a broken record: *information is used for decision-making*. In logistics and supply chain management, companies use information to make a wide range of inventory, transportation, and physical distribution facility decisions. When determining the optimal inventory levels to hold, companies need information on inventory holding and issuing costs, customer demand patterns, and ordering costs. When selecting transportation routes, modes, and vendors, companies need information concerning transportation costs for various options, shipment frequency and size, and customer delivery receipt locations. Finally, when determining the optimal location, layout, scheduling, and management of a warehouse or distribution center, companies need information regarding customer demand and locations, local regulations and taxes, and inventory type and quantity. Throughout the range of a company's inbound, internal, and outbound activities, information is truly the lifeblood of efficient and effective logistics management.

When there is insufficient information for decision-making within logistics and supply chain management, one possible result is the ***bullwhip effect***. In a supply chain, each member places an order for goods from its preceding member based on predicted demand. Companies calculate this anticipated demand using past sales patterns or estimated sales based on current or upcoming events. However, each chain member might act and think in isolation, creating an incorrect or incomplete picture of the *actual* product demand. As a result, the supply chain ends up first with too much inventory, then too little, then too much again, and so on. This repeating and fluctuating inventory pattern is due to a simple act of human nature when each person in the chain orders inventory without sufficient information about actual demand.

For example, let's say that an alcohol retailer called Brown Bottle Liquor Store orders its Bud Light beer from a regional distributor called Barry's Booze Distributors. Barry's orders its Bud Light from the regional Anheuser-Busch distribution center, which orders its Bud Light from the Anheuser-Busch manufacturing facility. Brown Bottle Liquor Store knows that the Super Bowl is a few weeks away and orders 500 cases, considerably more than its usual order. Barry's Booze Distributors sees this order and thinks that they should order a bit more Bud Light because this could be a new pattern for Brown Jug. They don't want to be out of supply, so they order 600 cases from the Anheuser-Busch distribution center, who sees that this is a larger than usual order and decides to increase it, so they don't run out of Bud Light for future orders. As a result, the Anheuser-Busch distribution center orders 750 cases from the manufacturer. Now that the orders have been placed and reversing the other direction in the supply chain, the manufacturer sends 750 cases down the supply chain, and everyone except Brown Bottle Liquor Store is stuck with more Bud Light than they need. Then, with the next order up the supply chain, everyone tries to correct this **_overage_**, an overstock situation in which an item's supply exceeds its demand. Whenever you see a store trying to sell off excess Halloween candy during the first few days of November at drastically reduced prices, the retailer likely had an overage of season-specific candy.

In our Bud Light story, supply chain members want to rid themselves of their excess stock in overage and begin ordering less than the desired quantity, not knowing that the other members of the supply chain are doing the same thing. Unfortunately, they wind up stuck with an **_underage_**, a shortage of inventory in which demand exceeds supply, because they have not ordered enough. Therefore, for the next Brown Bottle Liquor Store order, everyone orders too much again, and they're stuck with extra inventory, so they order too little for the cycle after that. This pattern repeats due to a lack of coordination and communication across the supply chain. However, the overages and underages decrease with each order until things normalize. The up and down pattern of the orders has the shape of a whip when cracked in the air.

FIGURE 7.6 - THE BULLWHIP EFFECT

To help reduce the bullwhip effect and other potential supply chain catastrophes, logistics and supply chain managers rely on shared information. To make suitable and productive decisions and avoid negative results such as the bullwhip effect, information must be:

- **Clear, complete, and accurate.** If information is incorrect or incomplete, decisions made will suffer a similar fate. Imagine placing a delivery order for eighteen pizzas for an office party and being misheard over the telephone, resulting in eighty pizzas landing at your office door!

- **Accessible in the right place.** When it can't be found, *useful* information is no better than *inadequate* information. A scene from the film *Zoolander*, a comedy about the world of male modeling, provides a great illustration of this point. While trying to stop an evil fashion designer from taking over the world, two heroic but less than computer-savvy male models are told that the files they need to find are "in the computer." As a result, the protagonists demolish the computer as they try to get the files they believe are literally "inside" the machine.

- **Accessible at the right time.** Information is of little use *after* a decision has been made. For example, a traffic light would be of little use if it were only visible from the middle of an intersection.

- **The kind of information needed.** If the information available is not relevant to the decision to be made or cannot be interpreted, it can be even more harmful than having no information. Imagine again that you are buying a car, and the only information you have about it is color and model name. You have no information about miles per gallon, safety features, and cost. Many of us might want to select a car based solely on its color and model name, but with this insufficient information, we might end up with a lemon that we can't even afford!

Logistics and supply chain management professionals must ensure that logistics information is clear, accurate, relevant, accessible at the right time, and in the right place. To help attain this goal, they turn to information systems and technology. ***Information systems*** are the systems and computer-based, internet-based, or cloud-based software programs that manage data flow in an organization. The data in information systems are managed systematically and methodically by collecting, storing, processing, analyzing, and distributing it to assist and organization in making decisions and planning, implementing, and controlling operations. ***Information technology*** is the use of computer hardware to collect, store, process, analyze, and distribute this data.

To make supply chain decisions and to help achieve supply chain efficiencies, companies rely on ***logistics information systems (LIS)***, which are the information systems that companies use to help efficiently and accurately record, analyze, and transmit logistics and supply chain information. In the next section, we will introduce a variety of logistics information systems.

7.3 LOGISTICS INFORMATION SYSTEMS

Within a logistics and supply chain setting, logistics information systems work together with a broader interacting structure of people, computer hardware, equipment, and procedures. Their collective goal is to make relevant and needed information available to logistics managers to plan, implement, and control activities related to the supply chain. These systems vary and fall into categories based on their use and the supply chain activities they support. This section will explore logistics information systems used for *records management, making decisions, purchasing, warehousing and transportation*, and *handling complex tasks*.

There is a lot of data to be recorded and managed when managing a company's logistics and supply chain activities. When computer-based, intranet-based, or cloud-based software systems manage these data records, this process is called ***ERM***, or ***Electronic Records Management***. Examples of ERM include:

- ***ERP - Enterprise Resource Planning.*** ERP is a type of information system used across an entire company for planning and managing its resources. It replaces a company's multiple and sometimes incompatible information systems with a single, integrated database system with seamless, real-time information sharing, storage, and retrieval. ERP systems play a large role in order receipt, shipments, and inventory management. ERP systems manage data within one company, although aspects of a system typically interface with customers and suppliers. The most commonly used ERP systems are those developed by SAP, Oracle, PeopleSoft, and BAAN.

- ***EDI - Electronic Data Interchange.*** EDI is a system of standards for structuring information for instantaneous transmission and receipt of data within a company, to its suppliers, and to its customers. EDI allows many processes and documentation to become automated, such as creating and completing purchase orders. EDI transmissions include only the data allowed by the pre-set structure, not accompanying words or messages. EDI is, however, the primary data transmission system used for e-commerce transactions around the world. Because of EDI's instantaneous data sharing, it can help companies avoid situations like the bullwhip effect.

- ***AIDC - Automatic Identification and Data Capture.*** AIDC is the process or system used to automatically and immediately identify items (also called ***Auto ID***) and collect and store information about the items in a company's information systems (also called Automatic Data Capture), all with little to no human interaction or involvement. For example, when goods leave a truck and enter a warehouse, they are typically scanned using AIDC before they are stored, so the company knows what items are in inventory. Items are again scanned using AIDC before leaving the warehouse. The company knows which items are no longer in inventory but are on their way to the next step in the supply chain. Three examples of technologies used as part of an AIDC system include bar codes, QR codes, and RFID. The next section of this chapter covers these technologies in greater detail.

An ERM system can help a company collect and manage data for supply chains and convey real-time information and real-time visibility regarding inventory and equipment. Once a company collects and stores information with ERM, it uses this information in a *DSS* to help make crucial decisions. A **DSS**, or **decision support system**, is an interactive information system used to provide information within a company to help it make more effective decisions. A DSS uses analytic models to solve complex problems. Its design is typically to suit a particular need or function. Ideally, a DSS in logistics and supply chain management should be intuitive, interpreting which information is meaningful and actionable. Within the world of logistics management, examples of DSS include:

- **WMS - Warehouse Management System.** A WMS manages warehouse business processes and directs warehouse activities, such as order receipt and shelving, order picking and shipping, inventory cycle counting, integration with RFID or voice recognition technology, and layout planning. A WMS can help a company make decisions about warehouse layout and flow, where to place which goods within a warehouse based on the frequency of issue, levels of stock to carry, and how to organize staffing based on warehouse human labor needs. Warehouse management systems use computers and scanning hardware within the warehouse, but the system's computing power is often cloud-based. For many companies, a WMS can also be a module or section of a more extensive ERP system.

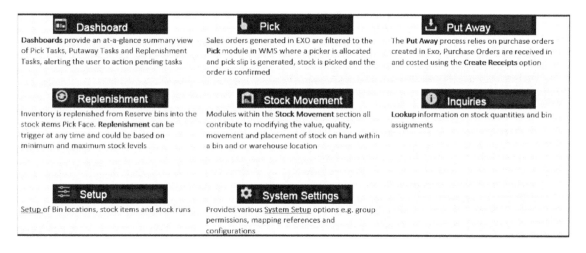

FIGURE 7.7 - SCREEN CAPTURE OF WMS FEATURES

- **TMS - Transportation Management System.** A TMS is a DSS used to manage and optimize transportation and labor planning, audit freight payments, manage carriers and third-party transport providers, coordinate shipment loading and scheduling, and manage transportation documentation and mileage. A TMS is typically housed within one company but may also involve information-sharing between multiple companies in the supply chain, such as suppliers, customers, and third-party transportation providers. Like a warehouse management system, a transportation management system can also be a module or section of a company's larger ERP system.

- *MRP - Material Requirements Planning.* MRP is a technique used for inventory control and production planning in the manufacturing process. An MRP system helps determine when and how much inventory a company should purchase to be used in or support its manufacturing activities.

- *DRP - Distribution Resource Planning.* DRP is a method of determining inventory demand at distribution centers and consolidating demand information into an organization's production and materials systems. A single company typically utilizes both MRP and DRP systems, but both may also interface with suppliers and customers.

Logistics information systems are also used to support a company's **purchasing** activities. A few examples of these systems used in the purchasing process include:

- *E-Commerce - Electronic Commerce.* E-Commerce systems are total supply chain information systems that conduct business electronically using EDI technologies to sell goods to other companies (*business-to-business* or *B2B*) or directly to consumers (*business-to-consumer* or *B2C*).

- *E-Tailing - Electronic Retailing.* E-tailing is a form of e-Commerce in which companies sell their goods via the internet. The online storefronts of many companies, such as walmart.com or homedepot.com, are e-tailing systems. While we are used to seeing e-tailing, not all e-Commerce is conducted over the internet. Many B2B sales interactions are conducted on internal systems that are not on the internet, with only the buyer and supplier granted access.

- *E-Auctions - Electronic Auctions.* E-Auction systems are those purchasing information systems that allow suppliers to conduct online live auctions of their goods for potential buyers. These systems allow greater flexibility and reduced cost for companies that typically auction their goods. They also have the benefit of providing convenience and instant results to buyers.

Logistics information systems used in a company's **warehouse** and **transportation** activities include:

- *EPOS - Electronic Point of Sale.* EPOS is an information system for recording retail sales by scanning products' bar codes at the cash register. Many retailers' EPOS systems are quite powerful and perform more complex tasks than recording sale information alone. They also link with or perform other functions, including inventory management, forecasting, customer relations and service management, and accounting. EPOS systems are useful for inventory activities because they know precisely how many types of goods are on the store shelves. Using this data, an EPOS system can provide real-time inventory counts of goods for retail stores. It can coordinate with automatic ordering processes with suppliers through EDI and e-Commerce systems. As shown in Figure 7.8, EPOS systems can be used in retail stores and restaurants for customer payments and keeping track of inventory.

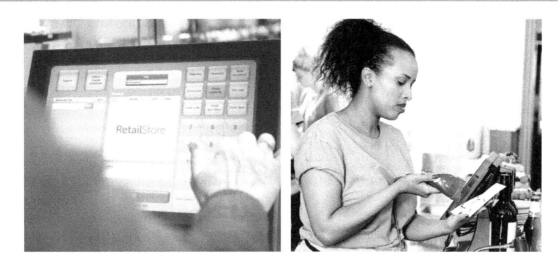

FIGURE 7.8 - AN EPOS SYSTEM TO RING UP A SALE IN A STORE AND MANAGE WINE INVENTORY IN A RESTAURANT

- ***VMI - Vendor Managed Inventory.*** VMI is the practice of a buyer allowing a seller, also called a vendor, to monitor product demand to forecast demand patterns and set product shipment levels and schedules. VMI systems may be part of larger ERP, EDI, or EPOS systems. Their ultimate goal is to ensure that the buyer has enough inventory needed while keeping inventory holding costs at a minimum. A supplier can also link its VMI systems to its own WMS and TMS systems to create efficiencies in distributing goods to customers. As shown in Figure 7.9, Some VMI systems are connected with wireless or cloud-connected vending machines to manage quantities of goods distributed to customers.

FIGURE 7.9 - VMI USING A VENDING MACHINE TO DISTRIBUTE GOODS

- ***LMS - Labor Management Systems.*** When goods come into and leave a warehouse, there are usually human labor hours involved handling the goods. Companies use labor management systems to create more efficient inventory handling. By recording and analyzing warehouse workers' movements, these systems identify when time is wasted on duplicative or nonessential tasks. The systems then find the most efficient way to handle warehouse tasks. Warehouse workers' movements can be manually logged in handheld systems or instantaneously recorded through geotracking devices.

- ***JIT - Just-in-Time.*** JIT is an inventory strategy in which inventory is moved along to the next segment of the supply chain, such as a manufacturing facility or a retailer's distribution center. It arrives at the exact time and in the exact quantity needed. JIT systems are utilized across multiple companies in a supply chain and dramatically reduce in-process inventory and associated costs. One component of JIT systems is ***real-time visibility***, which means that a company can immediately find any inventory item in a warehouse, any in-transit goods in the supply chain, and any vehicle used to move goods. This immediate access to supply chain goods' and transportation locations allows supply chain managers to immediately address any delays or complications that may slow down the supply chain.

- ***DFN - Digital Freight Network.*** Also called Digital Freight Matching, a Digital Freight Network is an online system that matches goods needing to be shipped with available trucks and truck drivers. Most companies that manufacture or sell goods do not own many or even any trucks themselves. Instead, they rely on freight companies with trucks to move their goods. They may even rely on freight brokers to find freight companies with available trucks to move their goods. Internet-based Digital Freight Networks use real-time visibility systems to show which trucks are available for use both when and where they are available. These networks will even show trucks en route transporting another company's goods with less than a truckload if they have space available for additional goods. Both freight brokers and companies wishing to transport goods can access these digital freight networks to find and book a freight company to move their goods. DFNs are considered the Uber of freight transportation and are becoming increasingly popular. Three of the biggest DFNs are Convoy, uShip, and, coincidentally, Uber Freight.

- ***Optimization Systems.*** EPOS and VMI can alert companies to inventory replenishment needs, and a TMS can assist companies in managing transportation needs. However, these systems may not be robust enough to help organizations determine how much inventory to hold, what safety inventory levels to set, or the best inventory levels for transportation or transportation times and routes. ***Optimization systems*** are information systems that use a company's structured data and big data. This data is used to forecast demand, set inventory and safety levels, classify and evaluate suppliers, provide information for inventory deployment to meet both customers' and the company's needs, established transportation routes and times, and much more. Optimization systems can help with complex decision-making in supplier chain management when looking for alternative and optimal solutions.

Finally, sometimes tasks are so complex that the logistics information systems covered in this section aren't enough. For highly complex tasks, companies are increasingly reliant upon *AI*, or ***artificial intelligence***, an area of computer science involved in the construction and research of machines that can do tasks that previously only humans could.

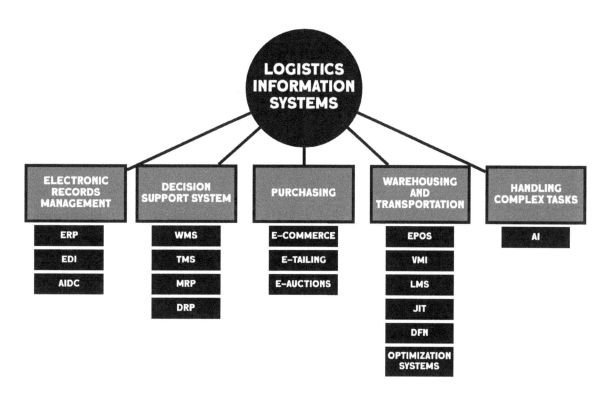

FIGURE 7.10 - EXAMPLES OF LOGISTICS INFORMATION SYSTEMS BY CATEGORY

7.4 SUPPORTIVE LOGISTICS TECHNOLOGY

A critical component of logistics information systems is the actual technology used to collect, house, sort, analyze, and distribute information needed by logistics managers and those handling logistics operations tasks. When we think of this technology used with logistics information systems, we typically think of computer hardware, such as CPUs, keyboards, and monitors. Additional forms of technology also play an important role in logistics, supply chain management, and supporting logistics information systems. These technologies that support logistics information systems include *labeling and tagging technology*, *handheld and wearable technology*, and *light-aided and voice-aided technology*.

With labeling and tagging technology, goods, vehicles, and even people in the supply chain are given a unique label or tag identifier. Information about an item or vehicle can be associated with a label or tag within an information system. Think about when you go to the grocery store and scan the barcode of your favorite brand of crunchy crackers. How does the grocery store cash register or scanner know what this item is or how much it costs? It is all

165

through an EPOS system, and information about your crunchy crackers is associated with the unique barcode you scanned for your brand, size, and flavor of crunchy goodness. Companies can gain information about items from labels and put new information into a system about the items. For example, the grocery stores in Alaska and Hawaii may need to add a 10% markup to the recommended cost associated with your crunchy crackers to account for the additional transportation costs to these more distant locations. When you are at a cash register in Akron, Ohio, it will show that your crunchy crackers cost $3.00, but when you visit Hilo, Hawaii, a cash register at the same grocery chain will show that the same crackers cost $3.30 when scanning the bar code.

Three of the most commonly used labels and tags in supply chain management are *barcodes*, *QR codes*, and *RFID tags*.

FIGURE 7.11 - LABELS AND TAGS IN SUPPLY CHAIN MANAGEMENT

A widely used form of technology-based item identification, **barcodes** consist of a series of bars and spaces printed onto a label, which is adhered to an item, a unit load, a vehicle, or even an employee's identification card or freight documentation. Information is associated with each unique arrangement and width of bars and spaces. A **barcode scanner** is an optical scanner that uses a light beam to read the label and then communicates the information to a central information system, like the EPOS system in our crunchy-crackers-at-the-grocery-store example. While some goods already have barcodes printed onto their packaging, barcode printers are used to print barcode labels at various locations, such as retail establishments, warehouses, and anywhere else that receives, stores, and distributes goods. To save time and labor costs, some locations that handle a high volume of goods use **print and apply labeling**. For example, let's imagine that a bulk order of packages of birthday balloons takes a long trip in a containership across the Pacific Ocean and a shorter trip by rail and then a trip by truck to arrive at a party supply distribution center outside Phoenix, Arizona. As the container is unloaded and the packages of birthday balloons travel by conveyor into the distribution center, barcode labels are printed and automatically applied to each package using machinery. No human hands are involved in peeling and sticking labels!

Thanks to a longer history, less expensive equipment, and its prevalence in retail, bar code technology remains one of the more commonly used forms of information technology in logistics and supply chain management. Companies use bar code technology in various settings, from extensive global supply chain networks to smaller local warehouses. Bar code technology is part of many logistics information systems, such as electronic point of sale and warehouse management systems. When we step into the self-scanning express aisle of a large grocery store, we become frontline users of barcode technology. Barcodes are also used for inventory visibility and traceability as barcodes are scanned when items enter and exit warehouses, vehicles, and customers' locations. Changes and improvements have occurred since the first barcode patent in 1951, railroad car use in the 1960s, and retail use in the 1970s. Barcodes are now *plug and play*, which means minimal set-up, configuration, or training is needed to use barcode devices as intended. Users simply plug them in and begin scanning!

OPTICAL BARCODE SCANNER   **QR CODE SCANNING APP**   **BARCODE/QR CODE OPTICAL SCANNER**

FIGURE 7.12 - BARCODE AND QR CODE SCANNERS

Similar to a barcode is a *QR code*, or *Quick Response code*, a two-dimensional and more complex barcode made up of black and white squares of different sizes on a grid and typically printed onto a label. Although initially developed in 1994 as a location tracker for automotive parts in car assembly plants in Japan, information on QR codes can be used for various purposes, such as website logins, counterfeit detection, and even obituaries on tombstones. Like barcodes, QR codes must be scanned by an optical scanner for interpretation. When you buy a large, packaged item, you may see both a barcode label *and* a QR code label on it. Each has a different purpose, such as the barcode is for retail pricing and information, and the QR code is for location scanning and information. Also, many optical scanners can scan both barcodes and QR codes, as shown in the example on the right in Figure 7.12.

Another popular form of labels and tags used within logistics information systems is RFID tagging. *RFID*, an acronym for *radio frequency identification*, is a technology that uses programmed transponder tags, which are attached to items, unit loads, or vehicles. The

167

transponder tags send out information about the items through radio waves. An RFID reader with an antenna reads this information and transmits it to a central information system, such as a transportation management system or an ERP system's inventory management section. Unlike bar codes, individual RFID tags can be programmed with additional information. Because they are read with radio waves and not an optical scanner's beam of light, RFID tags can be read when not in the line of sight, at distances of 90 feet or more, and even when the tagged item is in motion.

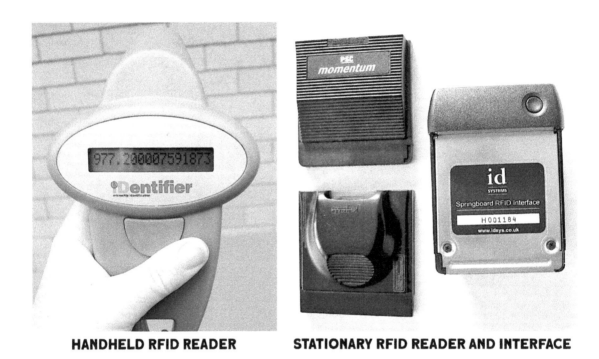

HANDHELD RFID READER   **STATIONARY RFID READER AND INTERFACE**

FIGURE 7.13 - RFID READERS

Highway borders between countries, territories, and states often have weigh stations for trucks that wish to continue their journey along the highway after crossing the border. These weigh stations weigh the trucks to ensure that they are within the weight limits for trucks carrying goods in that country, territory, or state. Originally at these weigh stations, truck drivers had to stop to provide information about their trucks, cargo, origin and destination, and other details while station officials weighed the truck. Thanks to RFID technology, all of that information can be read from an RFID tag on the truck by a weigh station RFID reader. At stations with weigh-in-motion technology, RFID tags send the required information, allowing the truck to be weighed without even coming to a stop!

Another way that RFID tags are used in the trucking industry is the combination of active RFID tags with GPS technology. A *passive RFID tag* is a tag programmed with information readable within the range of a powered RFID reader. These are the inexpensive tags that you might see in clothing, electronics, or books that act as theft deterrents because they are read and sound the alarm if you try to leave the store with them without paying. An **active RFID tag** is one with its own battery power source, and it transmits its unique signal periodically. **GPS**, or **Global Positioning System**, is a location tracking technology that used satellites to locate GPS tags and GPS-enables devices, such as mobile phones. When goods are in transit anywhere in the world, inventory visibility is possible by combining active RFID tags with GPS receivers. The RFID tag gets its location from the GPS receivers and sends it out on its periodic transmissions, allowing companies to see precisely where their goods are.

In addition to labeling and tagging technology, *handheld devices* and *wearable technology* also support logistics information systems. A **handheld device** is an item of portable computing technology that can be held in the palm of your hand. In logistics and supply chain management, handheld devices include handheld barcode and QR code scanners and RFID readers that logistics professionals use in warehouses and other locations along the supply chain to obtain information from labels and tags on goods. The next time you are in a large local grocery store, look for an employee picking an order for delivery or curbside pickup. When you find them, take a look at their hands. You'll likely see a handheld barcode scanning device that tells them what items to pick. To check if they picked the correct item for the order, the employee will scan the item's barcode. Some companies use rugged handheld devices designed specifically for inventory and warehouse tasks. Others use mobile phones and tablets, which are also handheld devices, with apps designed to take advantage of the camera and scanning capabilities built into these mobile devices.

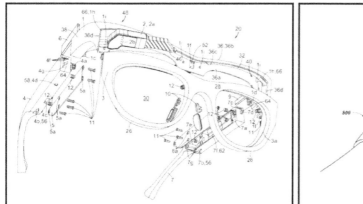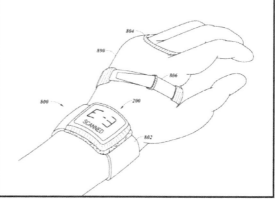

FIGURE 7.14 - AMAZON TECHNOLOGIES WEARABLES FROM AWARDED PATENTS

Wearable technology, also called a **wearable**, is an electronic device designed to be worn on the human body, often close to the skin. Much like handheld devices, wearable devices can send and receive information. Wearables are popular in the fitness and health industries because they instantaneously transmit information about the wearer's movements, heart rate, and blood pressure. Anyone who has a smartwatch already has a wearable device! In the world of logistics and supply chain management, the development and use of wearable devices are expected to grow dramatically in the 2020s. While handheld devices saved time compared to older methods and technology, wearables will save time compared to handhelds. For example, it may take someone in a warehouse five seconds to scan an item's barcode after picking it from a shelf. It may take only one second or less for the same data to be entered into an information system when someone is wearing a wearable technology wristband. The wristband reads the RFID tag of any item picked and automatically records and transmits the information that would previously have been scanned by a barcode reader. A leader in the supply chain wearables field, UPS has been using wearable wrist and ring technologies for a few years in picking, packing, and transportation. Amazon Technologies, Inc. has received multiple patents for wearables over the past decade, including patents for a wearable smart wristband in 2016, wearable eyewear in 2018, and a smart floor for wearables detection and information transmission in 2020.

Finally, along with labeling and tagging technology and handheld devices and wearables, another type of technology supporting logistics information systems is *light-aided* and *voice-aided technology*.

Light-aided technology is the use of electronic devices that utilize light to instruct someone what to do visually. Many warehouses have ***pick-to-light*** and ***put-to-light*** systems where a person picking an order or putting goods onto a shelf is directed to pick or put an item by a light illuminating directly above or below the item's location. Light-aided technology saves warehouse workers time and reduces errors because it is far easier to see a well-lit light than a number on a shelf.

Voice-aided technology uses voice-activated and voice-directed devices used in systems that guide users to complete specific actions using voice commands. For example, voice technology is gaining popularity in warehouse ***voice picking systems***, which are hands-free headset systems for pickers to listen to each item to be picked and its location. The order picker then uses voice commands to confirm that the correct items and quantities have been selected. This system has a bonus of allowing the picker to operate entirely hands-free without holding a handheld scanning device, a tablet, or even a clipboard. Commercial trucking also uses voice-aided technology, with truck drivers receiving and giving information vocally while still driving.

So how does voice-aided technology work? We have already mentioned that it is used in order picking systems, but how would it work, and how would it look? Here's a step by step example of voice-aided technology in order picking:

- **Step 1:** Armed with a hands-free, wireless headset, our fearless picker, Pauline Pettipot, enters the warehouse and listens to the system's command.

- **Step 2:** The system, usually in the form of a pleasant computer-generated voice, tells Pauline to go to location 1.1.2.4 in the warehouse.

- **Step 3:** Pauline goes to the location as instructed and reads a validation code found on the location racking through the microphone on her wireless headset. The system then confirms that Pauline is in the right spot or directs her to the correct location. The warehouse is quite large, and it took Pauline a few days until she was error-free when she started working at this warehouse.

- **Step 4:** Because Pauline is indeed at the correct location, the system then tells her through her headset the exact quantity of the item that she must pick at location 1.1.2.4.

- **Step 5:** Pauline then confirms the quantity picked by restating this quantity into her headset's microphone. She says, "Five picked." Luckily, that was the quantity desired. If the amount needed was not available, Pauline would state how many she actually picked, such as, "three picked," and the voice in the headphones might direct her to an alternate location for the remaining items or a suitable replacement.

- **Step 6:** After Pauline has confirmed that she has picked the correct quantity, the process starts over, and the system directs her to the next location for the next item.

7.5 AUTONOMOUS LOGISTICS TECHNOLOGY

In the previous section, we explored supportive technology in logistics, in which technology supports a human being's interactions with logistics information systems. For example, handheld barcode scanners do not operate on their own. They do not float around a warehouse like a friendly ghost, scanning barcodes as they wish. Instead, they require a human being to operate them. A growing trend in logistics is ***autonomous technology***, which are technological devices that do *not* require human operation. While this may sound sci-fi and futuristic to some, autonomous technology already exists in many supply chains, especially in the form of *robots*, *self-navigating drones*, and *automated trucking*.

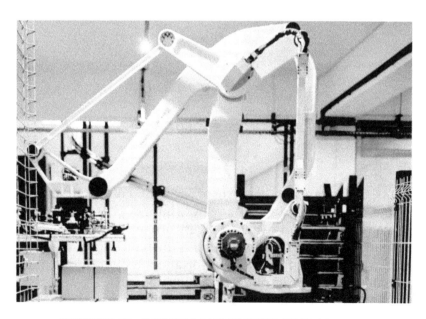

FIGURE 7.15 - ROBOTIC ARM PICKING HEAVY BOXES

A **robot** is a machine that can be programmed to complete complex actions and tasks autonomously or semi-autonomously. Some robots are designed to mimic human forms or actions, but not all robots do. Car manufacturing plants rely on robotic arms, which function like large human arms. The arms complete tasks under more extreme conditions or provide an accuracy that humans cannot deliver. Warehouses are becoming more fully automated with **autonomous mobile robots (AMR)**, which bear no resemblance to humans but instead appear as mobile, rolling machines with minds of their own. Amazon Fulfillment Centers extensively use Kiva Systems robots, which look like orange, oversized Roomba vacuums used to retrieve and put away bins of goods. Amazon's investment in robotics is a serious one, which was evident in their $777 million investment when they acquired Kiva Systems in 2012, making it the company's second-largest acquisition to date. Amazon is not alone in its extensive use of robots in supply chain functions. Since 2017, Walmart has been expanding its use of Bosa Nova robots designed solely for the onerous task of checking inventory. While robots are becoming highly visible in supply chains, you are more likely to see *cobots* in the future. **Collaborative robots**, also known as **cobots**, are designed to work alongside and interact with humans. Both DHL and Amazon are leaders in driving cobot initiatives for warehouse inventory or package picking.

FIGURE 7.16 - AUTONOMOUS MOBILE ROBOT MOVING PALLETIZED GOODS

In addition to robots, *drones* are another form of autonomous logistics technology. A **drone** is an uncrewed flying vehicle that can have a remote human pilot operating it or operate autonomously. You may have heard of regular delivery drone testing for last-mile deliveries. In logistics and transportation, **last-mile delivery** is the final step of the supply chain in getting goods to the consumer from the final transportation or distribution hub, such as a distribution center. In that last short leg of the supply chain journey, getting goods to the end user's door is often the most expensive, and many technologies are studied to look for more effective and efficient practices. Multiple companies across the world tested drones for last-mile deliveries throughout the 2010s, especially for medical and pharmaceutical deliveries.

In 2019, Walgreens was one of the first to test a drone delivery system for customers in a small area in North Carolina.

Delivery drones have been slow to adoption because of multiple and stringent Federal Aviation Administration (FAA) regulations over public airspace. While drones were being tested for last-mile deliveries, self-navigating drones were embraced and are now used regularly in warehouses. These autonomous drones in warehouses use vision sensing technology in conjunction with RFID and AI systems to complete various warehouse tasks, including picking and placing inventory, reaching heights and speeds that would be difficult for human workers. It has been much easier to establish systems of order picking drones than delivery drones because there are no FAA regulations governing warehouse interior airspace.

Finally, *autonomous trucking* is a third form of autonomous logistics technology. An **autonomous truck**, also known as a **self-driving truck**, is a truck that does not require a human to drive or operate it. The US military created the first self-driving trucks in the mid-1990s. Since then, many large companies have developed and tested autonomous trucks, including Caterpillar, Volvo, Daimler, and even Uber, who partnered with Anheuser-Busch to make a 120-mile beer delivery in 2016. Starsky Robotics was the first company to deliver goods with a completely crewless autonomous truck on a public highway.

Because of high insurance rates and potential safety issues, fully remote-controlled autonomous trucking has been slow to catch on. However, driver-assisted autonomous trucks are used in some supply chains. A company called Locomation has developed a form of autonomous trucking in which two trucks ride in a convoy. A human operates the first truck. The second truck, which is immediately behind it, is in autonomous mode and takes directions from the first truck's movements and wireless information. A driver is onboard the second truck, but this driver is resting instead of operating the vehicle. When the driver of

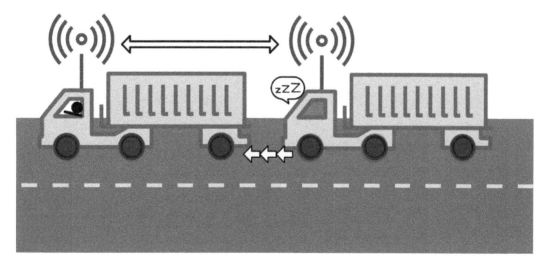

FIGURE 7.17 - FIRST TRUCK DRIVER-OPERATED AND SECOND TRUCK AUTONOMOUS

the first truck has driven for their daily limit, the second truck moves up into the first position, and the driver in the second truck drives. The driver in what was originally the first truck can now rest while their truck is in autonomous mode and taking orders from the other truck. This convoy system of one-operated-and-one-autonomous trucks is currently in use in supply chains in both Australia and the US.

Not just trucks but other autonomous vehicles have been in development and testing over the past five to ten years, especially for use in last-mile delivery. A leader in autonomous vehicles for small, last-mile deliveries called Nuro partnered with CVS in 2020 to deliver prescriptions and essentials to customers in Houston, Texas. With the successful test of a 30-car autonomous freight train in Colorado in 2019, we are also likely soon to see autonomous freight trains.

Some of the systems and technologies covered in this chapter may seem a few years away from everyday use. However, all logistics and supply chain managers, including those of smaller supply chains, must become familiar with both older and newer technologies to stay competitive in our rapidly changing world of logistics and supply chain management..

CHAPTER 7 REVIEW QUESTIONS

1. What is the difference between *data* and *information*?

2. What is *raw data*? Provide an example of a time you collected raw data, which was ultimately used to make a decision.

3. What is *big data*, and why has it become an important concept? How do companies handle big data?

4. In your own words, describe the *bullwhip effect*. Why might toilet paper be subject to the bullwhip effect in times of crisis, like the Covid-19 pandemic?

5. What is a *logistics information system*? When is an *LIS* used?

6. What is an example of an LIS you encounter regularly? Describe what it is and how it works.

7. What is *DFN*? In which situation would a DFN be useful to a company?

8. Why would an *optimization system* be necessary for a company's supply chain?

9. Describe how *RFID technology* works. What examples of RFID technology have you seen in everyday life?

10. What is your opinion of *autonomous trucking* and *autonomous vehicles* for delivery? What might the pros and cons of autonomous vehicles be?

CHAPTER 7 CASE STUDY

TECHNOLOGY INNOVATION AT WALGREENS

You may think of Walgreens as your neighborhood pharmacy. More than 75% of the US population lives within five miles of at least one Walgreens retail store. However, in the world of supply chain management, many think of this neighborhood pharmacy retailer and its parent company, Walgreens Boots Alliance, as pioneers and innovators in practical uses of technology in the supply chain.

Walgreens led the way with RFID implementation in 2008 when it began using RFID throughout its distribution operations to achieve its goal of 100% shipping accuracy between the distribution center and each retail store. They began using the Blue Vector RFID system in its 600,000 square foot South Carolina distribution center, which serviced over 700 retail locations in the southeastern United States at the time. The system is now used in all of its distribution centers and has dramatically reduced shipping errors and the time-consuming paperwork associated with errors. In the pharmacy business, accurate drug shipments can be a matter of life and death because some consumers cannot wait for critical lifesaving medications.

Walgreens was also one of the first stores in the US to accept Apple Pay and other forms of touchless payment, long before they became necessary during the Covid-19 pandemic. In 2015, Walgreens was the first retailer to integrated its payment system and loyalty program with Apple Pay for contactless rewards access and payments. Customers could use contactless technology to pay quickly and securely with Walgreens rewards points or their credit card using an iPhone or Apple Watch held near the scanner.

In 2019, Walgreens began extensively using Zebra tablets and handheld computers in its stores for team planning, looking up product information, and setting up orders. The Zebra handheld devices in Walgreens also improve the customer experience. For example, if a customer asks an employee with a Zebra handheld device if they have any peach flavored cough drops in stock, the employee can look it up. The employee can immediately tell the customer where the desired cough drops are, how much they cost, how many are in stock, and which nearby stores also have them in stock.

Going even further into the use of information hardware and wearables in 2019, Walgreens rolled out Theatro's SaaS Solution in almost 10,000 retail locations. The SaaS Solution is a hardware and software combination that lets Walgreens workers access over 80 voice-enabled apps and leverage the power of AI. Employees using the Theatro headset can access enterprise resource planning software data and functions hands-free through the Intelligent Assistant software. This technology is especially useful for store managers and inventory checkers who need to operate hands-free while having immediate access to inventory, store, and company information through a voice-enabled system.

In more cutting edge hardware developments, Walgreens has partnered with Wing, a drone delivery service owned by Google's parent company Alphabet. The two companies partnered to run a pilot program for drone deliveries of food, beverages, and health products in Christiansburg, Virginia, the first delivery program of its kind in the United States. On October 18,

2019, the first drone delivery occurred to a local couple who ordered cough drops, pain reliever, vitamin C, tissues, and bottled water.

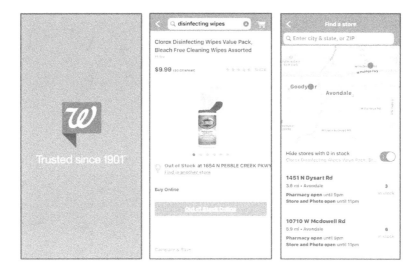

In 2020, Walgreens also upped their software game by partnering with Microsoft and Adobe to bring more personalized and engaging experiences to their customers, especially the 100 million members of the Walgreens Boots Alliance's loyalty programs. Walgreens is now able to give in-store and online customers a highly personalized experience through the Walgreens app, one of the most user-friendly online retail platforms that provide real-time data to customers on inventory availability. For example, disinfecting wipes were almost impossible to find during the Covid-19 pandemic. With the Walgreens app, you could check the Walgreens closest to you for item availability. If an item is not available, you can immediately see which store near you has any in stock with a real-time inventory count.

The next time you are in Walgreens, take a look beyond the pharmacy, photo center, and candy bars to check out their innovative use of information hardware and software.

References:
Berthiaume, D. (2019) History Made: Walgreens Takes Off with First Drone Delivery. Chain store Age. Retrieved from: https://chainstoreage.com/history-made-walgreens-takes-first-drone-delivery
Landi, H. (2020) How Walgreens Leveraged ItsMicrosoft Partnership to Respond to Covid-19. Fierce Healthcare. Retrieved from: https://www.fiercehealthcare.com/tech/how-walgreens-leveraged-its-microsoft-partnership-to-respond-to-covid-19
Landi, H. (2020) Walgreens Steps Up Microsoft Partnership, Adds Adobe Deal to Roll Out New Digital Tools. Fierce Healthcare. Retrieved from: https://www.fiercehealthcare.com/tech/walgreens-steps-up-microsoft-partnership-to-roll-out-new-digital-tools
McFarland, M. (2019) Alphabet's Wing to Make Drone Deliveries in small Virginia Town. CNN Business. Retrieved from: https://www.cnn.com/2019/09/19/tech/alphabet-wing-drone-delivery/index.html
Potter, P. (2019) Walgreens Adopts Dallas-Based Theatro's SaaS Solutions for Nearly 10,000 Stores. Dallas Innovates. Retrieved from: https://dallasinnovates.com/walgreens-adopts-dallas-based-theatros-saas-solutions-for-nearly-10000-stores/
Zebra Technologies. (2019) Zebra Mobile Computers Help Enable Walgreens to Bridge Digital and Physical Store Experience. Zebra.com. Retrieved from: https://www.zebra.com/us/en/about-zebra/newsroom/press-releases/2019/zebra-mobile-computers-help-walgreens-bridge-digital-and-physical-experience.html

Chapter 8

Finance in the Supply Chain

It is the job of logistics management to increase supply chain efficiency and effectiveness. Logistics managers must examine their company's current supply chain processes, procedures, and technologies in search of ways to improve them while saving the company money and increasing levels of service provided to customers. When changes need to be made, logistics managers must often face their stalwart peers and CEOs, who although working hard to improve the company themselves, may not want to hear about changing distribution center locations, using 3PLPs, or purchasing RFID technology. To an untrained ear, much of this may sound like expensive, convoluted logistics gobbledygook. How can a logistics manager speak the language of the CEO and the manufacturing, marketing, and finance decision-makers to get their attention? The answer to this question lies in one word: *money*.

BEFORE CHAPTER 8

AFTER CHAPTER 8

In the business world, money talks. At the core of decisions for most companies is how to improve the corporate bottom line. To be well equipped for discussing new ideas and potential changes with the top echelons of a company's management, logistics managers must know the basics of finance. They must know how to outline how changes in logistics management impact company profits. Throughout this chapter, you will be the logistics manager of a local toy manufacturer, Kearney's Crazy Kazoos. We will introduce a few core concepts of finance that will help you speak the language of the company's CEO, Crazy Jim Kearney, so that you can illustrate the positive impact of logistics management changes on Kearney's Crazy Kazoos' bottom line.

8.1 THE WHO AND WHAT OF FINANCE

The primary goal of a typical company is to make money while satisfying customers. A company needs to make money to pay its employees and continue to operate and grow. It also needs to make money so that the company's owners can earn a **profit**, which is the financial gain attained when the amount earned on producing, selling, operating, or servicing something is greater than the amount spent. But who are the owners of these companies?

Publicly traded companies are those companies whose ownership is divided into multiple pieces, called shares of stock, that are bought and sold on a stock exchange or other public market. Shares of stock used to be issued on paper, like the shares of Coca-Cola stock in Figure 8.1, but shares today are mostly electronic. **Privately owned companies** are companies that may also have their ownership divided into shares of stock, but they are not traded (bought and sold) on a stock exchange or other public market. Therefore, in all publicly traded companies and many privately owned companies, the owners are called **shareholders** or **stockholders** because they own one or more shares of stock in the company.

FIGURE 8.1 - TWENTY SHARES OF COCA-COLA STOCK FROM 1929

A company must make money from sales to new and existing customers to earn money for its shareholders. The same company is also responsible to its **stakeholders**, who are any other people or entities impacted by its actions. Examples of stakeholders include a company's shareholders, employees, suppliers, local community, professional associations, labor unions, the government, and even its competitors. Stakeholders are concerned with a company's financial health and rely on its success for their success.

A company, its shareholders, and its other stakeholders are all concerned with its finances. **Finance** is a broadly defined term that covers making, managing, and studying money and financial investments. **Corporate finance** is an area of finance that involves the finance of incorporated companies, single legal entities separate from their owners. Within the world of corporate finance, companies keep formal records of their financial activities and their overall long-term and short-term financial positions. These formal records are called **financial statements**. Companies generate various financial statements throughout the year, but most are issued periodically at regular intervals, such as annually or quarterly. Two commonly used financial statements that supply chain managers encounter are the income statement and the balance sheet. The next two sections explore *income statements* and *balance sheets*.

8.2 INCOME STATEMENTS

An **income statement** is a financial document that shows how much money an organization made or lost over a set period, typically over a financial year. For a manufacturing company, an income statement compares the sales value of the goods produced to its cost to produce these goods and operate the company. For a retail company, an income statement compares the sales value of the goods sold in retail stores to how much it cost to acquire these goods and operate the company. Income statements are also known by many other names, including **profit and loss statement**, **P&L**, **earnings statement**, **revenue statement**, **statement of financial performance**, and **operating statement**. For whatever company or industry you are in, make sure to know and use the correct terminology for this important document.

Let's now take a closer look at the annual income statement for Kearney's Crazy Kazoos and the role logistics-related expenses play in calculating the company's net profits. As shown in Figure 8.2, at first glance, the Kearney's income statement might seem a bit intimidating to the average logistics manager. It might be even downright horrifying to those with the slightest touch of numerophobia (fear of numbers). However, when broken down line by line, an income statement is quite simple to understand.

One thing to note when looking at an income statement is how numbers are represented. The numbers on the statement may be shown in an abbreviated format so that the numbers are not too long and confusing. For example, all of the numbers in the Kearney's income statement are represented "in millions of dollars." The first item, *net sales*, is not two thousand dollars but is instead two thousand *million* dollars, which is two *billion* dollars. Kearney's is indeed a highly successful kazoo company in net sales!

KEARNEY'S CRAZY KAZOOS, INC. Income Statement for Year Ending December 31, 2020 (in millions of dollars)	
1. Net Sales	$2000
2. Opening Inventory	($200)
3. Purchases	($890)
4. Closing Inventory	$210
5. Cost of Goods Sold	($880)
6. Gross Profit Margin	$1120
LOGISTICS OPERATING EXPENSES	
7. Transportation Expenses	($50)
8. Inventory Holding Expenses	($30)
9. Warehousing Expenses	($20)
10. Total Logistics Expenses	($100)
11. Other Operating Expenses	($220)
12. Total Operating Expenses	($320)
13. Net Profit Before Interest and Taxes	$800
14. Interest on Long Term Loan	($63)
15. Net Profit After Interest, Before Taxes	$737
16. Corporate Taxes Due, 40%	($294.80)
17. Net Profit After Interest and Taxes	$442.20

FIGURE 8.2 - INCOME STATEMENT FOR KEARNEY'S CRAZY KAZOOS 2020

Let's now break Kearney's income statement into three sections and examine each line to see what the item represents and how its value was calculated. As we look at each of the numbers, you might notice that some are in parentheses. Accountants often use either red ink or parentheses on financial statements to represent **outgoings**, the money the company spends. In the three sections below, we start with Kearney's net sales and, after factoring in all the company's outgoings, arrive at the final net profit.

How to Calculate the GROSS PROFIT MARGIN		
1.	Net Sales	$2000
2.	Opening Inventory	($200)
3.	Purchases	($890)
4.	Closing Inventory	$210
5.	Cost of Goods Sold	($880) ← line 2 plus line 3 minus line 4
6.	Gross Profit Margin	$1120 ← line 1 minus line 5

FIGURE 8.3 - CALCULATING THE GROSS PROFIT MARGIN ON AN INCOME STATEMENT

Line 1 shows the company's **net sales**, the total dollar amount Kearney's made from its products' sales throughout its 2020 financial year, also called the *fiscal year*. Net sales typically represent sales figures after deducting customer returns and discounts. They are dollar amounts from sales that have been finalized but may not have yet been paid by the customer. An unpaid amount for goods provided or services rendered is called an **outstanding** amount.

Line 2, **opening inventory**, represents the dollar amount of inventory Kearney's held in its warehouses at the start of the 2020 financial year. This inventory, left from 2019, was available for sale in 2020. The value of opening inventory is calculated from a physical inventory check of goods held in Kearney's warehouses at the end of the 2019 financial year.

Line 3, **purchases**, includes the dollar amount of inventory purchased by Kearney's from its suppliers. This inventory purchased may be actual kazoos and toys made by other manufacturers that Kearney's will resell. It may also be the raw materials and additional inventory needed to manufacture goods.

Line 4, **closing inventory**, is the dollar amount of inventory remaining in the Kearney's warehouse at the end of the 2020 financial year. Like opening inventory, the closing inventory value is calculated from a physical inventory check of goods at the end of the financial year. This 2020 closing inventory value will then be used as the opening inventory value for Kearney's 2021 income statement.

Line 5 represents the **total cost of goods sold**, i.e., how much it costs Kearney's to produce or buy the goods it sold. It is calculated by adding the opening inventory (*line 2*) and the purchases (*line 3*) and then subtracting the closing inventory (*line 4*).

Finally, line 6, the ***gross profit margin***, also known as the ***gross income***, is the difference between Kearney's sales and the cost of its sales. It is calculated by subtracting the cost of sales (*line 5*) from the net sales (*line 1*). A company's gross profit margin is an important figure because it indicates what resources it has available for other expenses, such as operating expenses, shareholder dividends, corporate expansion, and research and development.

How to Calculate the **INITIAL NET PROFIT**		
LOGISTICS OPERATING EXPENSES		
7.	Transportation Expenses	($50)
8.	Inventory Holding Expenses	($30)
9.	Warehousing Expenses	($20)
10.	Total Logistics Expenses	($100) ← line 7 plus line 8 plus line 9
11.	Other Operating Expenses	($220)
12.	Total Operating Expenses	($320) ← line 10 plus line 11
13.	Net Profit Before Interest and Taxes	$800 ← line 6 minus line 12

FIGURE 8.4 - CALCULATING THE INITIAL NET PROFIT ON AN INCOME STATEMENT

Let's now calculate Kearney's net profit from the sales after company operating expenses have subtracted. Some of these operating expenses include those related to logistics management, such as expenses for transportation (*line 7*), inventory holding (*line 8*), and warehousing (*line 9*). In some income statements, these expenses may be under just one heading, such as logistics costs. When these expenses are divided into different logistics categories in an income statement, companies can see how changes in specific areas can impact its bottom line, especially when comparing figures from year to year as category expenses increase or decrease.

Line 7, ***transportation expenses***, includes how much Kearney's spent in 2020 to transport goods into and out from its facilities. Transportation expenses might include shipping expenses for raw materials delivery, the use of 3PLP to deliver finished products to the customers' door, maintaining a fleet of delivery trucks, and customs brokerage charges for goods it imports from overseas.

Line 8, ***inventory holding expenses***, also known as ***inventory carrying costs***, represents the dollar amount it costs for Kearney's to hold its goods (lots and lots of kazoos) in inventory. These expenses do not include warehousing expenses, but they do typically include inventory damage, inventory becoming obsolete so that it can no longer be useful, inventory deterioration and spoilage, insurance, tax, and extra storage and handling expenses beyond standard warehousing expenses.

Line 9, **warehousing expenses**, represents Kearney's typical warehouse operating expenses, including those associated with inbound and outbound physical distribution activities.

Line 10, **total logistics expenses**, are all the logistics costs combined: transportation expenses (*line 7*) plus inventory holding expenses (line 8) plus warehousing expenses (*line 9*).

Line 11 includes all of Kearney's **other operating expenses**, such as administrative costs, facilities expenses, and employee salaries.

Line 12, **total operating expenses**, is the entire dollar amount Kearney's used in 2020 to run its business. It is calculated by adding the total logistics expenses (*line 10*) to the operating expenses (*line 11*).

Finally, line 13 shows Kearney's **initial net profit before interest and taxes**. This line represents the money the company has made after deducting all its operating expenses. It is calculated by subtracting the total operating expenses (*line 12*) from the gross profit margin (*line 6*) calculated at the end of Figure 8.3.

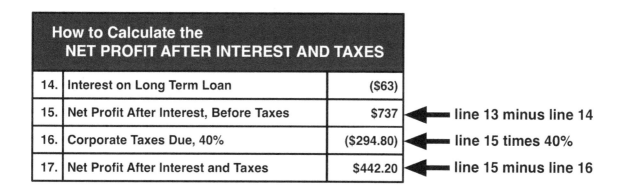

FIGURE 8.5 - CALCULATING THE NET PROFIT AFTER INTEREST AND TAXES

Line 14 represents the amount Kearney's Crazy Kazoos must pay the bank in **interest on a long term loan**. It is not located in the previous section of the income statement because, although it is an expense Kearney's incurs annually, it is not an *operating expense* for the company, i.e., a regular cost for operating a business. The bank calculates the interest on a long term loan based on the amount borrowed, the bank's interest rate, and how the interest is compounded.

Line 15, Kearney's ***net profit after interest, before taxes***, is calculated by subtracting the interest on the long-term loan (*line 14*) from Kearney's initial net profit (*line 13*). This is a significant amount for most companies because it is the profit value from which a company's taxes are calculated.

Line 16 indicates Kearney's ***corporate taxes due***. This value is calculated by multiplying the net profit after interest (*line 15*) by the tax rate, which happens to be 40% for Kearney's Crazy Kazoos.

Finally, the moment we have been waiting for is line 17, the ***net profit after interest and taxes***, which is calculated by subtracting the corporate taxes due (*line 16*) from the net profit after interest (*line 15*). This final amount represents the total profit or loss for Kearney's for 2020, which is how much the company made or lost overall. At the end of the financial year, the amount of net profit after interest and taxes can be placed into the shareholders' retained earnings account or shared among shareholders or owners as returns on their capital investment.

8.3 THE BALANCE SHEET

As previously mentioned, companies generate various financial statements, which are formal records of financial activities and their overall long-term and short-term financial condition. Along with income statements, another important financial statement for companies is the balance sheet. At its core, a ***balance sheet*** is a snapshot of a company's financial picture taken at a given time. It is a statement showing the company's ***assets***, which are everything the company owns, and its ***liabilities***, also called ***claims on assets***, which are all claims against the company, such as the money it owes. Unlike an income statement, which is calculated at specific annual intervals, a balance sheet can be calculated on any given day to get the financial "picture" of the company on that day. For example, it may be calculated quarterly for corporate investors or an any given time when the company is applying for a loan.

FIGURE 8.6 - ASSETS AND LIABILITIES MUST BALANCE IN A BALANCE SHEET

As we continue exploring Kearney's Crazy Kazoos' financial statements, we will look at its balance sheet. Like the balance sheets of most companies, it is divided vertically into two haves. The balance sheet's left side lists all the company's assets, and the right side lists all of its liabilities. As illustrated in the stick-figure form in Figure 8.6, both of these sides of the balance sheet must balance, which means that a company's total assets must equal its total liabilities. In this way, a company responsible to both shareholders and stakeholders can account for every penny, making sure that no loose change here or there is being siphoned off surreptitiously from somewhere in the company.

At first mention, this idea of a perfect balance between what a company owns and what it owes may seem preposterous. How on earth can a company ensure that its expenditures will equal the same amount as its net profits and assets? As we will see, this perfect balance is achieved when the owners or shareholders' investment in the company is brought into the equation. The dollar value difference between a company's assets and its liabilities is the amount owned by the company's owners or shareholders as a return on their investment in the company in addition to the amount of money a company will reinvest in itself. This difference is often called the ***shareholders' equity***. Therefore, if a company's assets are greater than its liabilities, shareholders own the difference. Suppose the company's liabilities are greater than its assets. In that case, shareholders do not actually owe the difference, but the company suffers the consequences of negative equity, typically resulting in decreased stock values. In the case of Kearney's Crazy Kazoos, note that shareholder equity is a positive number.

KEARNEY'S CRAZY KAZOOS, INC. Balance Sheet December 31, 2020 (in millions of dollars)						
ASSETS			**LIABILITIES/CLAIMS ON ASSETS**			
1.	CURRENT ASSETS			13.	CURRENT LIABILITIES		
2.	Cash	$80		14.	Accounts Payable	$220	
3.	Accounts Receivable	$160		15.	TOTAL CURRENT LIABILITIES		$220
4.	Inventory	$210		16.	FIXED LIABILITIES		
5.	TOTAL CURRENT ASSETS		$450	17.	Long Term Loan	$315	
6.	FIXED ASSETS			18.	TOTAL FIXED LIABILITIES		$315
7.	Land	$45		19.	TOTAL CURRENT & FIXED LIABILITIES		$535
8.	Plant & Equipment	$360		20.	SHAREHOLDER EQUITY		
9.	Buildings	$220		21.	Shareholder's Invested Capital	$53	
10.	TOTAL FIXED ASSETS		$625	22.	Retained Earnings	$487	
11.				23.	TOTAL SHAREHOLDER EQUITY		$540
12.	**TOTAL ASSETS**		$1075	24.	**TOTAL LIABILITIES**		$1075

FIGURE 8.7 - BALANCE SHEET FOR KEARNEY'S CRAZY KAZOOS 2020

Another thing to note when looking at the Kearney's balance sheet is that, like its income statement in Figure 8.2, the numerical amounts shown are in an abbreviated format so that the numbers can be easily represented and are not too long. In this case, all of the amounts are expressed "in millions of dollars." For line 2, the value of cash held by the company is not eighty dollars but is instead eighty million dollars.

Let's now take a look at the balance sheet of Kearney's Crazy Kazoos item by item, focusing on where logistics-related expenses come into the picture.

On the **left side of the balance sheet** for Kearney's Crazy Kazoos, as shown in Figure 8.8, the company lists its *assets*, which are all the company's money and everything else it owns, such as inventory, property, and equipment. The assets of a company fall into two categories: *current assets* and *fixed assets*. **Current assets** (*line 1*) are those assets typically used up within a financial period. These include all cash held and resources that will probably be converted into cash within the financial year, such as finished goods inventory. The value of a company's current assets fluctuates from day to day as money is spent and received.

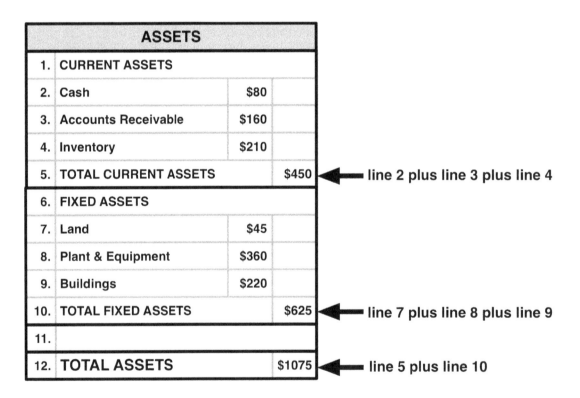

FIGURE 8.8 - THE ASSETS SIDE OF THE KEARNEY'S CRAZY KAZOOS BALANCE SHEET

Unlike these fluctuating current assets, *fixed assets* (*line 6*) do not fluctuate. These are the company's assets over a number of years to use in its efforts to generate profit. Fixed assets include the land, buildings, factories, and machinery the company owns. Let's now look at

Kearney's balance sheet's assets side line by line to see what the amounts mean and how they are generated.

Line 2, **cash**, is the money Kearney's has available for immediate spending. This cash may be kept in different locations, such as in a petty cash box in-house or in different bank accounts. To ensure that their balance sheets stay balanced, companies keep tight control of their cash and record even the smallest expenditures made from cash in office petty cash boxes.

Line 3, **accounts receivable**, is money owed to Kearney's by customers who have received goods but not yet paid for them. Even though the accounts receivable money is not yet in hand, a company must include these impending payments on the balance sheet to balance it. The goods received by the customers are no longer in the company's inventory, leaving a gap in the current assets that must be filled with the amount to be received.

Line 4, **inventory**, represents the value of the goods Kearney's owns that have not yet been sold to customers. This value is the estimated dollar amount of inventory remaining in the Kearney's warehouse when the balance sheet is calculated.

Line 5, **total current assets**, is the total amount of existing assets Kearney's has at the time of the Balance Sheet's calculation. This value is calculated by adding the cash value (*line 2*) to the accounts receivable value (*line 3*) and the inventory value (*line 4*).

Line 7, **land**, the first of our categories of fixed assets, is the value of the actual land that Kearney's owns. This is typically the land on which a company's factories, warehouses, and administrative buildings are located.

Line 8, **plant and equipment**, is the value of all the machinery and equipment Kearney's owns and uses to produce and distribute its products. This might include manufacturing machinery, forklift trucks, and computer equipment.

Line 9, **buildings**, represents the estimated value of all the buildings and facilities owned by Kearney's, such as its manufacturing facility, warehouses, and headquarters building.

Line 10, **total fixed assets**, is the total amount of fixed assets Kearney's has when generating the Balance Sheet. This value is calculated by adding the land value (*line 7*) to the plant and equipment value (*line 8*) and the buildings value (*line 9*).

Finally, line 12, **total assets**, is the dollar value of Kearney's current and fixed assets combined. This value is calculated by adding the total current assets (*line 5*) and the total fixed assets (*line 10*). The final amount must equal (or *balance* with) the total liabilities, calculated in the second half of the balance sheet (*line 24*).

On the **right side of its balance sheet**, highlighted in Figure 8.9, Kearney's lists its **liabilities**, also known as **claims on assets**, which are all claims against the company, such as the money it owes and will pay to banks and shareholders. The company's liabilities fall into three categories: *current liabilities*, *fixed liabilities*, and *shareholder equity*. **Current** *liabilities* (*line 13*) are liabilities and money owed that must be paid within a short period. This includes outstanding accounts payable owed to creditors that fall due and will be settled within the course of a normal business year, such as short-term loans, utility bills, rent, and corporate credit card debt.

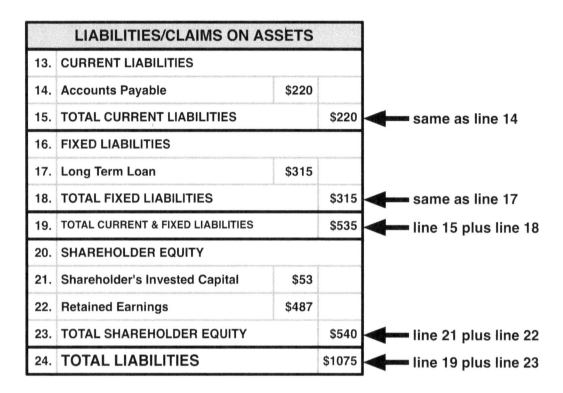

FIGURE 8.9 - THE LIABILITIES SIDE OF THE KEARNEY'S CRAZY KAZOOS BALANCE SHEET

Fixed liabilities (*line 16*) are liabilities and money owed over a term longer than the current financial year. This includes long-term loans and mortgages. *Shareholder equity* (*line 20*) is the company's net worth after all the money and inventory have been counted, and all the bills have been paid. It is essentially the claim the shareholders have on the business in the shares of stock they already own plus *retained earnings*, which are the company's earnings that are not redistributed to shareholders but are instead retained for reinvestment in the company. The value of shareholder equity is also called the *net worth* of the company.

Let's now look at the liabilities side of Kearney's balance sheet line by line, as shown in Figure 8.9, to see what each of the figures mean and how they are generated.

Line 14, *accounts payable*, is the money Kearney's owes immediately or in the short term to its creditors. For example, when Kearney's orders raw materials or office supplies from its suppliers, if it receives the items and has them in stock but has not yet paid for them, the amount owed would be counted as accounts payable.

Line 15, **total current liabilities**, is the value of all current liabilities added together. For example, a company may list various accounts payable and short-term loans on its balance sheet, which would be added to calculate the total current liabilities. In our example, however, Kearney's listed accounts payable (*line 14*) as its only category of current liabilities, making the total current liabilities (*line 15*) equal to accounts payable (*line 14*).

Line 17, **long term loan**, is the amount that Kearney's owes for loans taken out for longer than one year. The interest on this long-term loan is also included in the company's income statement. You can find it in line 14 of Kearney's Income Statement in Figure 8.2.

Line 18, **total fixed liabilities**, is the value of all fixed liabilities added together. For example, a company may include multiple long-term loans on its balance sheet, which would be added to calculate the total fixed liabilities. In our example, however, Kearney's listed one long-term loan (*line 17*) as its only category of fixed liabilities, making the total fixed liabilities (*line 18*) equal to the single long-term loan (*line 17*).

Line 19, **total current and fixed liabilities**, is the total of all that Kearney's owes to everyone except its shareholders. It is calculated by adding the total current liabilities (*line 15*) to the total fixed liabilities (*line 18*).

We now move into the realm of shareholders! Let's jump out of order a bit and first look at line 23, **total shareholder equity**. This is the dollar value difference between a company's total assets (*line 12*) and its total current and fixed liabilities (*line 19*). This amount is the shareholders' claim on the company after all of the bills have been paid. It is known as the company's **net worth**.

Line 21, **shareholders' invested capital**, also known as **capital stock**, is the current value of the shareholders' initial investment in the company.

As previously mentioned, line 22, **retained earnings**, represents the company's earnings that have not been redistributed to shareholders but are instead retained for reinvestment in the company. These retained and subsequently reinvested earnings are still technically owned by the shareholders because they are the owners of the company and its assets.

Finally, line 24, **total liabilities**, is the dollar value of Kearney's current liabilities, fixed liabilities, and shareholder equity combined. This value is calculated by adding the total current liabilities (*line 15*) to the total fixed liabilities (*line 18*) and the shareholder equity (*line 23*). This final amount must equal (or *balance* with) the total assets, calculated in line 12 in Figure 8.8 in the first half of the balance sheet.

8.4 FINANCIAL RATIOS

To better understand the implications of the amounts contained in income statements and balance sheets, corporate managers turn to financial ratios, many of which are extremely useful to logistics managers. As you may remember from way back when you learned pre-algebra, a ***ratio*** is a fraction or two numbers separated by a colon representing the amount or magnitude of one thing compared to the amount or magnitude of another thing. For example, if there are two cats and three ferrets in the room, the ratio of cats to ferrets is two to three, which can be written as 2/3 or 2:3.

In the business world, a ***financial ratio*** compares two numbers, and these numbers' values come from financial statements, such as balance sheets and income statements. Corporate managers use financial ratios to interpret information found on these financial statements by making comparisons that reveal if a company's operating expenses are too high, incur too much debt, or hold too much inventory. A company uses financial ratios to gain insight into its financial health by comparing its financial ratios to those of other companies and its own financial ratios from previous fiscal years. Like traditional mathematical ratios, financial ratios are expressed as fractions or as two numbers separated by a colon, but they can also be expressed as percentages and decimals.

Five commonly used financial ratios for strategic decision-making are: *net profit margin, asset turnover, return on assets, financial leverage,* and *return on net worth*. Let's now take a closer look at each of these ratios, what they mean, and how they can be calculated using data from our Kearney's Crazy Kazoos Income Statement and Balance Sheet.

FIGURE 8.10 - FIVE FINANCIAL RATIOS

The **net profit margin** is the first of our five financial ratios that tells a manager or stakeholder how much profit a company makes for every $1 it generates in sales. Therefore, the higher the net profit margin, the more profitable the company. Companies, investors, and potential investors will often compare a company's net profit margins to those of other companies in the same industry to see which company is more profitable. Companies can also compare their most recent net profit margin with those calculated in previous financial years to see how its profitability is changing.

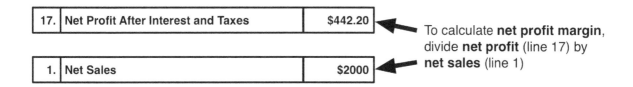

FIGURE 8.11 - CALCULATING THE KEARNEY'S NET PROFIT MARGIN (IN MILLIONS OF DOLLARS)

The net profit margin is calculated by dividing a company's net profit (after interest and taxes) by its net sales, both of which are on its income statement. In our Kearney's Income Statement, the net profit after interest and taxes (*line 17*) was $442.2 million. The net sales value (*line 1*) was $2000 million. We then calculate the net profit margin by dividing $442.2 million (*net profit*) by $2000 million (*net sales*), equaling a net profit margin of 0.2211 or 22.11%. Net profit margins are usually expressed with percentages.

The second of our five financial ratios is **asset turnover**, or the amount of sales a company generates for every dollar of its assets. The asset turnover ratio reveals how good a company is at using its assets to make sales. It is calculated by dividing the value of a company's net sales, found on its income statement, by its total assets, located on its balance sheet. In our Kearney's Income Statement, the net sales (*line 1*) was $2000 million. In our Kearney's Balance Sheet, the value of the total assets (*line 12*) was $1075 million.

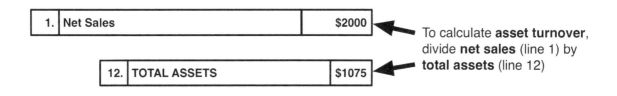

FIGURE 8.12 - CALCULATING THE KEARNEY'S ASSET TURNOVER (IN MILLIONS OF DOLLARS)

We can then calculate the asset turnover by dividing $2000 million (*net sales*) by $1075 (*total assets*), equaling an asset turnover of 1.86. The asset turnover ratio is typically expressed as a decimal number. This calculation means that for every $1 of assets Kearney's has, it generates $1.86 in sales.

Return on assets (ROA), the third of our five financial ratios, is a comparison that reveals how profitable a company is relative to its assets. This ratio is an important one for shareholders because it lets them know to what degree a company has taken their investment, which are now the company's assets, and turned them into profits. Return on assets also serves as an indicator for potential investors of how well a company can do with what it is given. It is calculated by dividing the value of a company's net profit, found on its income statement, by its total assets, located on its balance sheet.

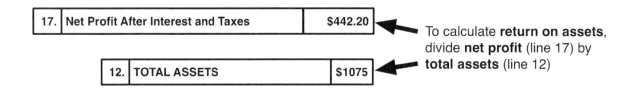

FIGURE 8.13 - CALCULATING THE KEARNEY'S RETURN ON ASSETS (IN MILLIONS OF DOLLARS)

In our Kearney's Income Statement, the net profit after interest and taxes value (*line 17*) was $442.2 million. In our Kearney's Balance Sheet, the value of the total assets (*line 12*) was $1075 million. The return on assets can then be calculated by dividing $442.2 million (*net profit*) by $1075 million (*total assets*), equaling 0.4113 or 41.13%. Return on assets usually appears as a percentage.

The fourth of our five financial ratios, ***financial leverage***, indicates the degree to which a company uses borrowed finances. Companies must perform a delicate balancing act when trying to achieve a good financial leverage ratio. Some financial leverage is desirable because

FIGURE 8.14 - CALCULATING THE KEARNEY'S FINANCIAL LEVERAGE (IN MILLIONS OF DOLLARS)

of the tax breaks it can bring, but too much leverage can place a company at risk of bankruptcy. Financial leverage is calculated by dividing a company's total assets by its net worth, also known as shareholders' equity, with both values found on its balance sheet.

In our Kearney's Balance Sheet, the total assets value (*line 12*) was $1075 million. The net worth (*line 23*), also called the total shareholder equity, was $540 million. The financial leverage can then be calculated by dividing $1075 million (*total assets*) by $540 million (*total shareholder equity*), equaling 1.99. The financial leverage ratio is typically expressed as a decimal number.

Our fifth and final financial ratio, ***return on net worth***, also called ***return on equity (ROE)***, reflects a company's ability to obtain a return on the capital invested by its shareholders. Shareholders typically compare a company's return on net worth ratio to those of the other companies in the same industry. The return on net worth is calculated by dividing a company's net profit after interest and taxes, found on its income statement, by its net worth, also known as total shareholder equity, located on the company's balance sheet.

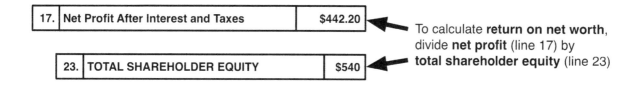

FIGURE 8.15 - CALCULATING KEARNEY'S RETURN ON NET WORTH (IN MILLIONS OF DOLLARS)

In our Kearney's Income Statement, the net profit after interest and taxes value (*line 17*) was $442.2 million. In our Kearney's Balance Sheet, the net worth (*line 23*), also called the total shareholder equity, was $540 million. The return on net worth can then be calculated by dividing $442.2 (*net profit*) million by $540 million (*total shareholder equity*), equaling 0.8189 or 81.89%. The return on net worth ratio typically appears as a percentage.

8.5 THE DUPONT STRATEGIC MODEL

A visual tool used to see a clear map of all of these ratios and the impact various line items on financial statements have on a company's bottom line is the ***DuPont model***, also known as the ***strategic profit model***. The model was created in 1914 by F. Donaldson Brown, a former electrical engineer who was working for the DuPont chemical company's Treasury Department. Brown developed the model after DuPont purchased 23% of General Motors Corporation when he was given the task of cleaning up GM's messy finances. The DuPont model continues to be used by companies today to get an instant overview of critical financial figures and ratios and to analyze their profitability. Logistics and supply chain managers

195

find the model extremely useful in illustrating the impact of logistics expenses on a company's bottom line and revealing the financial implications of changes to logistics expenditures and inventory holding. Shown in Figure 8.16 is an example of the DuPont model, modified to highlight logistics expenses.

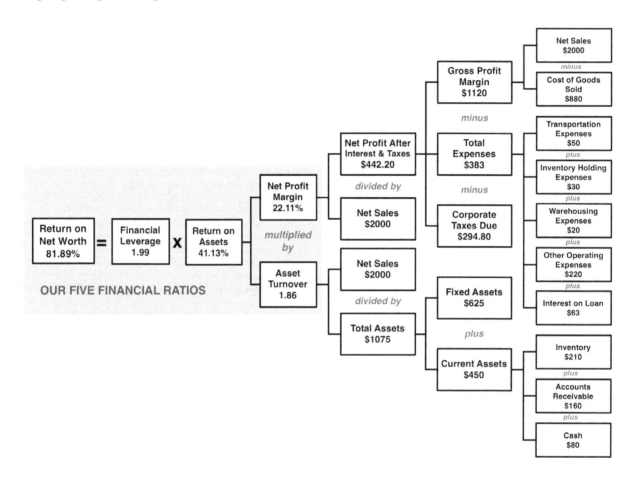

FIGURE 8.16 - DUPONT MODEL FOR KEARNEY'S CRAZY KAZOOS (IN MILLIONS OF DOLLARS)

But exactly where do each of the numbers come from in our DuPont model? The values used to calculate the model's ratios are from a company's income statement and balance sheet. The values on the top two-thirds of the DuPont model, such as the *net sales, corporate taxes due,* and *other operating expenses,* come from the income statement. The values on the bottom one-third of the model, such as *fixed assets, inventory,* and *cash,* come from the balance sheet. Compare the DuPont model in Figure 8.16 to the Kearney's Crazy Kazoo Income Statement in Figure 8.2 and its Balance Sheet in Figure 8.7. Can you find where each of the values came from in the DuPont model?

The DuPont model illustrates the mathematical relationships between various figures on an income statement and a balance sheet and how they create a company's financial indicators, such as our five financial ratios in Figure 8.10. The DuPont model is arranged so that values taken from the income statement are typically found in the top portion of the model and are used to calculate the *net profit*. The values taken from the balance sheet are usually found in the bottom part of the model and are used to calculate the *total assets*.

Logistics and supply chain managers can use the DuPont model when speaking with CEOs and upper-level company executives about logistics-related expenses. For example, they can use the model to show how changes they have made in logistics management have decreased logistics-related operating costs and positively impacted the company's financial bottom line, such as increased return on assets.

Logistics and supply chain managers can also use the DuPont model to convince CEOs and upper-level executives to make desired logistics management changes. To illustrate the impact desired changes could have on the company's financial ratios, the model can compare the current situation to the proposed one. For example, let's again consider the case of Kearney's Crazy Kazoos. You are again the Logistics Manager, and you would like to make a case for proposed changes to the CEO. Although the company is doing very well financially, you see significant room for improvement in inventory holding.

A year ago, you purchased a streamlined, top-of-the-line automatic storage/retrieval system that could cut your inventory holding expenses in half if installed. Your problem is that the Warehouse Manager, who happens to be the CEO's brother, refuses to install and use the system because he argues, "Things are just fine the way they are." You mentioned this to the CEO last year and told him about all the positive benefits the new systems would bring, such as faster order picking times and decreased costs. The CEO, usually an innovative thinker and receptive to change, simply replied, "Let's just wait and see what happens."

Now that a year has passed and the new inventory equipment is still uninstalled and unused, you decide again to approach the CEO about the automatic storage/retrieval system and the positive impact its use would have on Kearney's bottom line. This time, however, you crunch the numbers and draft a DuPont model to show the CEO the exact impact the Warehouse Manager's refusal to use the new system is having on the company's financial ratios.

Figure 8.17 shows the DuPont model with values from Kearney's current income statement, balance sheet, and financial ratios alongside the updated values resulting if the new inventory equipment were used and the inventory holding costs were cut in half. As seen in this reconfigured DuPont model, if the new automatic storage/retrieval system were installed and put to use, the 50% reduction in inventory holding costs would bring welcome ripples of change to the company's entire financial picture. Kearney's net profit would increase by a whopping $9 million, from $442.2 million to $451 .2 million! Three of its financial ratios (*net profit margin, return on assets*, and *return on net worth*) would also increase, with the ever-important return on net worth increasing by over 1.5%, from 81.89% to 83.50%!

After showing the Kearney's CEO your well-outlined DuPont model, he will immediately march straight down to the warehouse, have a heart-to-heart talk with his brother with your DuPont model in hand, and authorize immediate use of the new automatic storage/retrieval system.

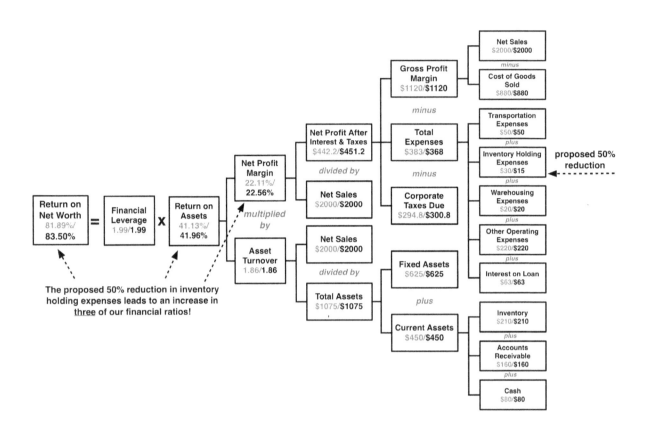

FIGURE 8.17 - DUPONT MODEL WITH ORIGINAL VALUES AND PROPOSED 50% REDUCTION IN INVENTORY HOLDING EXPENSE (IN MILLIONS OF DOLLARS)

8.6 THE INVENTORY TURNOVER RATIO

Although not found in the DuPont model, the *inventory turnover ratio* is another financial ratio of great interest to logistics and supply chain managers. The ***inventory turnover ratio*** is an indicator of how many times inventory "turns over" or is sold or used within a specific period. It is desirable and a sign of success for companies to have a high inventory turnover ratio because it means that the company more quickly sells or uses the inventory it produces or acquires. A lower inventory turnover means that inventory is sitting too long on warehouse shelves. Both the company's shareholders and the banks loaning it money want to see a high inventory turnover ratio. They want to see that the company can sell its inventory, which subsequently helps it turn a profit. What represents an adequate or desirable inventory turnover ratio is relative and will vary between companies and industries.

To calculate the inventory turnover ratio, divide a company's *cost of goods sold* (found on the income statement) by the *average inventory* for a specific period, such as a year, quarter, month, or week. As we will see below, values needed to calculate average inventory can also be found on a company's income statement. If a company has an inventory turnover ratio of 3 to 1, its inventory turned over (or had been used or sold) three times in the reporting period. The formula for the inventory turnover ratio is:

inventory turnover ratio = cost of goods sold / average inventory (by period)

Now it's time to get to work! Let's calculate the 2020 inventory turnover ratio for Kearney's Crazy Kazoos using the data already provided throughout this chapter. We can find the *cost of goods sold* in line 5 of the Kearney's Crazy Kazoos 2020 Income Statement in Figure 8.2. Therefore, the cost of goods sold in 2020 was $880 (in millions).

Let's now find the average inventory for 2020 for Kearney's Crazy Kazoos. To calculate the *annual average inventory*, we must find the average of the company's *opening inventory* and *closing inventory*. Both values can be found in the Kearney's Crazy Kazoos Income Statement for 2020 in Figure 8.2. The opening inventory, found in line 2, was $200 (in millions), and the closing inventory, found in line 4, was $210 (in millions). Therefore, the average inventory for 2020 is:

average inventory = (opening inventory + closing inventory) / 2

average inventory = ($200 million + $210 million) / 2

average inventory = $205 million

We now have all the data we need and are ready to calculate the inventory turnover ratio for Kearney's Crazy Kazoos for 2020.

inventory turnover ratio = cost of goods sold/average inventory

inventory turnover ratio = $880 million / $205 million

inventory turnover ratio = 4.2926, rounded to 4.3

Therefore, the inventory turnover ratio for Kearney's Crazy Kazoos for 2020 was 4.3, which means that the company's inventory turned over more than four times in the 2020 reporting period. As a current or future leader in logistics and supply chain management, you must understand the inventory turnover ratio, income statements, balance sheets, other financial ratios, and the DuPont model. This understanding will help you communicate effectively with a company's decision-makers, whose ultimate language is the language of money.

8.7 COST ACCOUNTING

This chapter has introduced you to *financial statements*, such as *income statements* and *balance sheets*. We also examined how information from financial statements allows corporate managers and shareholders to use *financial ratios* to compare their company's current performance to its past performance or the performance of other competing companies. In short, we learned the basics of *__financial accounting__*. Financial accounting is a branch of accounting that focuses on generating information in the form of financial statements for external purposes, such as demonstrating a company's performance and position to shareholders, lenders, and the government.

In addition to financial accounting, there are different branches of accounting, such as *cost accounting* and *managerial accounting*. Unlike financial accounting, which focuses on generating information to help those *external to a company* make decisions, both cost accounting and managerial accounting focus on generating information to help those *within the company* make decisions. Although cost accounting and managerial accounting are defined separately by accounting companies, many other companies use these two terms interchangeably.

FINANCIAL ACCOUNTING

GENERATE INFORMATION ABOUT COMPANY PERFORMANCE FOR EXTERNAL PURPOSES

MANAGERIAL ACCOUNTING

USE ACCOUNTING INFORMATION FOR INTERNAL DECISION-MAKING

COST ACCOUNTING

USE COST INFORMATION TO CONTROL AND REDUCE COSTS FROM WITHIN

FIGURE 8.18 - THREE TYPES OF ACCOUNTING

The goal of *__managerial accounting__* is to use and present financial accounting, cost accounting, and other related accounting information to help managers make effective decisions for their company. In our DuPont model example from section 8.5, remember that you were the logistics manager for Kearney's Crazy Kazoos. You could not convince the CEO to install the newly purchased automatic storage/retrieval system because the warehouse manager (who was the CEO's brother) didn't like change. You were able to use managerial accounting by showing the benefits of a new automatic storage/retrieval system on the company's bottom line, expressed in financial ratio terms with the DuPont model.

The goal of *__cost accounting__* is slightly different. Its primary goal is to determine the cost of a company's products or services and then use this information to help those from within the company control and reduce costs. With cost accounting, it's all about the costs! Having a fundamental understanding of cost accounting is very important to logistics and supply chain management professionals. One of the key objectives of logistics is to minimize costs and maximize customer service. Understanding where costs come from helps you as a logistics or supply chain manager make informed decisions that minimize costs without significantly impacting customer service levels. Let's look at an example in which understanding how holding inventory costs can reduce costs and ensure you have enough inventory to meet demand.

We've talked so much about Kearney's Crazy Kazoos this chapter that the kazoo factory employees have worked up an appetite! Across the street from Kearney's factory is Syracuse Sal's Sandwich Shop, where all the Kearney's employees love to go for lunch for Sal's famous Boston Beans on Texas Toast special. Coincidentally, one of the sandwich shop owners, Syracuse Sal, is the sister of Boston Bob, the notorious extreme couponer we met at the beginning of Chapter 4.

Both Sal and her partner Pat run the locally famous sandwich shop with a steady daily clientele and a fixed lunch menu. Sal does all of the cooking, which she loves, and all of the purchasing, which she hates. Unlike her frugally minded brother, Sal would rather spend time cooking and socializing with the regular customers. Sal's partner Pat, who operates the cash register and manages the wait staff, also does the business's record-keeping and pays all of its bills. Ever since they opened Syracuse Sal's Sandwich Shop, Pat has been frustrated with Sal because of her purchasing habits. As mentioned already, Sal deplores, detests, and hates purchasing. She thinks it is a waste of her time and talents, so she often buys overly large quantities so she won't have to go through the purchasing process as frequently. They no longer speak of the TP incident of 2014 in which Sal purchased three years' worth of toilet paper for the shop, which had to be stored in their garage, leaving no room for Pat's brand new scarlet Ski-Doo snowmobile.

Like other restaurants, Syracuse Sal's Sandwich Shop stores its inventory in the restaurant storeroom. Because of Sal's purchasing style, they also need to rent a space next door just to store the overflow of Sal's purchases. For years, Pat has tried to convince Sal to order in smaller quantities more frequently, but these pleas have fallen on deaf ears. Pat has even made the case that buying large quantities ties up their money and negatively impacts their small profit and that they would save money if they didn't have to pay for extra storage space. Unfortunately, Sal won't hear of it, often retorting, "You really think it will save us money if I stop buying in bulk? Then bring me the proof!"

You are one of the many happy customers of Syracuse Sal's Sandwich Shop and have a particular fondness for their famous Boston Beans on Texas Toast special. Pat gets to talking with you one day and learns that you are studying logistics and supply management. Pat is impressed and asks for your advice on convincing Sal that her overly large purchases are actually losing them money. To help Pat convince Sal, you simplify things and focus on just one of Syracuse Sal's Sandwich Shop's essential inventory items, the Boston Baked Beans. You decide to figure out what the total cost is to Syracuse Sal's Sandwich Shop for placing just one large order of beans per year. You decide to compare this amount to the total cost for placing multiple orders of smaller quantities of beans per year. You suspect this will give Pat all the proof needed to convince Sal.

To begin your calculations, you get the following information from Pat:

number of cans of beans used daily = 10 cans per day

number of days the cafe is open for lunch in one year = 300 days

annual order size = 3000 cans of beans (10 cans/day x 300 days = 3000 cans)

cost for one can of beans = $5 per can (assuming no bulk discount)

inventory holding cost percentage = 25% of annual inventory

cost of placing an order for cans of beans = $50 per order

You explain to Sal and Pat that your objective is to minimize the cost of holding inventory and the costs of ordering associated with their bean orders. You are trying to find a balance between the cost of holding inventory and the cost of ordering by finding that sweet spot at which the combined annual inventory holding cost and annual ordering cost is at its lowest amount. This sweet spot of lowest cost corresponds to an optimal number of orders per year of a set optimal quantity. In sum, you are looking for *how many orders* of *how many cans* of beans Sal should place to spend the *least amount of money* on ordering and holding costs combined.

You start by calculating the current total cost for bean orders for Syracuse Sal's Sandwich Shop using the following formula:

total cost = cost of orders + cost of holding inventory

The ***cost of orders*** is a fixed amount per order and accounts for the administrative cost that goes into placing an order, such as labor cost for the person placing the order. We already know the cost of orders is $50 per order because Pat had already calculated it based on actual ordering information.

To calculate the ***cost of holding inventory***, we multiply the *average annual inventory* by the *inventory holding cost percentage*. The inventory holding cost percentage lets us know what percentage of an item's cost is additionally needed to hold it in inventory. This percentage typically accounts for inventory damage, inventory becoming obsolete and no longer useful, inventory deterioration and spoilage, insurance, tax, and extra storage and handling expenses beyond standard warehousing expenses. Based on Pat's previous calculations, we already know that the inventory holding percentage is 25%, or 0.25 when expressed as a decimal number.

The formula you use for calculating the cost of holding inventory is:

cost of holding inventory =

value of average annual inventory x inventory holding cost percentage

The value of the average annual inventory is the cost per item, which we know is $5 per can of beans, multiplied by the average inventory. But how do we calculate the average inventory? Remember that you already learned the formula for this in Section 8.6:

average inventory = (opening inventory + closing inventory) / 2

The average annual inventory is the inventory held *on average* across the entire year. At the beginning of the year, there will be lots of inventory, which is 3000 cans of beans for **opening inventory**. In the middle of the year, 150 cafe days have gone by, and ten cans beans are used per day, which means that 1500 cans have been used (*150 days times ten cans per day*) and 1500 cans remain (*3000 cans opening inventory minus 1500 cans consumed*). All 300 cafe days have gone by at the end of the year, and all 3000 cans have been used (*300 days times ten cans per day*), and 0 cans remain for closing inventory (*3000 cans opening inventory minus 3000 cans consumed*).

Each Can of Beans Pictured Represents 10 Actual Cans of Beans

OPENING INVENTORY

ORDER RECEIVED
(beginning of the year)

3000 Cans of Beans in Inventory

0 Cans of Beans Used

SIX MONTHS LATER
(middle of the year)

1500 Cans in Inventory

1500 Cans Used

CLOSING INVENTORY

TWELVE MONTHS LATER
(end of the year)

0 Cans of Beans in Inventory

3000 Cans of Beans Used

FIGURE 8.19 - OPENING AND CLOSING INVENTORY TO CALCULATE AVERAGE INVENTORY

Therefore, when we plug in the values for what we know, we get:

average inventory

= (opening inventory + closing inventory) / 2

= (3000 cans + 0 cans) / 2 = <u>1500 cans</u>

value of average inventory

= average inventory x cost per item

= 1500 cans x $5 per can = <u>$7500</u>

cost of holding inventory

= value of average inventory x inventory holding cost percentage

= $7500 x 0.25 = <u>$1875</u>

Now for the grand finale in calculating current costs for ordering beans once per year:

total cost

= cost of orders + cost of holding inventory

= $50 (for one annual order) + $1875 = <u>$1925</u>

To find the sweet spot of the lowest combined order cost and inventory holding costs, you compare the final total costs of the current annual order to orders of smaller sizes placed more frequently throughout the year. To make this comparison, you create a spreadsheet for Sal and Pat with the information and formulas you now have, as illustrated in Figure 8.20. As seen in this spreadsheet, if one order of the needed 3000 cans is placed every year, the total cost to Syracuse Sal's Sandwich Shop, beyond the actual cost of the cans of beans, is $1925. If two orders of 1500 cans of beans were placed in one year, the total cost would go down by almost $900 to $1037.50. The sweet spot occurs if Sal were to place six orders of 500 cans of beans each time, bringing the total cost to its lowest point of $612.50.

Thanks to you, Pat now has all the information needed to convince Sal that Syracuse Sal's Sandwich Shop could reap significant potential savings by placing more orders of smaller quantities of beans throughout the year. In future studies or classes in logistics, supply chain management, or purchasing, you would learn how to calculate this optimal order quantity and order frequency quickly using a mathematical formula called the ***EOQ formula***, or the ***economic order quantity formula***.

NUMBER OF ORDERS	COST OF ORDERS $50 x number of orders	QUANTITY PER ORDER 3000 cans of beans/ number of orders	AVERAGE INVENTORY PER ORDER (opening inventory* + closing inventory**)/2	VALUE OF AVG INVENTORY PER ORDER average inventory per order x $5 unit price for each can of beans	COST OF HOLDING INVENTORY value of avg inventory x inventory holding cost percentage***	TOTAL COST cost of orders +cost of holding inventory
1	$50.00	3000	1500	$7500.00	$1875.00	$1925.00
2	$100.00	1500	750	$3750.00	$937.50	$1037.50
3	$150.00	1000	500	$2500.00	$625.00	$775.00
4	$200.00	750	375	$1875.00	$468.75	$668.75
5	$250.00	600	300	$1500.00	$375.00	$625.00
6	$300.00	500	250	$1250.00	$312.50	$612.50
7	$350.00	429	214	$1071.43	$267.86	$617.86
8	$400.00	375	188	$937.50	$234.38	$634.38
9	$450.00	333	167	$833.33	$208.33	$658.33
10	$500.00	300	150	$750.00	$187.50	$687.50

* opening inventory = quantity per order (the amount received is the new inventory amount)

** closing inventory = 0 (all cans of beans have been used)

*** inventory holding cost percentage = 0.25 (or 25%, which is information supplied by Syracuse Sal's Sandwich Shop)

FIGURE 8.20 - CALCULATING THE OPTIMAL NUMBER OF ORDERS AND ORDER QUANTITY FOR CANS OF BEANS FOR SYRACUSE SAL'S SANDWICH SHOP

CHAPTER 8 REVIEW QUESTIONS

1. What is the difference between a *publicly traded company* and a *privately owned company*? What are *shares of stock*, and which of these types of companies are divided into shares?

2. What are *financial statements*, and why might they be necessary?

3. In an *income statement*, how are *purchases* different from the *total cost of goods sold*?

4. What is the bottom line (or last line) of an income statement? Why is this information useful to a company?

5. What is a *balance sheet*? What is on each half of a balance sheet?

6. To "balance" a balance sheet, what should the difference between the *total assets* and *total liabilities* always be? What role does *shareholders' equity* play in getting a balance sheet to balance?

7. What is the difference between *current assets* and *fixed assets*? Provide a specific example of each from a company other than a kazoo company.

8. What is a *financial ratio*? What is its purpose?

9. Select one of the five financial ratios covered in this chapter and describe it in your own words. To whom might this ratio be especially useful? Why?

10. What is the *inventory turnover ratio* and how a business might use it? Describe how it is calculated.

CHAPTER 8 CASE EXERCISE

WORKING WITH FINANCIAL STATEMENTS AND RATIOS

Throughout this chapter, you became quite the expert in financial statements, ratios, and the DuPont model for Kearney's Crazy Kazoos. You even put on your cost accounting hat to help Kearney's employees' favorite lunch hot spot, Syracuse Sal's Sandwich Shop. Because you've become quite famous for your financial prowess and understanding of logistic and supply chain management, you have been offered a job as Logistic Manager by Toby's Troublesome Toys, which happens to be the oldest competitor of Kearney's Crazy Kazoos.

Part 1: The Toby's Troublesome Toys Income Statement

You have just learned the following facts about your new employer:

- *Toby's Troublesome Toys made $1000 million in sales in 2020.*

- *The company's opening inventory at the beginning of 2020 was $100 million, and its closing inventory at the end of 2020 was $200 million.*

- *Throughout 2020, Toby's made $500 million in purchases.*

- *The company spent $30 million on transportation, $30 million on inventory holding expenses, and $40 million on warehousing expenses.*

- *Toby's also spent $300 million on other operating expenses.*

- *Toby's does not have any long-term loans, and its corporate tax rate is 30%.*

TASK #1: Using the information provided and the format shown in Figure 8.2 earlier in this chapter, prepare a 2020 Income Statement for Toby's Troublesome Toys.

Part 2: The Toby's Troublesome Toys Balance Sheet and DuPont Model

As the Logistics Manager of Toby's Troublesome Toys, you have learned a few additional facts about your new employer:

- *Toby's Troublesome Toys currently has $50 million in cash, $50 million in accounts receivable, and $200 million in inventory.*

- *The company's buildings are worth $400 million, its land is worth $100 million, and its facilities and equipment are worth $200 million.*

- *Toby's currently has a whopping $800 million due in accounts payable.*

- *The company has no long-term loans.*

- *Toby's has $50 million in shareholder's retained earnings and $150 million shareholders' invested capital.*

TASK #2-A: Using this new information you have acquired, prepare a Balance Sheet for Toby's Troublesome Toys following the format shown in Figure 8.7 earlier in this chapter.

TASK #2-B: Using the values you have already calculated on the income statement and balance sheet for Toby's Troublesome Toys, now complete a DuPont model for the company following the format shown in Figure 8.16.

Part 3: Impact of Reducing Logistics Costs on Net Profit

As the new Logistics Manager for Toby's Troublesome Toys, you are responsible for all the logistics functions of Purchasing, Warehousing, Inventory Management, and Transportation. You have proposed implementing new systems that will reduce inventory holding costs by 20%, warehousing costs by 15%, and transportation costs by 10%. The CEO of Toby's Troublesome Toys, Samuel Stuckinthemud, is reluctant to make any changes and believes that the proposed reductions would have little impact on the corporate bottom line.

TASK #3: To convince the CEO of Toby's Troublesome Toys to make your proposed changes, create a new "proposed" income statement in the same framework of the actual 2020 Income Statement. Your goal is to highlight how these reductions would have impacted the company's 2020 bottom line if were changes made at the start of the 2020 fiscal year.

Part 4: Working with Ratios and Creating a DuPont Model for TT Toys

Although he is a stuck-in-the-mud, as his name suggests, the CEO is intrigued by the savings to be reaped from your proposed. He tells you what he really wants to see is how these changes could impact the return on net worth, as shown in a DuPont model.

TASK #4: Using the DuPont model you created for Task #2-B, create a new DuPont model that will show previous 2020 calculations alongside calculations with the proposed reductions in logistics expenses. Use Figure 8.17 as a framework for how to complete this.

Part 5: Comparing Inventory Turnover Ratios

Toby's Troublesome Toys suspects that they generate more sales and turn over inventory quicker than their competitor, Kearney's Crazy Kazoos. They're not sure and need to find out this information for potential investors.

TASK #5: Using the information already provided, calculate the inventory turnover ratio for Toby's Troublesome Toys. Assess how it compares with the inventory turnover ratio calculated for Kearney's Crazy Kazoos earlier in this chapter.

Part 6: Sal's Needs More Beans - Revisiting Cost Accounting

Since Toby's Troublesome Toys has been taking such a close look at Kearney's Crazy Kazoos, they have also been looking at where they go to lunch, too. As a result, Syracuse Sal's Sandwich Shop has become the favorite lunchtime hangout for Toby's Troublesome Toys employees, too. Their favorite meal is Boston Beans on Texas Toast. Sal and Pat now know that they will need to order 5000 cans of beans in 2021 to accommodate their newfound customers.

TASK #6: Using all of the sandwich shop data from 2020 in Section 8.7, figure out how many orders of what quantity will be needed in 2021 when the bean quantity is increased from 3000 cans to 5000 cans to minimize ordering and holding costs.

Chapter 9
Global Supply Chain Management

Right now, take off one of your shoes. Take a deep breath, hold your nose, and venture to take a look at the "Made In" label inside it. I'd be willing to bet a good spaghetti dinner that they were not made in your city or even your country! Now for the rest of the day, ask everyone you meet to take off a shoe to see where it was made. Although some countries make more shoes than others, you are likely to find an entire United Nations of footwear. But why aren't our shoes made by a local neighborhood cobbler anymore? Why aren't 99% of the durable goods around us made in our hometowns?

Our world has become a global marketplace. Most of the goods we buy and use every day are from different parts of the world. Most large US manufacturers generate significant portions of their sales and purchases overseas. Even companies that we have traditionally associated with the culture and history of one country have "gone global" in both their manufacturing and sales efforts. For example, Deere & Company, the manufacturers of John Deere agricultural equipment associated with farmers in America's heartland, employs approximately 74,000 people in more than 30 countries worldwide and has factories overseas in Canada, Argentina, India, Germany, and Russia.

As companies "Go Global," the role of logistics and supply chain management moves from *very important* to *absolutely critical*. Greater geographic, political, legal, and cultural distances and differences must now be traversed to move goods along a supply chain from raw materials to finished goods to consumers, making logistics and supply chain costs a significant portion of overall product costs. Therefore, logistics and supply chain professionals must understand the global market environment and how to manage their logistics and supply chains effectively to minimize cost, minimize delivery time, maximize handling conditions, and increase customer service.

9.1 INTERNATIONAL MARKET ENTRY

The sale of goods and services across countries' borders, known as ***international trade***, has become a fact of life for large businesses. According to the World Trade Organization's *World Trade Statistical Review 2019*, over $19 trillion of merchandise was exported from countries worldwide in 2018, representing a substantial increase of more than $2 trillion from the previous year. But why do companies choosing to leave the safety and security of their home markets and venture into the vast, unknown waters of the global arena? Companies choose to expand their operations from domestic to global for a variety of reasons, including:

- **Access to more consumers.** Expanding from a local or domestic customer base to a global one can dramatically increase the number of customers who buy a company's products. For example, an American soft drink manufacturer's domestic market is the US population of over 328 million people. Although this may sound like a large enough market, why stop there when the soft drink company could expand its market to the entire world's population, which, as of 2020, the United Nations Population Division estimates to be 7.8 billion. For the US soft drink manufacturer, that's almost seven and a half billion potential new customers!

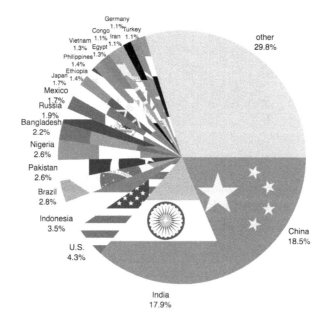

FIGURE 9.1 - WORLD POPULATION PERCENTAGE BY COUNTRY FROM 2017 DATA

- **Less expensive production costs.** Many countries worldwide have lower production costs because of lower cost-of-living and standard-of-living, making labor costs much lower. Countries may also have lower production costs because of their proximity to raw materials or national financial incentives to set up manufacturing facilities. Companies often choose to relocate their production facilities to countries with lower production costs to get a greater return for their shareholders and pass savings on to their customers.

- **Product interest waning in domestic market.** Companies may sometimes have to expand their market globally because their domestic customers are no longer interested in their product. For example, Fresca was a grapefruit-flavored diet soda produced by The Coca-Cola Company and very popular in the US in the 1960s and 1970s. Lyndon Johnson drank it and even the 1980's comedy film *Caddyshack* featured a joke about the drink. For a few decades, Fresca was a part of American culture. As healthier diet and zero-calorie drinks entered the US market, Fresca's popularity waned, and Coca-Cola focused on producing it in other countries. It quickly became highly popular in some markets. Interestingly, because of Fresca's popularity in global markets, Coca-Cola decided to reintroduce the drink back into the US in 2018 (decades later) with new flavors and packaging.

- **Increased foreign competition in company's domestic market.** A company may also find that its domestic market's customer base is dwindling because foreign competitors have moved in. For example, in the latter part of the twentieth century, Mars, Inc., a US-based chocolate candy manufacturer, began to move into various world markets, including the United Kingdom. Because it offered a variety of new products, Mars became quite successful in the UK, hurting the sales of local candy manufacturer, Cadbury Schweppes. Cadbury then decided to regain its solid customer base by moving into international markets, including the United States, the home turf of Mars. As a result, both candy companies became highly successful and had high brand recognition levels in both the US and UK markets.

Now that you know *why* companies enter global markets, let's look at *how* they enter them. When a company decides to enter a new foreign market, it selects a ***market entry strategy***, the mode of ownership and operations when entering this new market. A company's market entry strategy may vary according to the politics, culture, market size, location, geography, and transportation infrastructure of that country. As the company continues to operate in the market, it develops its ***market operating strategy***, the mode of ownership and operations to continue functioning in this market after entering. A company may use the same market entry and operating strategies. After entering the market with one strategy, it may also find a different strategy more beneficial to continued operations in that market.

Five examples of market entry and operating strategies are:

- ***Indirect exporting.*** When a company's goods are sold in another country through an independent intermediary, it uses the market strategy of ***indirect exporting***. A company representative may never even set foot in the target country where its goods are sold. Compared to the next four strategies, this market entry strategy requires the least cost and risk for the company and typically produces the lowest overall profit levels. For example, in a small country or a new, untested market, a company may choose to use indirect exporting to "test the waters" to see how its product will do in that new market before placing any of its valuable financial assets or resources there. When shopping in smaller countries, such as island nations tourists visit on a summer vacation, you might notice that stores' durable goods are significantly more expensive than in larger countries. For example, the price of a washing machine or coffee maker might be 50% more than you have seen elsewhere. This price increase is partly because these goods have probably made it to the store shelves by going through an indirect exporter. It is too expensive for Maytag, LG, or Samsung to set up operations in every country worldwide to sell washing machines. Instead, they sell their products to or through an indirect exporter to get them to smaller countries where customers still have the means and desire to buy quality appliances. These indirect exporters and any other middlemen involved in this supply chain must also make a profit, which leads to a higher price tag to end users. Another form of indirect exporting is **online sales**, in which the company uses an online platform as its intermediary to sell its goods in another country. For example, when Chinese companies that do not have a physical presence in the US sell their goods to American customers on amazon.com, they are engaged in indirect exporting.

- **Licensing.** The market entry strategy of **licensing** occurs when a company decides to grant a license to another company to: produce the original company's product, use its production processes, or use its brand name. With licensing comes low cost and low risk, but the main company (the **licensor**) often has little control over strategy, marketing, and manufacturing. It also cannot benefit from experience curve effects or location economies. For example, Harvard University enters into licensing agreements with various clothing manufacturers overseas who wish to sell sweatshirts and t-shirts with the Harvard name or university trademark. Harvard, an academic institution, has no desire to set up apparel businesses worldwide. Instead, the university can protect its trademark and make some money by entering foreign markets through a licensing strategy.

- **Direct exporting.** When a company decides to export its products on its own to the desired foreign market, it engages in the somewhat riskier and potentially more profitable market entry strategy of **direct exporting**. When engaging in direct exporting, a company may use: a *domestic-based export division*, an *overseas sales branch or subsidiary*, *traveling export sales representatives*, or *foreign-based distributors or agents*. Companies with large, expensive products often use direct exporting for smaller and newer markets. In these situations, a company might find it too costly to set up extensive production or distribution operations. Still, it would benefit from having highly knowledgeable sales reps to market and represent its products in these markets. For example, luxury American electric automotive manufacturer Tesla entered new markets worldwide in the mid-2010s using direct exporting through overseas sales branches. This way, Tesla can sell to new customers in locations where buyers have large amounts of disposable income, such as the United Arab Emirates, before deciding if setting up manufacturing facilities there would be profitable.

- **Joint venture.** A **joint venture** occurs when two or more otherwise independent companies join to form a new company, sharing knowledge, cost, risk, and profits.

Joint ventures with local partners often ease a company's entry into foreign markets, providing political advantage and access to local market knowledge. Large consumer goods companies that need to produce a large volume of products and get them to customers in a new market may use this strategy. For example, both The Coca-Cola Company and PepsiCo frequently form joint ventures with local enterprises when entering new foreign markets. Although the companies import some ingredients, soft drink bottling is far more cost-effective when accomplished as close to the customer as possible. Therefore, both companies typically set up full-scale bottling plants when entering a new market. Partnering with a local enterprise for a joint venture helps them defray costs, minimize risk, and get immediate knowledge of the local market.

- ***Wholly owned subsidiary.*** If a company sets up an operation in a foreign country and owns 100% of the stock, it is a ***wholly owned subsidiary***. The company may set up a new operation or purchase an existing operation to produce or promote its product. With wholly owned subsidiaries, companies have complete control over strategy, marketing, and manufacturing. Although the wholly owned subsidiary strategy presents a company with the highest cost and greatest risk of all market entry and operating strategies, it also provides the potential to reap the greatest profits. For example, the famous global chain of Swedish furniture stores, IKEA, is really owned by a Dutch conglomerate, INGKA Holding BV, and has large retail locations worldwide. When entering new markets, INGKA Holding BV uses the wholly owned subsidiary strategy and owns all facilities and operations for each store in each new country.

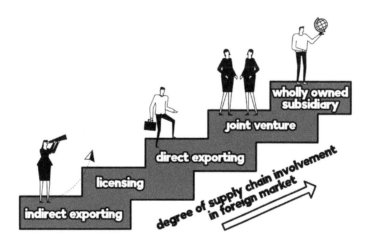

FIGURE 9.2 - RELATIONSHIP BETWEEN MARKET STRATEGY AND SUPPLY CHAIN INVOLVEMENT

The nature and complexity of a company's supply chain within a foreign market are related to its market entry and operations strategy. For companies that are *less* directly involved with a foreign market, such as those with *exporting* and *licensing* strategies, their supply chains are shorter and logistics operation simpler. For companies that are *more* directly involved with a foreign market, such as those with *joint venture* and *wholly owned subsidiary* strategies, their supply chains are longer and their logistics operations more complex.

9.2 THE GLOBAL SUPPLY CHAIN ENVIRONMENT

In global logistics, companies often deal with countries and cultures quite different from their own. When a company expands its operations from domestic to global, it faces many new challenges. Examples of these challenges include country-to-country differences in culture, language, politics, economics, currencies, business practices and norms, time zones, attitudes toward time, required documentation, contracts, security, and legal recourse options when infractions occur. Even two countries with the same language and relatively similar cultures can send confusing and conflicting messages through differences in word choice, demeanor, tone of voice, and body language. English-speaking logistics managers in both the United States and England sometimes use very different words to describe the same thing, as in the case of "18-wheeled tractor-trailer" in the US versus "articulated lorry" in the UK.

Before engaging in international logistics and supply chain relationships, it is imperative to learn as much as you can about the many countries and regions through which your supply chain passes. It is also essential to consider how the practices, procedures, customs, and capabilities of these countries and regions impact your company's logistics and supply chain management. A useful framework for outlining country-specific factors that can influence a company's logistics and supply chain management is the PESTEL market analysis tool used in strategic management. A **PESTEL** framework is used to outline a country's environmental factors that can impact business operations and decisions. Originally referred to as PEST but changed after two additional factors were later added, PESTEL is an abbreviation for the six factors outlined for a country examined using the tool: *political, economic, social, technological, environmental,* and *legal.* All six factors can influence a company's supply chain operations and management when operating in another country.

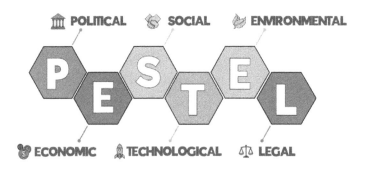

FIGURE 9.3 - THE PESTEL MARKET ANALYSIS FRAMEWORK

Political factors that can influence the management of global supply chains in a PESTEL analysis include a country's:

- **Political climate.** When a country is in political turmoil, this wreaks evident havoc on supply chains. After the dissolution of the Soviet Union in 1991, many Russian-foreign joint ventures quickly formed and folded because of the difficulty of getting goods to customers, mainly because the foreign partners did not understand the nature and location of Russia's political power at the time. The political climate of the relationship between two countries can also significantly impact global supply chains. The tumultuous relationship between the US and China beginning in 2017 has led to a trade war and tariffs imposed by both sides that made importing and exporting some goods between the countries more challenging and more expensive.

- **Attitude toward foreign trade.** Countries with an open and positive attitude toward foreign trade generally create a much easier operating environment for international companies with local supply chain operations. These countries have considerable economic support, often from the IMF (International Monetary Fund) and other economic communities. Countries with a more skeptical and negative attitude toward foreign trade don't have this economic support. They often impose restrictions on foreign companies, including license requirements, tariffs, taxes, quotas, complicated customs procedures, and discriminatory government and private procurement policies, all of which make supply chains far more expensive and challenging to operate. According to the World Bank website, as of July 2020, the countries imposing the highest tariffs on goods imported into their countries are Palau, Solomon Islands, Bermuda, and Libya. These four countries had tariff rates of at least two to three times greater than other countries measured.

- **Political stability.** The stability and reliability of a country's election process and the consistency and predictability of its policies and practices (e.g., regarding taxes, profits, and ownership rights) can also influence international supply chains. For example, when a nationwide referendum resulted in a 52% vote for the United Kingdom to leave the European Union, a move since known as **Brexit**, there was a perceived lack of political sta-

FIGURE 9.4 - BILLBOARD IN NEWCASTLE, UK AND THE IMPACT OF BREXIT

bility in the eyes of foreign businesses operating in the UK. As a result, many businesses have moved either all or most of their operations out of the UK and into other countries in Europe or Asia. A few of these companies include Ford, Honda, Dyson, Panasonic, Sony, HBSC, UBS, Body Shop, and Michelin.

Economic factors that can influence the management of global supply chains in a PESTEL analysis include a country's:

- **Economic orientation.** Often, the degree to which a country embraces a capitalist economic orientation has a significant influence on supply chain operations in that country. People in many of the world's developing, transitioning, and less-developed economies are more worried about product availability and less accustomed to stream-lined logistics management practices, such as just-in-time. As a result, companies in these countries sometimes use hoarding to ensure supply, resulting in production delays for other companies due to material shortages because materials are being hoarded, which means longer lead times and late deliveries for all.

- **Geography.** A country's physical barriers and geographic distances can also influence the speed and cost of its supply chains. For example, the cost and speed of getting goods manufactured in Japan to a remote village in the Himalayas would be far greater than getting the same goods to a port city in India, even though the distances to the two locations would be the same.

- **Location and concentration of buying power.** The goal of a supply chain is to get goods to customers. When many customers live in or near the same place, companies can achieve economies of scale and supply chain costs can decrease. As a fun little experiment, start in a large metropolitan area and note the price of a gallon of milk. Then, take a drive further and further from the city into a remote area. Stop at a store every thirty miles or so, and notice how the price of milk increases.

Social factors that can influence the management of global supply chains in a PESTEL analysis include a country's:

- **Language differences.** Language difference is one of the most apparent external influences on international business. Similar words in the languages of two different countries can mean entirely different things. For example, the American baby food company Gerber has to be careful when entering French-speaking countries because "gerber" is slang for "to vomit" in some contexts. Companies also find that language differences are a barrier to effective international logistics management. As early as 2013, when Inc.com called Mexico "the New China," and with increased tariffs between the US and China beginning in 2017, some manufacturers producing goods for the US market have shifted their operations from China to Mexico. US companies have embraced this decision because the language barrier between English and Spanish is much smaller than the language barrier between English and Mandarin Chinese.

- **Values and customs.** Differences between values and customs often pose complex problems for effective logistics and supply chain management. Even something as simple as a business card can confound logistics managers when working abroad. For example, an American logistics manager, who typically travels with approximately 20 business cards, may unknowingly insult Korean, Chinese, and Japanese suppliers when accepting their business cards in typical American fashion. Americans usually grasp the center or center edge of the business card between the thumb and edge of the forefinger. The customary Korean, Chinese, and Japanese fashion of accepting a business card is to grasp each of the two bottom corners of the business card using the thumb and forefinger tips.

FIGURE 9.5 - CULTURAL DIFFERENCES IN HOW BUSINESS CARDS ARE ACCEPTED

Technological factors that can influence the management of global supply chains in a PESTEL analysis include a country's:

- **ICT infrastructure.** The energy, transportation, information communication technology, and other organized sets of facilities and systems allowing people and companies to operate within a country are examples of *infrastructure*. Acting as the backbone that enables businesses and individuals to operate as quickly, conveniently, and easily as they do, a country's infrastructure has an enormous influence on international supply chains. A country's *information communication technology infrastructure*, or *ICT infrastructure*, has become more important over the past couple of decades. Countries with an inadequate or outdated ICT infrastructure can cause significant supply chain delays and increased costs, especially when just-in-time, inventory visibility, and cloud-based systems are needed. When entering new countries, companies can look to the United Nations International Telecommunications Union (ITU) for useful information about a country's overall ICT infrastructure. The ITU publishes an annual ICT Development Index, also called the IDI, which measures countries' ICT development. These measurements are based on fourteen indicators of information communication technology access, use, and skills, including the percentage of households with a computer and internet access, mobile phone subscriptions per 100 residents, and percentage of the population with ICT skills. As reported in the ITU's *Measuring the Information Society Report 2017*, Iceland, Korea, and Switzerland topped the IDI list of the 176 countries listed with the United States in 16th place between France and Estonia.

- **Personnel preparedness.** The degree to which a country's workforce is educated and prepared for information communication technology (ICT) tasks can substantially influence its logistics and supply chain management. Most global companies rely on hiring local mid-level to lower-level logistics managers because of their understanding of the local workforce, infrastructure, and economy. These local managers must also be ready to learn and operate complex information and communications systems necessary to manage the supply chain. The ITU's *Measuring the Information Society Report 2018* found that many developing countries have had substantial growth in mobile-cellular networks and broadband internet access. However, it also found that a significant impediment to people accessing the internet was a lack of ICT skills. The more complex online and mobile telephone activities have become, the larger the learning curve for those new to them. Even if the technology is there, understanding local levels of ICT knowledge is essential when hiring local supply chain managers and operators.

Environmental factors that can influence the management of global supply chains in a PESTEL analysis include a country's:

- **Climates and climate change.** When a company's supply chain crosses countries worldwide, it crosses various climates and must be prepared. Climate and weather events can slow down and even halt supply chains when companies are not prepared. A company should know when the hurricane, monsoon, and snowstorms typically occur in countries their goods move through to adjust transportation needs and times accordingly. Companies should also consider and prepare for the climate change impacts in these countries, such as rising sea levels, erratic weather patterns, and more frequent avalanches in snowy areas. The climate-related wildfires in California and Australia from 2018 through 2020 had an enormous impact on local and global food supply chains. Companies impacted are taking this knowledge to plan for the future to minimize supply chain risks by planning alternate routes, suppliers, and production locations. Companies should also consider how their supply chains impact climate change in the countries where they do business. They must plan to: minimize this impact through reduced carbon emissions, streamline supply chains to reduce waste, maximize cargo container capacity for optimal loads, and optimize cargo transport routes for fuel-efficiency.

- **Recycling requirements**. Different countries handle recycling differently and have different degrees of regulation and law surrounding recycling requirements. *Recycling*, which is converting trash and waste products into reusable material, prevents pollution and conserves energy and natural resources by reusing materials. When a company's supply chain operates within a country, the company needs to know the laws and requirements related to recycling. When in Azerbaijan or Andorra, where there is little to no recycling, a company must plan to utilize and recycle goods in an environment that does not make it easy. When in Germany or Singapore, two countries with high household and corporate recycling levels, companies must understand how to follow national laws for recycling their supply chain waste and produce products and packaging that are recyclable. Countries may also have regionally-specific recycling initiatives, such as collecting and recycling food waste that cows can eat in India.

FIGURE 9.6 - RECYCLING AWARENESS POSTER IN INDIA

Legal factors that can influence the management of global supply chains in a PESTEL analysis include a country's legal understanding and accountability, protection of patents and trademarks, freedom in market competition, recourse for dispute adjudication, and adherence to international laws. One of the most commonly cited legal factors affecting international logistics management in many emerging and developing economies around the world is:

• **Corruption and the lack of legal recourse** of companies to counteract it. In these countries, companies' distribution channels are competing against an array of informal vendors. These informal vendors, often selling smuggled goods, can make consumer demand almost impossible to estimate. They also pose particular problems for strategic planning, alliances, and corporate control of global brands and pricing. In these markets, the same global brands can be competing alongside one another, with only their means of distribution, *traditional distribution* versus *smuggling*, separating them. For example, a Snickers bar marketed and distributed by Mars, Inc. might be competing side-by-side in a Kazakhstan market stall against a Snickers bar that disappeared from a distribution channel in Russia and smuggled into Kazakhstan. This parallel competition of the same goods from the same company makes it difficult for companies to evaluate consumer demand and build a legitimate and substantial presence in a new market.

9.3 TRADE AGREEMENTS AROUND THE WORLD

As defined earlier in this chapter, *international trade*, also called **overseas trade**, is the sales of goods and services across countries' borders. International trade relationships are the connection between **imports** (goods and services flowing into one country from another) and **exports** (goods and services flowing out from one country into another). To promote and protect international trade, countries set up trade agreements with other countries around the world. A **trade agreement**, also known as a **trade pact**, is a contractual agreement concerning the trade relationship between nations. Trade agreements may be **bilateral**, between two countries, or **multilateral**, between more than two countries.

Bilateral and multilateral trade agreements often establish areas of trade covered under the agreement. A **free trade area** is a set group of countries that have agreed to eliminate or minimize tariffs, product quotas, and other restrictions for goods traveling across the countries' borders. Its goal is to stimulate trade between the countries that are members. A free trade area is established under a **free trade agreement**, or **FTA**, which is the multinational agreement signed between these countries outlining the terms of this free trade area. Some free trade areas have existed for decades, such as the European Free Trade Association (EFTA) or the Common Market for Eastern and Southern Africa (COMESA). A more recently established FTA is the Comprehensive and Progressive Agreement for Trans-Pacific Partnership, or CPTPP, which became effective in December 2018 after the United States withdrew from signing the original Trans-Pacific Partnership, or TPP, agreement in 2016. The CPTPP is the third-largest free trade area globally and covers significant tariff cuts and eliminations between the member countries.

FIGURE 9.7 - COUNTRIES OF THE CPTPP FREE TRADE AREA

One subset of a free trade area is a ***trade bloc***. A trade bloc is a large free trade area of member countries, typically in the same region, joined together in a common agreement to reduce or eliminate barriers to trade throughout the entire bloc of member countries. These agreements to reduce or eliminate trade barriers include any range of formal trade, tariff, customs, and tax agreements across the trade bloc. The previously mentioned EFTA, or European Free Trade Association, is an example of a trade bloc. Its four members are Iceland, Liechtenstein, Norway, and Switzerland, and, as a bloc, these four countries have entered into a variety of trade agreements with non-EFTA countries around the world.

A ***regional trade agreement***, or ***RTA***, is a term used by the World Trade Organization when two or more countries enter into a reciprocal trade arrangement of rules that apply for all of its members. This reciprocal arrangement might present more favorable trade conditions between the countries, such as minimization or elimination of tariffs, quotas, and other restrictions. Although originally regionally based, members of an RTA do not have to be from the same region. The sea of politics and economics gets a bit murky because the terms free trade area, trade bloc, and regional trade agreement often mean the same thing or apply to the same relationships. It all depends on the agreement and whom you ask!

The ***World Trade Organization***, or ***WTO***, defines itself on its website, wto.org, as "the only global international organization dealing with the rules of trade between nations... The goal is to help producers of goods and services, exporters, and importers conduct their business." As of June 1, 2020, the WTO reported 303 active RTAs around the world. All RTAs in the WTO have in common that they are reciprocal trade agreements between two or more partners.

Some of the more widely known RTAs or regional groups established by RTAs include:

- **EC Treaty**, or **Treaties of the European Union**, which is a collection of treaties among currently 27 counties in Europe to establish and provide a working constitution for the European Union (EU) and its current member states. The earliest of the treaties dates back to 1957, and multiple counties have been added to the EU since. With Brexit, i.e., the UK's withdrawal from the EU in 2020, this marked the first time a member state had left the European Union.

- **United States-Mexico-Canada Agreement (USMCA)**, which replaced the North American Free Trade Agreement (NAFTA) on July 1, 2020. Not surprisingly, its members include Canada, Mexico, and the United States.

- **Southern Common Market (MERCOSUR)**, whose members include Argentina, Brazil, Paraguay, and Uruguay. Venezuela is also a member but has been suspended since December 2016.

- **Association of Southeast Asian Nations (ASEAN)**, whose members include Singapore, Brunei, Malaysia, Thailand, Philippines, Indonesia, Vietnam, Laos, Myanmar, and Cambodia.

- **Common Market of Eastern and Southern Africa (COMESA)**, which is a large free trade area in Africa whose members currently include Djibouti, Eritrea, Ethiopia, Somalia, Egypt, Libya, Sudan, Tunisia, Comoros, Madagascar, Mauritius, Seychelles, Burundi, Kenya, Malawi, Rwanda, Uganda, Eswatini, Zambia, Zimbabwe, and the Democratic Republic of the Congo.

There are also many RTAs between these regional groups and other countries, such as EU-Vietnam, MERCOSUR-Israel, and ASEAN-Republic of Korea. Finally, some RTAs are between two individual countries, such as India-Malaysia, Panama-Peru, Japan-Australia, and United States-Oman.

Another international trade factor with implications for logistics in the US are maquiladoras in Latin America. A *maquiladora* is a foreign factory in Mexico, Nicaragua, Paraguay, El Salvador, and other Latin America areas that imports materials and equipment duty-free and tariff-free, assembles or manufactures goods, and then exports them, typically back to the company's home country. Most Mexican maquiladora factories are owned by US companies from various industries, including transportation, electronics, textiles, and machinery. Maquiladoras can be 100% foreign-owned, but they can also be a joint venture between foreign and local companies.

Along with RTAs and the maquiladoras, another important element of trade arrangements is the *special economic zone* or *SEZ*. An SEZ is a clearly defined area of a country where trade laws are different from the trade laws in the rest of the country. The trade laws in special economic zones can impact tax, trading, customs, labor regulations, and investing in that area. There are currently over 5000 SEZs in the world.

FIGURE 9.8 - AERIAL VIEW OF THE COLÓN, PANAMA FREE TRADE ZONE

Two types of special economic zones are the *free trade zone* and the *export processing zone*. Also called a **foreign trade zone** or an **FTZ**, a **free trade zone** is an area within a country where tariffs, quotas, and bureaucratic requirements have been eliminated or minimized to provide incentives for foreign companies to do business there. FTZs are beneficial to the countries because they generate employment opportunities and foster the development of export-oriented industries. There are currently almost 300 FTZs in the United States, with many located near land, air, and sea borders at border crossings, international airports, and cargo ports. FTZs worldwide produce a variety of goods, including electronics, clothes, shoes, and toys. Examples of these FTZs are the Waigaoqiao FTZ in Shanghai, China and the Colón FTZ in Panama at the Atlantic gateway to the Panama Canal.

Another type of special economic zone is the **export processing zone**, also known as an **EPZ**. An EPZ is an area dedicated to improving and increasing exports from a country by encouraging foreign companies' investment. Like an FTZ, an EPZ removes barriers for foreign companies, often by providing tax exemptions. EPZs are generally found in developing countries and began as processing and assembly areas. They have grown to include technology parks, finance zones, logistics centers, and tourist resorts in more than 100 countries.

9.4 INTERNATIONAL TRADE DOCUMENTATION

As a supply chain grows across an increasing number of countries, a growing amount of paperwork is required. In the world of international trade, this paperwork is a necessity. Without accurate and timely documentation, companies would not be permitted to trade outside their own countries. Exporters, importers, shipping companies, freight forwarders, banks, insurance companies, the regulating authorities of the countries both importing and exporting the goods, consular offices, chambers of commerce, and a massive battery of attorneys are all involved in ensuring that a global supply chain's complex network of documentation is completed and completed correctly.

While thousands of different trade documentation forms vary from country to country and from company to company, global logistics and supply chain managers must understand six primary trade documentation categories. These six categories of international trade documentation are:

- **Transaction documents.** Also found in domestic trade, *transaction documents* are exchanged between a buyer and a seller as part of the agreement to sell or purchase goods. Examples of transaction documents include *RFPs, proposals, purchase orders, sales contracts*, and *commercial invoices*. Remember from Chapter 3 that an *RFP* is a *request for proposal* and that RFPs, proposals, purchase orders, and contracts are all vital documents in the *purchasing process*. In international trade, a **commercial invoice** is a legal document from a seller of goods (the exporter) to the buyer of goods (the importer). It is an essential document because it is contractual proof of the sale between the seller and buyer.

- **Export documents.** Documents required by the export authority of a country are called *export documents*. When completed and approved, these documents allow goods

1. Goods consigned from (Export's business name, address, country).

2. Goods consigned to (Consignee's name, address, country).

MINISTRY OF TRADE
OF THE REPUBLIC OF INDONESIA
CERTIFICATE OF ORIGIN

FORM B

Reference No. :

3. Means of transport and route (as far as known).

Shipped by :

From :

To :

Date of shipment :

4. For official use.

5. Item number.	6. Marks and number of packages	7. Number and kind of packages; description of goods.	8. Gross weight or other quantity	9. Number and date of invoices

10. Certification.

It is hereby certified, on the basis control carried out, that the goods stated above were produced in Indonesia.

11. Competent authority (name, full address).

....

(Signature) (Stamp)

FIGURE 9.9 - EXAMPLE OF A BLANK CERTIFICATE OF ORIGIN FROM INDONESIA

to leave a country. Export documentation varies according to the country of export and the goods involved. Examples of export documents include *export licenses and permits, Bill of Lading, export declaration and inspection certificates,* and *Certificate of Origin.* An ***export license*** is a document from a government licensing agency that allows the exporter to engage in specific export transactions. Different agencies in the same county may issue export licenses. For example, in the United States, the Drug Enforcement Agency controls export licenses for controlled substances, while the Food Safety and Inspection Service of the Department of Agriculture controls export licenses for meat and egg products. A ***Bill of Lading***, also referred to as ***BOL*** or ***B/L***, is a document issued by a carrier that acknowledges that specific, listed goods have been received as cargo for conveyance to a particular, listed place for delivery to an identified consignee. Translated into non-logistics human-speak, a transportation service company states on a BOL that it received goods and knows where to deliver them and to whom. An ***export declaration*** is submitted by an exporter at the port just before goods leave a country. And finally, a ***Certificate of Origin***, also referred to as ***C/O*** or ***CO***, is a document an exporter completes to demonstrate that the goods being exported originate in the country stated. A Certificate of Origin is necessary when countries have restrictions on imports from other countries. This document will allow the exporter to bring goods into the importer's country as long as they originate from an approved country. For example, cigar smokers in the United States cannot legally buy Cuban cigars in the US because they cannot be imported into the US and would not have a valid Certificate of Origin when entering the country.

- ***Carrier documents.*** *Carrier documents* are issued and used by a carrier or transportation provider, such as a barge, shipping line, railroad, airline, international trucking company, freight forwarder, or 3PLP. Examples of carrier documents include a *Bill of Lading* and *insurance and inspection certificates*. In a nutshell, a ***carrier's insurance certificate*** is written or electronically documented proof that a carrier has insurance for the vehicles they operate and the goods they transport.

- ***Import documents.*** Those documents required by the import authorities of a country are called *import documents*. When completed and approved, these documents allow goods to enter a country. Import documentation varies according to the country of import and the goods involved. Examples of import documents include *import licenses and permits, commercial invoices, Bill of Lading, Certificate of Origin, import or customs declaration*, and *inspection certificates*. In some countries grouped into trade zones through regional trade agreements, a common set of documentation and rules may be used across all countries. For example, the required customs import declaration document to import goods into any European Union country is called the ***SAD***, or ***single administrative document***.

- ***Banking documents.*** *Banking documents* are those documents required by the banks participating in international transactions. The types and degree of banking documentation required are influenced by the importing and exporting countries' regulations and banking practices. Examples of banking documents include all documents associated with company credit issues.

- ***Goods-specific documents.*** Finally, *goods-specific documents* are required for import or export based on unique requirements for the nature of the items traded. Goods-specific documents are often required for international trade of goods such as arms and ammunition, radioactive materials, animals, and food products. Have you ever moved with a dog or cat from one country to another? Some countries require little to no documentation, while others require extensive documentation, medical exams (for the pet), quarantine (for the pet), and microchipping (again, for the pet, but hopefully that one was obvious).

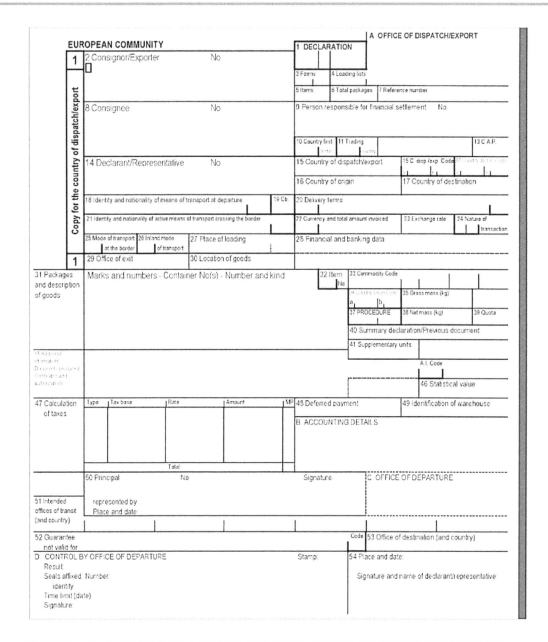

FIGURE 9.10 - EXAMPLE OF A SINGLE ADMINISTRATIVE DOCUMENT FROM THE EU

Some forms of documentation may span two or more of these six categories of international trade documentation when used by multiple parties for multiple functions. For example, you may have noticed that the *Bill of Lading* and *Certificate of Origin* made multiple appearances across the six categories. Also, the amount of documentation required may vary according to the nature of the goods and the regulations of the countries importing and exporting the goods.

9.5 INCOTERMS AND ISO 9001

In the world of international trade and documentation, global logistics and supply chain managers should know **INCOTERMS® rules**, the set of eleven standardized international terms that describe both the buyers and the sellers' obligations under a contract of sale. Each of the eleven INCOTERMS® rules represents a specific set of trade conditions that the buyer and seller agree to, clearly outlining and allocating the costs, risks, customs, and insurance responsibilities of each party in an international transaction.

INCOTERMS, an abbreviation for International Commercial Terms, are created and published by the International Chamber of Commerce (ICC), the world's largest international professional business organization. The ICC focuses on rule setting, dispute resolution, and policy advocacy in international trade. They are accepted by governments and other legal entities worldwide for terms used in international trade. By themselves, INCOTERMS® rules are not contractually or legally binding. Still, they are regularly included in buyer and seller contracts worldwide as a quick means of describing who is responsible for what in international sales.

Each of the eleven INCOTERMS® rules is referred to by a three-letter abbreviation. According to the IC's most recent update in 2020, the complete list of INCOTERMS® rules, along with a brief explanation of each, is:

1. **EXW** or **Ex Works** *(for any mode of transport)*: The seller makes the goods available for collection from its premises or another named location where the buyer or the buyer's agent will collect them and prepare them for export to the buyer's location. The seller generally has the goods packed ready for shipment. The seller does not load the goods or clear them for export.

2. **FCA** or **Free Carrier** *(for any mode of transport)*: The seller delivers the goods to a carrier or at another mutually agreed location where the seller will consolidate the goods into a larger consignment ready for shipment by an intermodal carrier.

3. **CPT** or **Carriage Paid To** *(for any mode of transport)*: Similar to FCA, the seller delivers the goods to a carrier or at another mutually agreed location, but the seller pays the freight, and the risk passes to the buyer once the goods are delivered to the first carrier, regardless of the type of transportation used.

4. **CIP** or **Carriage and Insurance Paid To** *(for any mode of transport)*: With CIP, the terms are the same as in CPT, but the seller also has to insure the goods for all modes of transportation to the buyer's destination. The risk transfers to the buyer when the goods are given into the first carrier's custody, after which point the insurance policy covers the risk.

5. **DAP** or **Delivered at Place** *(for any mode of transport)*: The seller pays for delivery to the named place or destination in the buyer's country, not including import clearance costs, and assumes all risk until the goods are ready to be unloaded by the buyer.

6. **DPU** or **Delivered at Place Unloaded** *(for any mode of transport)*: The seller pays for delivery to and unloading at the buyer's named location, not including import clearance costs, and the seller assumes all risk until the goods are ready to be received and unloaded by the buyer.

7. **DDP** or **Delivered Duty Paid** *(for any mode of transport)*: This term represents a maximum commitment from the seller and a minimum one from the buyer. With DDP, the terms are the same as in DAP, but the seller delivers goods to the buyer unloaded after paying the import duty to the destination country.

8. **FAS** or **Free Alongside Ship** *(for waterway transport only)*: The seller delivers the goods alongside the ship that will carry the goods overseas. The responsibility of the seller ends here. The buyer bears all costs and risks from this point on.

9. **FOB** or **Free on Board** *(for waterway transport only)*: The seller delivers the goods to the port of export, where they then become the buyer's responsibility as soon as they are loaded over the ship's side rail. The buyer bears the loss if the goods should fall and become damaged after being loaded onto the ship.

10. **CFR** or **Cost and Freight** *(for waterway transport only)*: The seller pays the costs and freight as far as the port of destination in the buyer's country, but the risk passes to the buyer as the goods cross the ship's rail in the port of shipment in the seller's country.

11. **CIF** or **Cost, Insurance and Freight** *(for waterway transport only)*: The seller is in the same position as in CFR but must also provide marine insurance during the carriage. The risk passes to the buyer as the goods cross the ship's rails, but the insurance policy covers the buyer's risk.

Another concept in international trade and documentation that global logistics and supply chain managers should know is *ISO 9001*. The **International Organization for Standardization**, or **ISO**, is an independent, nonprofit, international organization made up of 165 standards organizations from around the world, such as the American National Standards Institute in the United States and the Standardization Administration of the People's Republic of China (SAC) in China. In the ISO, these 165 worldwide standards organizations work together to create sets of unified international standards in various areas that impact our lives, such as credit card technology protocols, country codes for telephones and banking, food safety rules and practices, and guidelines for standard paper sizes. One of the sets of ISO standards that impacts supply chains is the ISO 9001 series, formerly known as the ISO 9000 series. The **ISO 9001 series** provide standards and requirements for companies' quality management systems. When companies purchase goods, they hope to purchase goods of adequate and consistent quality levels. If a supplier meets ISO 9001 requirements, buyers can be confident in the quality levels of their purchases.

FIGURE 9.11 - ISO 9001 CERTIFIED GM ASSEMBLY PLANT IN UNITED STATES

FIGURE 9.12 - ISO 9001 CERTIFIED RESTAURANT IN INDIA

FIGURE 9.13 - ISO 9001 CERTIFIED FISH MARKET IN JAPAN

CHAPTER 9 REVIEW QUESTIONS

1. What benefits does *international trade* offer a company? List five companies you buy products from that are engaged in international trade.

2. What is a *joint venture*? In what situations do companies form joint ventures?

3. What is a *wholly owned subsidiary*? What are the risks and benefits of forming a wholly owned subsidiary?

4. What is a *PESTEL analysis*? What are the six factors in a PESTEL analysis?

5. Select one of the factors of a PESTEL analysis. Write a brief analysis of that factor that would help a foreign company considering doing business in your country.

6. What is a *free trade area*? What is a *free trade agreement*? How are the two related?

7. What are two of the types of *special economic zones*? What is the difference between the two?

8. In your own words, describe one of the six categories of *international trade documentation*.

9. What is the purpose of the *INCOTERMS® rules*? Who uses them?

10. What is the *ISO*? Why is it important for supply chain management?

CHAPTER 9 CASE STUDY

DISASTER EVENTS AND GLOBAL SUPPLY MANAGEMENT

When small disasters happen, there are supply chain consequences. Imagine that you have just used the UberEats app to order an extra-large Sicilian style pizza from Pittsburgh Paulie's Pasta and Pies. Because the UberEats app has a real-time vehicle visibility function, you can see that the driver picked up your pizza ten minutes ago. Even though the driver is only twelve minutes away, the car hasn't moved for eight minutes. Your pizza is getting colder and colder by the minute. You look outside and see that it's a stormy day. High winds knocked down some trees in your area only eight minutes ago, causing immediate gridlock traffic that will not budge. This small weather disaster has harmed your pizza supply chain, destroying your weekly family pizza-and-games night or perhaps your blissfully-alone-Netflix-and-pizza night that you have looked forward to all week.

Although it disrupted the supply chain and was disastrous to your perfect pizza plans, this high wind disaster was a small, local event. Imagine events that happen on a larger scale and the impact they have on supply chains. On March 11, 2011, an earthquake in Japan and its subsequent tsunami resulted in catastrophic conditions for Japanese automobile manufacturers. With many of its automobile and parts manufacturing facilities and its suppliers' facilities destroyed, Toyota lost production of an estimated 400,000 vehicles worldwide, resulting in a loss of almost $2 billion in its second financial quarter. The company's operations and supply chain didn't return to normal until the end of 2011. The company had also lost many customers, which had a longer-lasting effect on its operations, its hundreds of thousands of employees, and the Japanese economy. From this regional disaster, automakers learned not to rely on one supplier or one set of suppliers set in one geographic region. Having multiple suppliers located in different areas can offset the hurt of regional disaster events.

The earthquake, tsunami, and the bulk of impact were localized to one geographic area. Now imagine a disastrous event of global proportions. We don't have to imagine such an event because we have all experienced one recently: the Covid-19 pandemic. A virus that stretched across even the farthest reaches of the globe, Covid-19 had a swift impact on global supply chains. China's supply chains stalled as the virus spread through the country, and workers were under quarantine. There were shortages of truck drivers to pick up and deliver cargo containers, cargo ships canceled sailings, and cargo sat backlogged at Chinese ports. India had over 50,000 containers backlogged and sitting in its ports as many truck drivers, and port workers could not work during the country's lockdown. As the virus spread through Europe, borders closed, and trucks lined up for miles and miles at national borders. In the United States, railroad cargo transportation decreased by approximately 20% in the first half of 2020, and ocean shipping decreased by almost 25%.

During a global pandemic like Covid-19, there is the obvious impact of the reduced workforce on the global supply chain. Many who work in manufacturing or logistics are sick, under quarantine, or under a regional or national lockdown, which slows down supply chains or even brings them to a standstill. People become worried about much-needed goods still being available at their supermarket or drug store. As a result, the term *supply chain* is heard from more politicians' mouths than ever, and there is an uptick in commercials and ads showing the strength of companies' supply chains. Everyone is telling people not to worry. But what do we do? Worry. This further complicates supply chains.

Because people worry about supply chain problems, they think about what they cannot do without and thus begins what appears to be a period of frenzied panic buying, or as described by Germans, *hamsterkauf*. People stock up on what they view as essential items with a long shelf life to get them through a period of crisis. What is essential varies from country to country, however. It's canned tuna fish and cereal in the US, pasta in Italy, garlic in Moldova, boxed wine in Finland, and marijuana in the Netherlands. One item that was viewed as absolutely essential in multiple countries during this period of hamsterkauf was... Can you guess? Toilet paper! People across the world were buying it up until the shelves were empty, and it was nowhere to be found along the supply chain.

TOILET PAPER AISLE OF GROCERY STORE IN TOWNSVILLE, AUSTRALIA ON MARCH 11, 2020

People were not using more toilet paper due to the coronavirus but were instead engaging in the rational practice of *forward buying*, purchasing goods in advance of requirements. As is often the case with forward buying during disaster events, people know that they will be at home longer than usual, so they stock up on essential goods for a longer timeframe. However, retail stores and online sellers only hold a few weeks of inventory. When people see items on store shelves diminishing, they are more likely to buy them and buy them in greater quantities. In the United States, toilet paper sales were up 734% on March 12, 2020, compared to the same day in 2019. By March 23, 70% of retailers and online sellers in the US reported that they were out of toilet paper. Even commercial toilet paper used for office buildings, restaurants, and other workplaces should have been plentiful because of stay-at-home and quarantine orders. However, commercial toilet paper and toilet paper from online Chinese suppliers began to run out in late March. The US wasn't alone in this massive forward buying of toilet paper. In the first few months of the global pandemic, Australia held the lead for toilet paper sales, sometimes at levels four or five times higher than countries hit harder by the virus.

This forward buying behavior during a disaster event leads to a *bullwhip effect*, as described in Chapter 7, and *overage* results. By July 2020, there was more than enough toilet paper to go around, with sales dipping lower than 2019 levels because many people didn't need to buy toilet paper anymore because they had months worth of inventory in their garages and basements.

Sometimes, there is a skewed perception of demand during disaster events, even though the supply should match standard demand patterns. People aren't using more goods but are instead buying more because of a perceived change in the environment. Supply chain professionals must perform a challenging balancing act between volatile and fluctuating demand patterns in these situations. In the case of toilet paper during the early days of Covid-19, there could have been a disastrous global bullwhip effect. Rather than ramp up production to levels to meet perceived demand, toilet paper executives focused on transferring commercial toilet paper inventory to domestic use. They also improved logistics and shipping practices to get inventory to customers quicker, and they reworked product packaging for customers' new needs of larger sizes with longer-lasting rolls.

The actual demand for some items increases during disaster events, however. After hurricanes, floods, and tsunamis, local water supplies can become compromised, and demand for bottled water skyrockets. During the Covid-19 global pandemic, the demand for items used in hospitals to handle the increasing number of sick and dying patients increased dramatically, such as the need for medical masks, respirators, ventilators, and oxygen. For people at home, who were told to use hand sanitizer and wash their hands with soap, the demand for hand sanitizer and liquid soap increased.

There seemed to be enough soap to satisfy the increasing demand, but soap manufacturers reached a problem with product packaging. There just weren't enough pumps produced for pump dispensers of liquid soap. Most pumps were made in China, but production could not be ramped up because employees were under stay-at-home orders. As already mentioned, manufacturing and outbound transportation in China had slowed because there were not enough employees working to keep the global supply chain moving.

Pumps were also far more complicated to reproduce than the soap itself. Many tiny parts are needed to create a soap dispenser pump. India even banned exporting pumps to meet local demand. In this case, supply chain and manufacturing professionals had to be flexible and reconsider product packaging. Unilever PLC began to move to squeeze bottles, and Colgate-Palmolive Co. used more screw tops. Companies in many countries embarked on advertising campaigns to encourage consumers to save pump top bottles for reuse. In London, firefighters got creative with reverse logistics and worked with a *Tops Off* campaign, in which they collected pump and spray tops for recycling and reuse.

During the global coronavirus pandemic, hand sanitizer was another item with increased demand and limited supply. Sales of hand sanitizer increased dramatically by 73% in March 2020, and stores were out of supply by the end of March. Hospitals and public buildings also had a significantly increased need but were having difficulty finding available supply. Some suppliers on Amazon engaged in price gouging, where the price of twelve 8oz bottles of Purell hand sanitizer jumped from $30 to almost $160 overnight. Even Amazon workers themselves in both the US and UK reported to CNBC in March 2020 that they were afraid to come to work because of what they perceived as unsafe working conditions, especially because of a shortage of hand sanitizer in the workplace. Employees in at least one Amazon Fulfillment Center in the US have since sued their employer after 44 cases and one fatality related to COVID-19.

The demand had increased and would continue to grow. The hand sanitizer industry predicted overall annual growth of 20% from 2019 to 2025. Manufacturers had to adapt. Local alcohol distilleries across the world began switching machinery settings to manufacture hand sanitizer for local customers. The World Health Organization published guidelines to help local businesses produce hand sanitizer. The US government even eased regulations to allow for more impurities in hand sanitizer sold.

Other companies that used similar ingredients and packaging began making hand sanitizer for the first time on a large scale. Starbucks reached out to Soapbox, one of its liquid soap suppliers, and asked them to supply hand sanitizer. Pharmacy chains and grocery store chains quickly followed suit. As a result, Soapbox invested time and trust in their supply chain relationships. It could source sanitizer ingredients and the much-coveted lids and pump tops when other companies could not. The company produced its first 3 million bottles of a brand new product line of hand sanitizers in less than two weeks, thanks to preexisting relationships with suppliers and creating ties with new supply chain partners. Because distilleries and soap companies were able to step in and assist with the increased demand, hand sanitizers were regularly back on store shelves by the summer of 2020.

So what lessons can we learn from disaster events and global supply chain management?

1. **Don't put all your eggs in one basket.** Like automobile manufacturers learned from the Japanese earthquake and tsunami, using multiple suppliers located in different parts of the world can offset the risk of localized disaster events.

2. **The bullwhip effect is a reality and will happen.** Supply chain managers need to be ready for variations in demand based on how human beings respond to disasters. Don't necessarily ramp up production to unrealistic levels and exaggerate the bullwhip effect's impact. It's more cost-effective to maximize the impact of the supply chain and get produced goods more quickly to consumers who need them.

3. **Identify real increases in demand during disaster events and consider the packaging.** Inexperienced companies may think only of the product they need to pro-

duce when genuine surges of demand happen during a disaster event. Sometimes it's harder to increase production or supply of the item's packaging. Supply chain managers should be ready with contingency plans for increased demand for goods *and* packaging.

4. **Utilize the power of reverse logistics.** When packaging sometimes just isn't available, consider how to utilize existing packaging. In the case of London and soap pumps, even the fire department might be willing to help.

5. **Look to alternate suppliers and maintain good supply chain relationships.** Starbucks couldn't find hand sanitizer, so it encouraged one of its soap suppliers to produce the much-coveted product. Because Soapbox already had strong relationships with its suppliers, it quickly adapted and produced hand sanitizer in a market with limited product supplies.

References:
Almeida, I. and de Sousa, A. (2020) Countries Starting to Hoard Food, Threatening Global Trade. Bloomberg. Retrieved from: https://www.bloomberg.com/news/articles/2020-03-24/countries-are-starting-to-hoard-food-threatening-global-trade

Altman, S. (2020) Will Covid-19 Have a Lasting Impact on Globalization? Harvard Business Review. Retrieved from: https://hbr.org/2020/05/will-covid-19-have-a-lasting-impact-on-globalization

Beauty Packaging. (2020) Updates on the Hand Sanitizer Shortage & FDA's New Guidance for Manufacturers. Retrieved from: https://www.beautypackaging.com/contents/view_breaking-news/2020-03-27/more-on-the-hand-sanitizer-shortage-fda-which-work-best-for-covid-19/

Dalavagas, I. (2020) The Impact of Japan's Disaster on Toyota, Honda, and Nissan. ValueLine.com. Retrieved from: https://www.valueline.com/Stocks/Commentary.aspx?id=10972#.XxhUIS2z1DM

Nickelsburg, M. (2020) Warehouse Workers Sue Amazon over COVID-19 Exposure After Death of an Employee's Relative. GeekWire.com. Retrieved from: https://www.geekwire.com/2020/warehouse-workers-sue-amazon-covid-19-exposure-death-employees-relative/

O'Brien, M. (2020) How Soapbox Pulled Off a COVID-19 Sanitizer Supply Chain Miracle. Multi Channel Merchant. Retrieved from: https://multichannelmerchant.com/news/soapbox-pulled-off-covid-19-sanitizer-supply-chain-miracle/

Palmer, A. (2020) 'They're Putting Us All at Risk': What It's Like Working in Amazon's Warehouses During the Coronavirus Outbreak. CNBC. Retrieved from: https://www.cnbc.com/2020/03/26/amazon-warehouse-employees-grapple-with-coronavirus-risks.html

PR Newswire. (2020) Hand Sanitizer Market in US - Industry Outlook and Forecast 2020-2025 Retrieved from: https://www.prnewswire.com/news-releases/the-us-hand-sanitizer-market-is-expected-to-grow-at-a-cagr-of-over-20-during-the-period-20192025-301046930.html

Twinn, I., Qureshi, N., López Conde, M., Garzón Guinea, C., and Perea Rojas, D. (2020) The Impact of COVID-19 on Logistics. International Finance Corporation World Bank Group. Retrieved from: https://www.ifc.org/wps/wcm/connect/industry_ext_content/ifc_external_corporate_site/infrastructure/resources/the+impact+of+covid-19+on+logistics

Wall Street Journal. (2020) Soap Makers Are Cleaning Up Amid the Pandemic, But Can't Get Enough Hand Pumps. Retrieved from: https://www.foxbusiness.com/features/soap-makers-are-cleaning-up-amid-the-pandemic-but-cant-get-enough-hand-pumps

Wieczner, J. (2020) The Case of the Missing Toilet Paper: How the Coronavirus Exposed US Supply Chain Flaws. Fortune. Retrieved from: https://fortune.com/2020/05/18/toilet-paper-sales-surge-shortage-coronavirus-pandemic-supply-chain-cpg-panic-buying/

Zhou, N. (2020) Off the Chart: Australians Were World Leaders in Panic Buying, Beating UK and Italy. The Guardian. Retrieved from: https://www.theguardian.com/world/2020/jun/03/off-the-chart-australians-were-world-leaders-in-panic-buying-beating-uk-and-italy

Chapter 10

Customer Service and the Supply Chain

Think back to some of the best and worst experiences you've had as a customer. Perhaps you were staying at home during a global pandemic and ordering your food through online and grocery store delivery services. After a month of sticking with just the basic staples of your diet, you decide to treat yourself and order a box of mint chocolate chip frozen Greek yogurt bars. You can almost taste their chilly yumminess as you put them in your virtual shopping cart. It's the middle of the summer. The average daytime temperature is above 104 degrees Fahrenheit, which is steamy 40 degrees Celsius. You live twelve miles away from the online grocery distribution center, and your house is usually the fifth or sixth stop in the delivery route, so you know that ordering frozen Greek yogurt bars is a bit of a gamble. The first time you receive them, you are ecstatic! The online grocer has delivered your frozen yogurt bars in a padded freezer bag accompanied by two frozen bottles of water to keep them cool. The box arrives with every mint chocolate chip Greek yogurt bar still frozen, intact, and indescribably delicious.

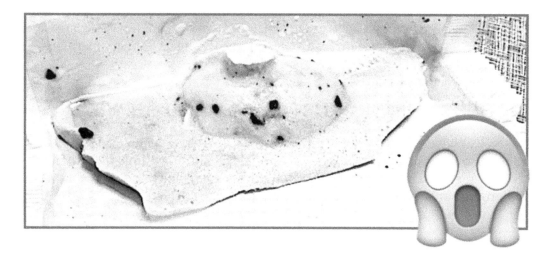

ATTEMPTED RE-FREEZING OF MELTED FROZEN YOGURT BAR

Because you had a good experience in the past, you decided to order your favorite box of mint chocolate chip frozen Greek yogurt bars again on a particularly hot day. You follow the grocery delivery route with the visibility function on its mobile phone app. As usual, your house is the fifth one in its delivery route. You wait patiently until... It arrives! Your scrumptious, frozen goodies are here! However, the yogurt bars that arrive are not frozen. Contained in each package within the box is a soupy mush. You notice that the frozen bars were not in a freezer bag. Instead, they were delivered in an ordinary shopping bag next to a ten-pound sack of potatoes, a pint of strawberries, and ten cans of tuna fish. On the way to your house without protection, your yogurt bars turn from solid to liquid. As a result of this highly disappointing experience, you vow to never shop with this online grocer again. Ever.

However, that is not the end of our story. There has to be a happy ending, right? You find out that the company has an online "no-hassle" return policy. Because the item is a food item, no actual return of goods is required because of the risk of introducing food that has been handled by others back into the supply chain. Instead, you select the item on your online shopping receipt that you want to return. You then choose the reason for your dissatisfaction from a drop-down list provided and are automatically refunded the amount paid onto the credit card used for the original payment. Although you are still disappointed not to have your yummy box of mint chocolate chip frozen Greek yogurt bars, you are happy the refund process took less than five seconds. You decide that, although you had a bad experience with your second attempt at ordering the world's yummiest frozen treat, you are satisfied with the service the online grocer provided overall, so you continue to use them for your online food shopping.

Although it may not be immediately apparent, this story shows how the customer experience and the world of logistics are inextricably linked. The logistics management decisions a company makes can directly influence the customer service and the quality of the customer's experience. In this case, the company provided good service with inventory and delivery visibility and bad service with inadequate packaging. It also provided a solution to a logistics-related problem through good reverse logistics in handling product returns. This chapter will explore the relationship between logistics and customer service and how a logistics manager can measure and analyze logistics performance to improve the customer experience.

10.1 UNDERSTANDING CUSTOMERS AND SERVICE

Before we look at how logistics and the customer experience are related, let's explore what we mean by *customer* and *customer service*. Although we usually think of customers as people, customers may also be companies. A **customer** is a person or company that receives a requested product or service. For example, Walmart is one of Coca-Cola's many customers. Customers are either *external* or *internal* to the company providing the product or service.

External customers are private individual end users or organizations that receive a product or service from a company *other than* their own company. For example, you buy a bag of tortilla chips from the grocery store, and the Taco House Restaurant chain buys the same chips from the manufacturer. You are both *external* customers because you are not part of North of the Border Snack Foods, the tortilla chip manufacturer. When we think of the word *customer*, we typically think of external customers.

Internal customers are the individuals or departments within a company who receive goods or services from within that same company. For example, at North of the Border Snack Foods, the production department creates, fries, and salts the chips, which they send to their *internal* customer: the packaging department. After the packaging department places the chip into bags and seals them, it sends the bags of chips to its internal customer: the finished goods warehouse. This process of sending goods from internal customers to internal customers continues until the product reaches the external customer and eventual end user. It is essential to be aware of the existence and importance of internal customers. However, for the remainder of this chapter, we will use the term *customer* to refer to external customers.

A product or service's ultimate success occurs when customers spend their hard-earned cash to buy that product or service. In most cases, external customers have a choice between different brands offered by competing companies. These customers make their choice based on how well a product or service meets their needs. Can the product or service be acquired easily and readily in the needed quantity and quality at the right time and place? Does the product or service meet their perception of a fair price? These questions are all being asked and answered while competitors are also trying to get their business. Customers almost always have choices, so they are continually evaluating one company's products and services against its competitors. In the case of our melted frozen yogurt bar, you (the customer) could switch to any number of competing online grocery delivery services for your frozen treat needs. However, the company with the melted bars retained you as a customer because they handled the melted product issue using swift and effective *customer service*.

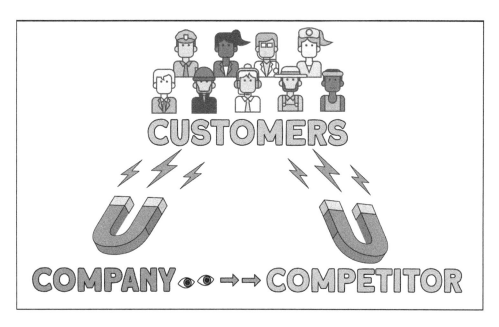

FIGURE 10.1 - COMPANIES, COMPETITORS, AND CUSTOMERS

A company wants to attract and retain customers, but so do its competitors. Therefore, as illustrated in Figure 10.1, the company must keep an eye on its competitors' practices and prices while adjusting its own to attract new customers and retain existing ones to achieve financial success. But what makes a company stand out from its customers? Decades ago, companies relied on lower prices to attract new customers, but customers today want more. They want a company that will meet their needs before, during, and after the sales transaction. All of a company's plans and actions to meet or exceed customers' needs before, during, and after a sale is called **customer service**. Many people, teams, and departments within a company and third-party service providers may all be involved in providing customer service in the hopes of attracting and retaining customers. When developing products, selling them, distributing them, and handling after-sales support, an effective company focuses on customer satisfaction and good customer service. Highly effective companies create and use customer service policies and standards to ensure consistent service levels to customers. In the case of our melted frozen yogurt bars, the online grocer appears to have adequate policies and standards for item refunds but no consistently practiced policy or standard for packaging frozen goods.

Below are a few definitions offering a basic understanding of some terms you may encounter in the world of customer service:

- **Customer Relationship Management**, also known as **CRM**, is an organization's department or approach used to meet customers' needs before, during, and after sales transactions. The primary functions of CRM are *marketing* (pre-transaction), *sales* (transaction), and *service* (post-transaction).

- **Customer Service and Support**, also known as **CSS**, is the department or function within an organization to whom customers turn for immediate help with a product or service after delivery. Typically, Contact Centers or Help Desks are part of CSS. Marketing, Sales, and CSS are often the three primary branches of a Customer Relationship Management department.

- A **customer service policy** is a written statement concerning how an organization or department will treat its external or internal customers and what customers can expect from the relationship. Many organizations post their customer service policy in the location visible to the customer during the sales transaction. For example, when you buy items in a clothing or electronic goods store, you will likely see the customer service returns policy printed on the receipt.

- **Customer service procedures** are the actual physical routines and detailed steps an organization or department uses to provide customer service to its external or internal customers. Many organizations develop these procedures as situations arise and do not put them in writing. However, far more effective companies record their customer service procedures in writing and make them available to all who provide or impact the organization's customer service. This practice allows for consistent customer service with all parties working toward the same customer service goals, such as putting yoghurt bars into freezer bags.

10.2 THE CUSTOMER EXPERIENCE

Over the past decade to decade and a half, there has been a gradual shift in focus in the world of companies and customers. Companies were originally focused on the *service* they provide to customers. Wanting to meet customers' needs, companies focused on their actions and the policies, procedures, and standards they establish to meet these needs. While there is still a focus on customer service, effective companies now have an additional focus: the *customer experience*. Rather than use a strictly linear approach by targeting a customer's need and addressing it through a customer service policy or practice, companies now use a holistic approach and consider the entirety of a customer's experience with the company and the product.

The **customer experience**, also called **CX**, is the customer's perception of a company based on all interactions with a company and its products. In our melting frozen yogurt bar example, the customer experience was a positive one when:

- *the bars were easy to order online, and you knew if the desired quantity was in stock and you could read nutritional information and reviews about them;*

- *there was inventory visibility on the company's app during delivery so that you knew exactly when your bars would arrive (and you even knew your driver's name and vehicle type); and*

- *the bars arrived on time and were left right at your front door in the shadiest spot.*

The customer experience became a negative one when you found that the bars had melted to a green, gooey liquid because the delivery packaging was inadequate for frozen goods. However, the customer experience had a happy ending when the refund process was online, easy, and immediate, and all future orders had adequate packaging so that your yogurt bars stayed frozen, even on the hottest and sunniest days.

The customer experience has become even more important than price for companies trying to distinguish themselves and stand out from their competitors. In a 2020 report called "Experience Is Everything," accounting firm PxC surveyed 15,000 people from 12 countries around the world. They found that customers' experience was overwhelmingly the primary deciding factor for people's purchasing decisions. They also found that a third of the respondents reported they would walk away from a brand they loved after a single bad customer experience and that the experience is more influential than advertising. Despite a positive customer experience being something respondents were willing to pay a higher price for across all industries studied, just less than half of US customers reported that companies provide good customer experiences.

Companies know that how customers perceive the customer experience with their company is important. Most effective companies try to manage this perception generated by the customer experience. Their goal is for customers to have a positive customer experience and thus continue to buy their products. Even better, companies want to create such a highly positive customer experience that customers become informal marketers for the company.

When customers tell their friends, family, and coworkers about a great experience they had with a company, that company is more likely to gain new customers than through advertising and expensive marketing campaigns. To manage and cultivate a positive customer experience, companies consider the customer journey.

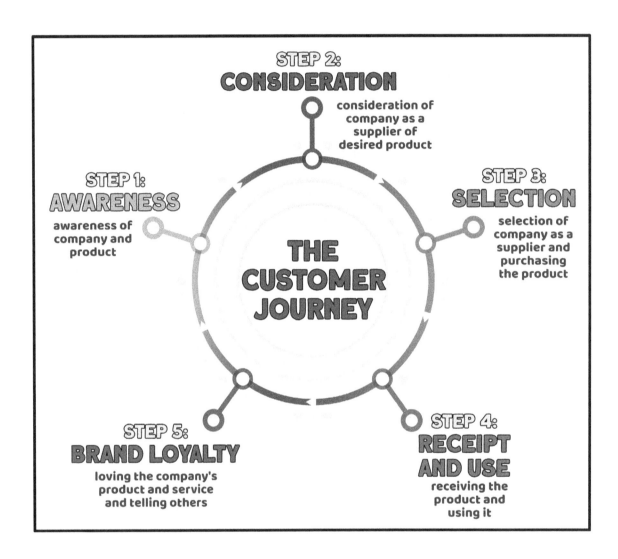

FIGURE 10.2 - THE CUSTOMER JOURNEY

When a customer buys or considers buying something from a company, they embark on the **customer journey**, as shown in Figure 10.2. A customer or potential customer can go through steps with a company, including

- **awareness** of the company and product,

- **consideration** of the company as a supplier of the product,

- **selection** of the company and purchasing the product,

- **receipt and use** of the product, and

- experiencing **brand loyalty** and advocating for the company and product.

When trying to improve the customer experience, companies create customer journey maps in which they map out the current stages of a customer's journey and explore opportunities for improvement. Even though we have been focusing on companies that sell products, companies that provide services also use customer journey maps, like the segment shown in Figure 10.3 from a larger Rail Europe Customer Journey Map.

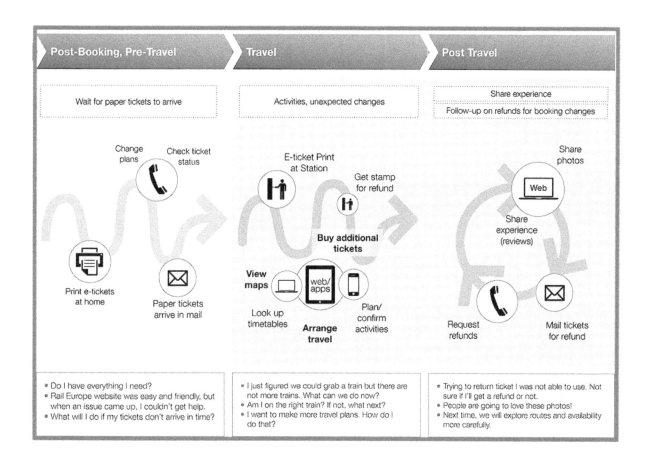

FIGURE 10.3 - CUSTOMER JOURNEY MAP EXCERPT FOR RAIL EUROPE

10.3 CUSTOMER SERVICE AND LOGISTICS MANAGEMENT

The goal of customer service is to meet customer expectations and produce customer satisfaction. Coincidentally, this is related to the concept of *utility* that we covered way back in Chapter 2. Utility is an economics term referring to the satisfaction or happiness customers experience when they consume a company's goods or services. The four primary types of utility are *form*, *time*, *place*, and *possession*.

Remember that ***form utility*** is the value added to products as their form changes, such as when raw materials are transformed or manufactured into finished goods. ***Place utility*** is the value added to products when they are at the right place within the supply chain, from the receipt of raw materials from suppliers to the distribution of finished goods to external customers. ***Time utility*** is the value added to products when they are available when both internal and external customers desire them. ***Possession utility*** is the value added to products when a desire to possess them has been created in consumers' minds and is further enhanced through customers' ease of owning the product.

In the relationship between a customer and a company providing a product or service, the company attempts to add value to the customer's experience using all four types of utility. First, when the company produces the product, its manufacturing or production department works to ensure that it will be of good quality and meet customers' expectations. This stage creates *form utility*.

Next, the logistics or physical distribution department works to ensure that the product is available where and when the customer wants it. This task includes ensuring that a delivery van is loaded on time and arrives at the end user's home at the correct time. It also includes using marketing forecasts of customer demand to ensure that the right quantity of goods is readily available through warehouses, distribution centers, or JIT systems at any given time of the year. This logistics-driven stage creates both *time* and *place utility*.

Finally, the marketing department is hard at work before the customer even places an order for the product by creating a desire for the product. They educate customers in what the product does. They also inform customers of its customer service policies, delivery, and corresponding service. This stage creates *possession utility*. If done correctly, the customer will evaluate whether the company and product have lived up to expectations after delivery. The customer then forms an evaluative judgment about whether they have received satisfactory customer service and are satisfied with their customer experience.

In many companies, the marketing department and its customer service arm then call, mail, or email customers to determine if they are satisfied with the product and each of the four types of utility the company has attempted to provide. Think about the last time you took your car to a large dealership's department for a routine service. Chances are, you received a follow-up telephone call or email a few days later asking you questions about your degree of customer satisfaction. Some companies even opt to get immediate feedback from customers, while customer service judgments are still fresh in their minds. For one furniture company in Alaska, immediate customer feedback is standard procedure. Immediately after Furniture Enterprises delivers and sets up a piece of furniture, its delivery crew provides a feedback section on the delivery bill, which must be signed by the customer. It contains a few brief questions asking customers about their degree of satisfaction with the furniture delivery and setup process. Regardless of how and when customer feedback on a company's utility provided is obtained, it is valuable knowledge that all departments within a company should use to continue to evaluate customer service and work to improve the customer experience.

Two of the four types of utility, *time* and *place*, are added by logistics and supply chain management activities, which means that the relationship between logistics management and a company's customer service is important. Logistics also plays a role in creating *form* utility by ensuring that the purchasing department purchases and gets the right production inputs to the company's manufacturing department. Finally, logistics plays a role in rounding our the four types of utility by establishing highly efficient and effective distribution processes, which makes potential customers want to do business with a company and purchase/possess their products, thus contributing to *possession* utility.

Logistics management also plays a critical role in all three stages of the customer service process. The **customer service process** has three primary phases that cover the entirety of the relationship between the customer and the company supplying the desired goods or services. The phases are *pre-transaction*, *transaction*, and *post-transaction*. Logistics plays a significant role in providing effective customer service during all three of these phases.

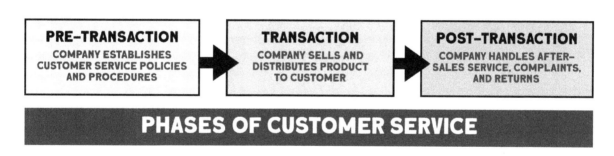

FIGURE 10.4 - THE CUSTOMER SERVICE PROCESS

The **pre-transaction phase** of a customer service relationship occurs *before* the sale has happened, often before the customer has gone anywhere near the supplier. During this initial phase, a company's Marketing department establishes its customer service policies and procedures, working closely with the Physical Distribution department or third party providers to ensure that these policies and procedures are realistic and consistently delivered to customers. For example, you might initially attract customers with a customer service policy that states, "We promise to deliver your order to you less than one hour after you have placed it." Unless you a company like are amazon.com, this highly unlikely for your physical distribution department to carry out. In the end, you might be left with some very unhappy, dissatisfied customers.

During the pre-transaction phase, companies also ensure that they are ready for potential upcoming sales by forecasting customer demand and maintaining enough inventory or immediate access to inventory to fill future orders. Companies also ensure that all of their information technology and communication systems are in place and in working order for upcoming sales to easily find and track products as orders are filled and delivered. In our age of immediate gratification and rapid advances in information technology, a critical element of customer service is **inventory visibility**. Inventory visibility is the ability of a company and its customers to know exactly where a specific product is in the supply chain at any time as it is being delivered. Because companies know exactly where their products are during the distribution process, they can inform customers of delays and early deliveries.

FIGURE 10.5 - INVENTORY VISIBILITY IS CRITICAL TO GOOD CUSTOMER SERVICE

The **transaction phase** of the customer service relationship is the *actual* sales transaction: the customer placing an order for a product or service and the company delivering that product or service to the customer. When a customer places an order for goods with a company, the order flows through the company's Finance and Marketing departments. However, it is essentially the company's logistics-related departments that fill the order. The order is picked from the warehouse, packaged for delivery, and transported to the customer. Although a company's marketing department typically makes the sale, it is the warehousing and physical distribution departments that do all the heavy lifting during this phase.

Finally, the **post-transaction phase** of the customer service relationship between a customer and a supplier takes place *after* the sale has occurred, and the product or service has been delivered. This phase is largely the domain of a Customer Service and Support department, which handles customer complaints, returns, recalls, customer satisfaction surveys, and post-sales service, including warranties and repairs. However, logistics-related departments such as Physical Distribution and Warehousing also play a significant role during this phase, especially in dealing with the reverse logistics aspects and physical handling of goods. Remember from Chapter 5 that **reverse logistics** is a specialized area of logistics concerned with the backward or reverse flow of goods up the supply chain. It involves moving goods from the customer back to the supplier due to product returns and safety or quality recalls.

In examining the three phases of the *customer service process* in Figure 10.4, you may have noticed that they are related to the five steps of the *customer journey* in Figure 10.2. Both occur simultaneously, but the customer journey's focus is the action a customer takes, and the focus of the customer service process is the action the supplier takes. Figure 10.6 illustrates the overlap in time between the phases and steps of each.

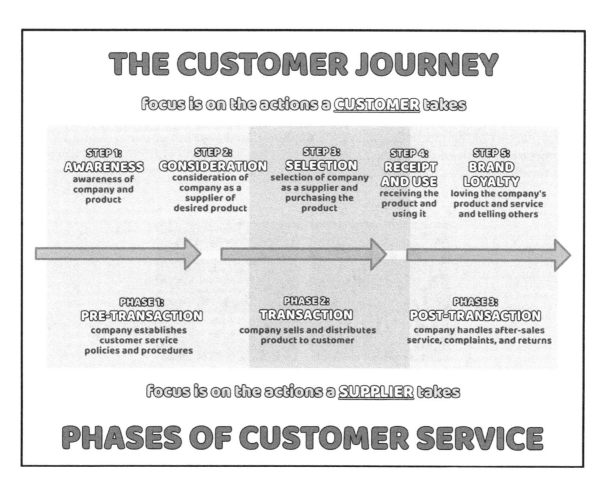

FIGURE 10.6 - CONNECTION BETWEEN THE CUSTOMER JOURNEY AND CUSTOMER SERVICE

10.4 THE MARKETING-LOGISTICS RELATIONSHIP

In Chapter 5, we learned that a company's Marketing department determines the nature and structure of its product's *distribution channel*, which is the marketing term for the flow of goods from the company to its customer. It also determines the *level of customer service* the organization provides throughout the channel. The Marketing department selects and designs the distribution channel, such as when, where, and to whom goods are delivered. It is then the mission of the organization's logistics operations departments, such as Warehousing, Physical Distribution, and Transportation, to carry out the Marketing department's plans and strategy. These logistics operations departments physically move goods through the distribution channel, ensuring that all of Marketing's distribution channel goals and promises to customers are met. In simpler terms, *Marketing* makes the customer service promises, and *Logistics* must keep them.

Marketing departments often establish their organization's customer service goals and promises based on the *marketing mix.* A term commonly used by marketing academics and professionals, the **marketing mix** is the mix of variable factors that a company controls and adjusts to achieve its desired level of sales and customer service while maintaining the desired level of profitability. The most commonly used classification of variable factors within the marketing mix is known as the **Four Ps of marketing**: *product, price, place,* and *promotion*. Companies make adjustments to their own decisions and levels of effort within each of these 4P categories to simultaneously maximize sales, service, and profitability. Logistics management is heavily involved in the *place* factor, but it also plays a significant role in all four factors of the marketing mix. Let's explore the 4Ps and their connection to logistics using our example of the online grocer and the Greek frozen yogurt bars from the beginning of the chapter.

FIGURE 10.7 - THE 4 PS OF THE MARKETING MIX

The ***product*** factor of the 4Ps focuses on getting the exact product customers want. It involves decisions regarding the product itself, such as *is this the product customers want,* and *is its construction both of sufficient quality and profitable*? While this is primarily the domain of the manufacturing or production department of an organization, logistics management also has an impact on the product factor in the following ways:

- **product availability:** Logistics managers must ensure that the products customers want will be available *when* they want them, either by forecasting demand and keeping products in inventory or by keeping the product readily available through just-in-time systems. With our online grocer, logistics managers must ensure that additional quantities of the frozen yogurt bars are held in inventory in the hottest summer months when customers want more frozen treats to cool them off. Customers logging on to the online grocer's app want to see that they can get one, two, three, or even ten boxes of frozen yogurt bars if they want them.

- **product quality:** Purchasing manager ensure that the quality of products purchased are up to the desired specifications and then, all of those in the Warehousing, Physical Distribution, and Transportation departments must ensure that the products are kept safe with the appropriate packaging and held securely during storage, handling, and transportation. This attention to product quality throughout the supply chain keeps our fragile frozen yogurt bars from melting. Sadly, there was a lack of attention to packaging for transport in our earlier example because the frozen bars were not placed in a freezer bag for delivery, resulting in poor product quality and a melted mess when our delivery arrived.

- **order accuracy:** Logistics managers must also ensure that customers get the exact products and quantity of products they want by paying close attention to the order picking stage of the logistics chain. If there are mistakes in the order picking stage and customers receive the wrong product, such as 300 boxes of green tea frozen yogurt bars instead of 300 boxes of mint chocolate chip ones, customers will be unhappy and unlikely to become repeat customers. The frozen yogurt bar company must also incur the added reverse logistics expense of collecting the wrong products and redelivering the right ones. Even worse, imagine if you have a nut allergy and receive pistachio-peanut frozen yogurt bars instead of mint chocolate chip ones. Because they are both sold in green packaging, you don't notice until you take your first bite, which nearly lands you in the emergency room because of your nut allergy!

The ***price*** factor focuses on setting a price good for the customer and the company's bottom line. It involves setting the right price for the product, which will generally be acceptable for the cost-conscious customer and the profit-focused supplier. In the case of our Greek frozen yogurt bars, you, as a customer, might be willing to pay $3.95 for a box of four bars, putting the price per bar at under a dollar. If the company were to raise the price to $5.25 per box, customers like you might not be willing to pay, especially if other brands are available in your desired price range. The Marketing department must find a balance in price between what is acceptable to the customer and profitable to the company.

While a company's marketing department is the major player in setting product prices, its logistics costs significantly impact these prices. Streamlined and efficient logistics processes reduce operational costs, which allows the marketing department to set lower product prices. Conversely, logistics inefficiencies and errors can significantly increase product prices. If customers' orders are filled incorrectly or incompletely, delivered late, or damaged in transit, additional logistics costs are incurred. Companies must correct orders and handle returns, such as in the case of the customer that ordered 300 boxes of mint chocolate chip frozen yogurt bars and received green tea flavored bars instead.

The **place** factor concerns getting the product to a customer *where* it is needed *when* required, which is the responsibility of the company's Logistics department or supply chain managers. Warehousing, Order Picking, Physical Materials Handling, and Physical Distribution departments or sections all work together to ensure a correct, on-time delivery and a reduced overall order cycle time. The **order cycle time** is the time it takes for a company to fill an order, from the time the customer places the order to the time the customer receives shipment of the product. Because we live in a world of instant gratification, the shorter the order cycle time, the greater customer satisfaction levels.

When placing an order with an online grocer for frozen yogurt bars and other needed foods and household products, most customers like to have the same flexibility in selecting a delivery time they have if they choose to go to a grocery store themselves. Customers are more likely to use a particular online grocer as a supplier if they can get immediate or same-day delivery rather than wait three or four days for the next delivery window. Customers also like to know *where* their groceries are while traveling en route and receive a notification when delivered, allowing customers to understand delivery delays due to traffic or bad weather. They can see these delays happen in real time through the delivery inventory visibility function of the online grocery store's app.

Finally, the **promotion** factor of the 4Ps focuses on educating consumers about the product and all of its wonderful qualities, existing incentives to purchase the product, and how and where they can buy this amazing product. This task of educating customers is handled by a company's Marketing department, which attempts to create a desire for the product in the consumer market and then sell it to customers. Although its role may be less evident in this part of the marketing mix, the Logistics team plays a significant role in the informal promotion of a company's product to potential repeat customers.

When customers order a product, they do not usually meet anyone from the company selling the product until it is delivered onto their doorstep or into their loading bay. A company's physical distribution employees, professionalism and courtesy, and accuracy and timeliness with which it fills an order are all part of its product promotion efforts. When a company handles physical distribution well, customers feel more inclined to purchase its products again. If a company handles physical distribution poorly through late deliveries or impolite employees, customers are likely to look elsewhere when purchasing similar products in the future. With our melted frozen yogurt bar example, if the online grocer had not quickly fixed the problem with its easy online refund process, you might be tempted to explore other online grocery suppliers for your future frozen treat needs - and for all other groceries and household items as well.

THE EXTENDED MARKETING MIX

The traditional marketing mix includes the 4Ps: *product, price, place*, and *promotion*. However, some companies use the ***extended marketing mix*** when setting their customer service and marketing goals, which includes seven factors that start with the letter P. The 7Ps are the original four (product, price, place, and promotion) plus *people, physical evidence*, and *process*.

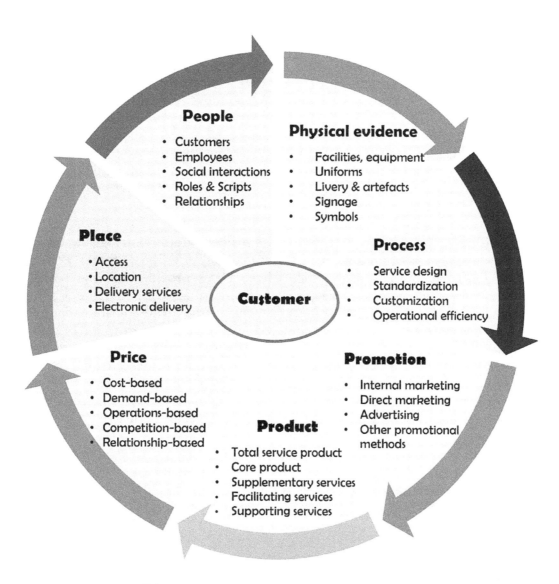

FIGURE 10.8 - THE EXTENDED MARKETING MIX

Now that we understand the role logistics management plays in marketing and customer service, let's look at a few fundamental, bare-bones rules logistics managers follow to help their organization provide exceptional customer service. While most of these may seem obvious, they sometimes get forgotten or neglected as managers become occupied with immediate tasks and putting out fires in their day-to-day operations.

The basic rules for exceptional logistics management customer service are:

- **Fill the order correctly.** It is essential to deliver the customer *what* they want in the right *quantity* and of the right *quality when* and *where* they want it. Performing this first step keeps customers happy and avoids costly reverse logistics corrections. In our case of the melted frozen yogurt bars, the online grocer loses the cost of the box of bars every time there is a melting incident.

- **Address mistakes immediately and professionally.** No matter how well you follow the first rule, mistakes do happen. When they do, a company's logistics management must address these mistakes immediately and professionally while keeping the customer informed throughout the process. When considering your company for repeat business, customers are more likely to remember how well a mistake was addressed rather than remember the mistake itself. In the case of our melted frozen yogurt bars, the company's immediate and easy refund process keeps customers coming back.

- **Consider how to provide added value and service.** Good logistics teams are always on the lookout for how to improve what they offer the customer. For example, companies may find ways to decrease delivery times, provide additional packaging to minimize product damage, or keep customers informed of product location through visibility functions in apps while in transit. During the Covid-19 pandemic, Amazon Fresh, the grocery arm of amazon.com, received so many orders that it couldn't keep up with demand. Amazon Fresh decided to first focus on its regular, pre-existing customers. Most of these customers would stick around if they received the same quality of service before, during, and after the pandemic. To continue to provide the same steady quality and immediate service to their regular customers, Amazon Fresh temporarily halted accepting new members during its busiest period.

- **Perform customer service audits.** Logistics managers can gain much insightful information on how to improve customer service through customer service audits. In these audits, external and internal customers are questioned about their degree of satisfaction with specific logistics-related elements of the transaction in ordering and receiving the product.

- **Develop repeat customers.** Above all, logistics managers and operators must remember that their primary goal is not merely to fill an order and deliver it. Their goal is also to provide an exceptionally-good experience for the customer, which will make them want to do business with the company again. Many organizations spend a lot of money attracting customers, only to lose them by poor customer service.

10.5 CUSTOMER SERVICE INFORMATION AND METRICS

Throughout this chapter, we have established that logistics plays a significant role in customer service. To maintain and increase customer service levels, logistics and supply chain managers first *isolate each of the logistics elements* that impact customer service. Next, they *measure and analyze these elements* based on preset standards to see if their department's contribution to the company's overall picture of customer service is sufficient.

Let's now look at how logistics managers measure and analyze the elements of their company's logistics performance needed to maintain acceptable customer service levels. As shown in the table in Figure 10.9, these logistics performance elements can be categorized and sorted into each of the three phases of customer service: *pre-transaction, transaction*, and *post-transaction*. Once sorted into their customer service phase, these logistics elements are then measured by logistics managers and their staff. These measurements are analyzed and compared to preset standards based on what the company believes is acceptable to achieve desired customer service levels.

For example, in the pre-transaction phase of customer service, logistics managers are concerned with assessing the logistics element of *product availability*. These managers want to be certain that they are prepared for customers' orders by holding or having ready access to enough finished product to meet customer demand and thus provide an adequate level of customer service. They can use product demand forecasts to set the desired inventory level to hold to meet potential customer needs. Logistics managers can then periodically measure the actual inventory percentage to see if it matches the preset level desired.

In the table in Figure 10.9, logistics elements that impact customer service, such as product availability, are examined across each of the three phases of customer service. The table then provides questions logistics managers ask about each logistics element related to customer service and how to measure this element's performance. Larger companies use customer relationship management (CRM) systems or modules within their ERP systems. Remember from Chapter 7 that an ERP system, or enterprise resource planning system, is a type of information system used across an entire company for planning and managing its resources.

As long as a company has a customer service policy and procedures, understands the role of logistics in customer service, and understands the impact of logistics performance, nothing else can go wrong for a logistics manager wanting to provide exceptional service, right? Wrong! No matter how well a company and its managers understand the impact logistics management has on customer service and how to measure and assess logistics performance, something can still get in the way: human behavior. In the next chapter, we will explore how to address the unique, unpredictable, and sometimes-disruptive human side of the logistics-customer service interface through leadership in the supply chain.

		LOGISTICS	OVERVIEW	PERFORMANCE MEASURE
Phase of Customer Service	**Pre-Transaction**	**PRODUCT AVAILABILITY**	Will the product be ready and available, even before the customer's order has been placed? Demand forecasts are used to determine the stock levels of products that should be held. The product availability is the percentage of product currently held compared to these predetermined levels.	% of product available compared to predetermined level desired
		INFORMATION AND COMMUNICATION SYSTEMS	Are the information technology and communication systems adequately prepared for future transactions? Can the systems get accurate and timely information to customers?	1. % of systems functioning correctly 2. Tests and spot checks of systems for speed and accuracy of information transfer
		CUSTOMER SERVICE POLICY CONSISTENCY	Do the current customer service policy and standards set by the organization match its logistics capabilities?	Comparison of company customer service policy with realistic order picking and distribution standards
	Transaction	**STOCK LEVELS**	Is enough stock available to fill a customer's order?	% or amount of desired product in stock
		ORDER CYCLE TIME	How long does it take to fill a customer's order from the time the order is placed until the customer receives the goods? Was the delivery early, on time, or late?	Speed and historical consistency of both the entire order cycle and its individual segments
		DAMAGED SHIPMENTS	Are the goods damaged during order picking, packaging, or in transit?	% or number of goods damaged in shipment to the customer
		ORDER ACCURACY	Is the order sent to and received by the customer accurate? Have the correct types, quantities, and qualities of the item been received?	1. % or amount of current order filled correctly 2. Number of mistakes in order filled
		ORDER INFORMATION AVAILABILITY	Is product information readily available to the organization, such as in-stock availability? Is delivery information such as inventory visibility readily available to both the organization and the customer?	1. Number of occurrences of unavailable information per transaction 2. Customer evaluation of quality and content of information available
	Post-Transaction	**POST-SALES SUPPORT**	How quickly and professionally are customer complaints handled by the logistics department? How quickly are product returns picked up?	1. Response time to customer complaints 2. Customer evaluation of quality of response to complaints
		POST-SALES SERVICE	How quickly and professionally are warranty and repair service matters handled by the logistics department? Are customers satisfied with the quality of reverse logistics service they receive?	1. Response time and quality in handling warranty service and repairs 2. Customer evaluation of quality of post-sales service
		RECALLS	Are product recalls handled rapidly and professionally? Are all product owners reached?	1. Recall scope & response time 2. Customer evaluation of recall process

FIGURE 10.9 - MEASURING LOGISTICS PERFORMANCE IN THE CUSTOMER SERVICE PROCESS

CHAPTER 10 REVIEW QUESTIONS

1. What is the difference between an *internal customer* and an *external customer*? Provide an example of each.

2. What is *customer service*? Who is responsible for the customer service provided to a company's external customers?

3. What is the role of *Customer Relationship Management* in a company? What is the connection between *CRM* and *CSS*?

4. What are the four types of *utility*? What do they have to do with customer service?

5. What is the first phase of the *customer service process*? What role does logistics play in this phase?

6. What are some examples of *reverse logistics*? During which phase of the customer service process do they occur?

7. What is a commonly used classification of the *marketing mix*? What does each of the four letters represent?

8. What role does logistics play in one of the letters of the marketing mix?

9. Why do logistics managers perform customer service audits?

10. How is *order cycle time* used as a performance measure of the transaction phase of customer service?

CHAPTER 10 CASE STUDY

SELF-SERVICE IN THE CUSTOMER EXPERIENCE

An increasingly important element of the customer experience is **self-service**, the practice of companies allowing customers to handle the selection, picking, and payment of goods or services themselves without human assistance from employees during the sales process. As twenty-first-century consumers, we want to be able to walk into a store and get information about products or pay for a purchase with no human interaction. We want to be able to shop from the comfort of our own home in the middle of the night in our pajamas if the mood strikes us. And when things go wrong, we want an immediate and seamless customer service resolution process that doesn't involve the time and stress of real people asking us questions.

We have grown accustomed to self-service since the invention of the vending machine in 1833, the installation of the first self-service gas pumps in 1964, the creation and rapid growth of ATMs in the 1990s, and the continued use of service kiosks and self-checkout stands across stores, airports, and restaurants throughout the 2000s. In their 2019 Annual Connected Retailer Survey, technology solutions company SOTI found that 73% of shoppers preferred to use self-service technology in brick-and-mortar stores to improve their shopping experience and minimize human interactions with store employees.

GROCERY STORE SELF-CHECKOUT IN BERGEN, NORWAY

It's not that shoppers don't want other humans in their customer experience, however. A PWC study found that 82% of US consumers believe that human interaction is an integral part of the customer experience. As consumers, we want a combination of technology and social interaction, with technology to provide immediate service where it can, like providing information or handling the checkout process instead of waiting in line for a human to handle it. In some stores, you may have to wait 15 minutes for a human being to find out if a desired item is in stock, while in other stores, you may be able to open the store's app and see how many items are available in the store and other nearby locations. Which store do you think is more likely to result in a positive customer experience?

When we desire human interaction in our shopping experiences, we typically have more complex problems or immediately need to address issues and fix problems that technology cannot. For example, what if an app tells you that a store has ten items in inventory, but you cannot find them, even when looking in the location described in the app. Rather than go to a customer service desk where an employee looks it up and tells where you might be able to find the item, a more desirable customer experience would be for any available employee to walk you to the item. The employee would make sure it is there and that they have fully resolved your problem, and that they have answered all your additional questions.

To free up employee time for more complex and meaningful customer interactions, companies understand the importance of a self-service customer experience. They also know they must do it correctly and without flaws. The PWC study found that 32% of consumers worldwide will walk away from a favored brand after a single bad customer experience. Imagine that you are in a grocery store and decide to pay using self-checkout because you think it will save you time. However, depending on when and where you shop, you may end up waiting in a self-checkout line 10 minutes or more. This is just as long as you would wait for a human-manned checkout, but you then have to do your own work in checking yourself out, which can be onerous if you've purchased lots of vegetables and bulk items without bar codes!

To improve customer service and allow for immediate checkout and payment, some grocery and retail locations have begun to implement Scan & Go technology, where customers use their own devices. For example, in Walmart-owned Sam's Club locations, customers can use the Sam's Club app on their mobile phones to scan items, pay for their purchases, and show an employee their resulting QR code to be scanned as they leave the store. No waiting in a single line! This is an example of *__frictionless shopping__*, in which a retailer sets up an in-store customer experience that is not impeded or slowed down by any unnecessary actions. Customers can select items and walk out of the store with them as quickly as they desire.

To make the customer experience even more frictionless, Amazon has created brick-and-mortar stores called Amazon Go. In these stores, customers scan their app as they enter, select items from the shelves as they would in any other grocery store, and then walk out with no scanning and no additional payment action. Amazon Go uses a Just Walk Out system, a combination of 3D vision cameras, deep learning algorithms for product identification, and software systems to tie it all together for a seamless and frictionless customer experience. In 2020, Amazon licensed the Just Walk Out system and began selling it to other retailers who wanted to provide faster and frictionless shopping experiences for their customers.

Companies like Amazon and Walmart have invested a lot in technology software and hardware to enhance the customer experience and negate time-consuming human engagement when it's not needed. But what about companies that sell products that typically involve lots

AMAZON GO GROCERY STORE IN SEATTLE, WASHINGTON

of human interaction? Can these companies create opportunities for self-service in the customer experience? Let's imagine that you have to buy a pair of eyeglasses. Do you think an eyeglasses company could build a successful self-service customer experience? How about a self-serve experience in which customers don't have to leave the comfort of their own homes to buy a pair of prescription spectacles?

In 2008, four MBA students at the Wharton School of Business asked themselves those very questions. Two years later, they launched their website, WarbyParker.com, which has grown into a highly popular online **D2C (*direct to consumer*)** business selling prescription eyeglasses, sunglasses, and contact lenses. The company has crafted a customer experience that combines both high-tech and old school techniques. On the fun and user-friendly Warby Parker app, customers can take a photo of themselves and virtually "try on" all the frames the company sells. There are even quizzes with fun illustrations to help customers select the frames that will fit and look the best on them. Then, when a customer has selected the top five frames, they place an order through the app or on the company's website, and the frames are sent to the potential customer for a "Home Try-On." Customers have an old-school mail-order experience of trying on the frames in the comfort of their own homes before making a decision or before placing an order for five more new frames to try on. There is lots of sophisticated technology behind Warby Parker's customer experience. However, the company's goal is to make the entire experience a fun, useful, inexpensive, and meaningful one, with paired donations of glasses and personal protective equipment to those in need. All accomplished when and where the customer wants to with human interaction only when it's needed.

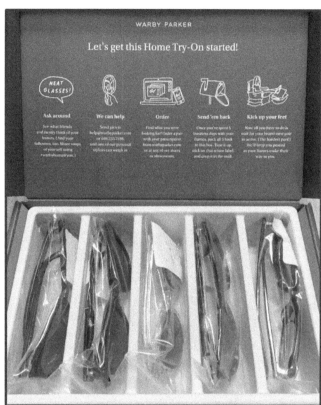

WARBY PARKER IN-APP VIRTUAL TRY-ON (LEFT) AND MAILED HOME TRY-ON (RIGHT)

References:

Almeida, I. and de Sousa, A. (2020) Countries Starting to Hoard Food, Threatening Global Trade. Bloomberg. Retrieved from: https://www.bloomberg.com/news/articles/2020-03-24/countries-are-starting-to-hoard-food-threatening-global-trade

Carroll, J. (2017) Computer Vision and Deep Learning Technology at the Heart of Amazon Go. Vision Systems Design. Retrieved from: https://www.vision-systems.com/non-factory/article/16750602/computer-vision-and-deep-learning-technology-at-the-heart-of-amazon-go

Convenience Store News. (2020) Amazon Selling 'Just Walk Out' Frictionless Checkout Platform to Retailers. Convenience Store News. Retrieved from: https://csnews.com/amazon-selling-just-walk-out-frictionless-checkout-platform-retailers

PWC. (2018) Experience Is Everything. Here's How to Get It Right. Retrieved from: https://www.pwc.com/us/en/advisory-services/publications/consumer-intelligence-series/pwc-consumer-intelligence-series-customer-experience.pdf

QikServe. (2018) The Evolution of Self-Service Technology. QikServe.com. Retrieved from: https://www.qikserve.com/self-service-tech-a-history/

SOTI. (2019) Annual Connected Retailer Survey: New SOTI Survey Reveals U.S. Consumers Prefer Speed and Convenience When Shopping with Limited Human Interaction. SOTI.net. Retrieved from: https://soti.net/resources/newsroom/2019/annual-connected-retailer-survey-new-soti-survey-reveals-us-consumers-prefer-speed-and-convenience-when-shopping-with-limited-human-interaction/

Winfrey, G. (2015) The Mistake That Turned Warby Parker into an Overnight Legend. Inc. Retrieved from: https://www.inc.com/magazine/201505/graham-winfrey/neil-blumenthal-icons-of-entrepreneurship.html

Chapter 11

Leading and Managing in the Supply Chain

Since the early 2000s, Canadians have been crossing the US border to buy milk, household items, and fashionable clothing for tweens at big-box retailer Target, known for its one-stop-shopping and affordable merchandise. Because Canadians seemed to love the US stores and its competitor Walmart was successful in Canada, the Target retail chain entered full force into the Canadian market, opening an impressive 133 stores in a short time between 2013 and 2014. As Canadians began to shop in their new local Target stores, they noticed that many shelves were empty. Perhaps worse, there were almost no locally produced goods or even any Canadian goods. And worst of all, most items were more expensive than in the US stores. Unfortunately, Target had expanded too quickly in Canada. The company did not take the time to develop its distribution channels and a base of local suppliers. Before opening its stores, Canadian Target employees warned company leaders about problems with distribution and glitches in the new technical system, hoping to delay the scheduled store openings. The Target Canada leadership team, comprised mostly of American Target executives, decided to push on and keep the original store launch dates. This team was led by a less experienced American CEO who had never led a store launch in another country before. All of this resulted in brand new Target stores in Canada with empty shelves and many expensive imported goods that customers were accustomed to purchasing from local producers at lower prices. Some potential Canadian customers stayed away from Target stores while others kept crossing the border to shop in US Target stores for better bargains. After losing a staggering $2.1 billion in these first two years with no hopes of reaping a profit until 2021, Target decided to close all 133 of its Canadian stores in 2015 and filed for Canadian bankruptcy protection.

KFC, the current moniker for Kentucky Fried Chicken, is a US-based fast food restaurant chain known for its fried chicken. KFC, the second-largest restaurant chain in the world, opened its first overseas restaurant in England in 1965. The UK's KFC operation has become a finely tuned machine and has grown to over 900 restaurants. However, in February 2018, the thriving fast-food chain had to close over three-quarters of its restaurants because it had run out of chicken! KFC had a new logistics service provider in the UK who had just one warehouse in the entire country. A series of traffic accidents occurred, slowing down and stopping traffic in the three major highway junctions near the warehouse. Trucks were backed up in the traffic and eventually could not leave the warehouse, causing a few days of delivery delays and leaving KFC restaurants across the UK without chicken for a few days in mid-February. Rather than panic or shut down restaurants and wait for the problem to go away, the company's leadership trusted a unique and bold idea championed by the KFC UK Chief Marketing Officer. The company immediately addressed the problem and informed the public through a humorous social media campaign and full-page newspaper ads with an empty chicken bucket labeled FCK instead of KFC, and read, "A chicken restaurant without any chickens. It's not ideal." The company also apologized to customers and let everyone know that employees would continue to be paid, even if their restaurants were closed. Customers may have been initially upset by the supply chain disruption but were won over by the honest, humorous apology campaign. As a result, KFC remains a staple of the UK fast-food dining scene today and consistently ranks among the UK's highest-earning restaurant chains.

Target in Canada and KFC in the UK are examples of two supply chain failures but with two very different outcomes. Why did one story have a happy ending and the other a tragic ending? It all came down to differences in the management and leadership of these companies during a supply chain crisis. This chapter will explore the concepts of management and leadership and their implications for logistics and supply chains.

11.1 THE PEOPLE CHAIN

Even if you have never worked in the logistics field, after reading the first ten chapters of this book, you now have a pretty good idea of what logistics is and how supply chains function. When we think of supply chains, we generally think of a *flow of goods*. We think of a flow initiated by a user's need, moving seamlessly from raw materials' suppliers to factories to warehouses to distribution centers, finally reaching the eventual retailer or end user. We think of physical goods, transportation equipment, and advanced IT systems. However, when most of us think of supply chains, we often overlook the tens, hundreds, or even thousands of people involved. There are people who place the orders, people who receive the goods, people who check the order after it is received, people who store and issue the goods, people who drive the truck and pilot the ships to get the goods where they need to go, people who set prices, people who keep information systems running, people who make the big corporate decisions, and so on, almost ad infinitum! Figure 11.1 shows an example of where some of the people are in the Orange-U-Yummy simple supply chain from Chapter 1.

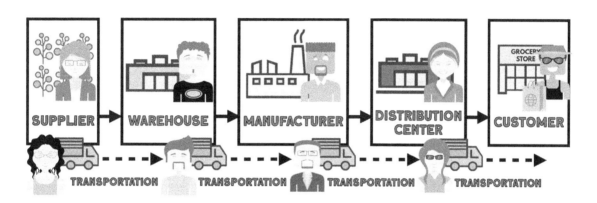

FIGURE 11.1 - SOME OF THE PEOPLE IN THE ORANGE-U-YUMMY SIMPLE SUPPLY CHAIN

But isn't a supply chain really about the physical supply? Why mention all of these people? In a supply chain, there is work to be done. Goods must be moved and handled, and decisions must be made. So who does all this work in the supply chain? While there are a few robots and some automation in supply chains, *people* do most of the work in supply chains. According to a 2018 *Harvard Business Review* article titled, "The Supply Chain Economy and the Future of Good Jobs in America," 37% of all jobs and 44 million people are part of supply chains in the United States. Figure 11.2 highlights where people are in the complex supply chain from Chapter 1.

People in a supply chain do not act independently or simply work at tasks as they see fit. Instead, there is a coordinated work effort between tens or hundreds or even thousands of people who must work together and communicate to keep supply chains flowing quickly, smoothly, and efficiently. In their various roles, such as purchasers, suppliers, warehouse managers, and customers, *people* are the supply chain's links. Their relationships are the essential solder of the supply chain's links. If even one relationship is weak, the entire chain can fail.

To assign, maintain, and optimize the work that keeps a supply chain running, both *management* and *leadership* are required. Also, to ensure that supply chain relationships are functioning well and providing an optimal output for supply chains to flow smoothly, people in the supply chain will need to understand management skills and management principles.

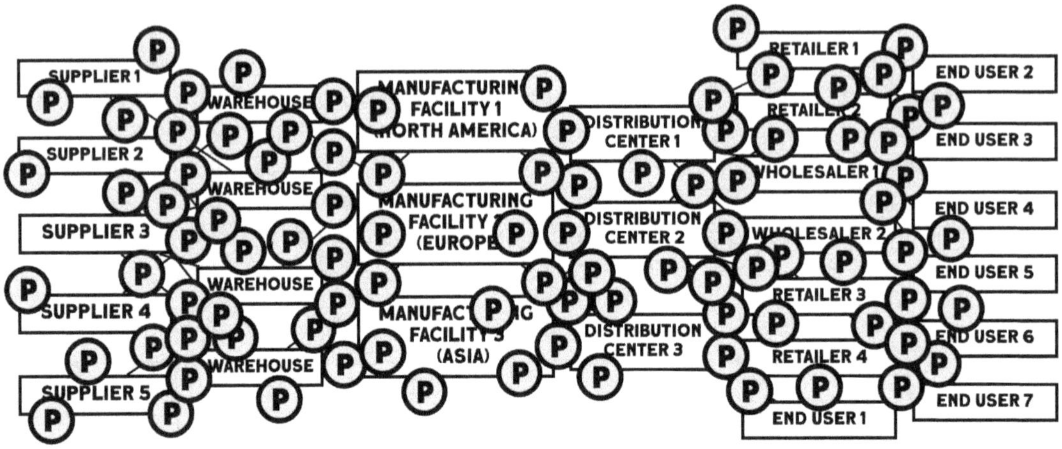

FIGURE 11.2 - SOME OF THE LOCATIONS OF PEOPLE IN A COMPLEX SUPPLY CHAIN

For example, when members of a supply chain do not focus on developing their interpersonal skills for open and friendly communications with their internal and external customers, even the smallest differences of opinion or break in communication can stop a supply chain dead in its tracks. In the case of Target's expansion into Canada, according to "The Last Days of Target" in the journal *Canadian Business*, many Canadian Target employees read the signs locally before stores opened. They knew that there were severe problems with distribution and the new IT system. Although the Target Canada executive team listened to employees who highlighted the many risks of sticking to the store launch dates, they did not appear to appreciate the message or read the fear and apprehension in the messengers' tone of voice. Instead, the executive team remained optimistic and pushed ahead with the launch dates, resulting in one of the most significant retail failures in the 21st century.

11.2 MANAGEMENT VERSUS LEADERSHIP

When a group of people works together to complete a task, such as a group of people moving goods across a supply chain, someone must

- *oversee the tasks,*

- *assign parts of the work to different people,*

- *follow up with workers to provide support and make sure the work is being completed, and*

- *be ultimately responsible for the successful accomplishment of the task.*

This person is called a ***manager***. There are multiple managers in any supply chain, ensuring the work is getting done in each of the supply chain's many segments. For example, there is a Head Elf in the toy production workshop in Santa Claus' supply chain to make sure toys are getting manufactured. There is another Head Elf to make sure the worker elves load all of the toys on the sleigh. Finally, there is a Head Reindeer to ensure all of the other reindeer stay on course during their long journey around the world to deliver toys. Each of these Head Elf and Head Reindeer positions performs the role of a *manager* within the toy delivery supply chain. In medium-sized and large-sized organizations, there are senior managers who manage the work of managers. Depending on the organization's size, there can be multiple layers of managers between an employee and a CEO. For example, at Amazon, there are formally numbered employee and manager levels. The first four levels are non-management employees with varying levels of education and experience, and the subsequent levels are hierarchies of managers, with CEO Jeff Bezos at Level 12.

We know that companies have managers, but what exactly do they do? The essence of what managers do is called ***management***, which is getting work accomplished through other people. One of the founders of modern management was a French mining engineer and executive from way back in the late 19th and early 20th centuries named Henri Fayol. He published works on management theory that continue to guide how management is defined today. Fayol divided *management* into five essential functions:

- ***Planning*** is seeing the big picture of the work to be accomplished and deciding how to get the work accomplished using systems, materials, and people. It involves developing an over-arching plan of action for what needs to be done and how to get there.

- ***Organizing*** is putting the systems, materials, and people in place to get tasks done. It involves utilizing the plan of action and breaking up the work into a series of tasks that can be accomplished by specific roles within departments or teams within particular timeframes. Organizing can include ***staffing***, which is finding the right people for each role or task from within the organization or from new hires to the organization.

- ***Commanding***, now more commonly called ***directing***, is making sure people in the organization know what to do in what timeframe to achieve the organization's broader goals. It involves communicating each required task and its importance to people and seeing if they need additional support or materials when embarking on their task.

- ***Coordinating*** is using the plan of action to create a set of systems, guidelines, and rules for people accomplishing the work. These all provide structure for those doing the work and serve as a roadmap for performing work.

- ***Controlling*** is keeping people on task as they accomplish the work, typically through measuring performance against standards and communicating these performance results. It involves checking timeframes and people who may need additional support, materials, or time to accomplish assigned tasks.

267

In our North Pole toy workshop, the Head Elf in charge of Outbound Toys and Sleigh Loading is a manager. The Head Elf knows that toys must be moved from the workshop to the sleigh every day, so she creates a plan of action to utilize the elf workers best and materials handling equipment assigned to her department. She organizes the elves into work units and assigns each the materials handling equipment they need and provides them timeframes and work goals. The Head Elf also directs her department by training elf workers how to do their required tasks. She also directs by establishing and using dependable communication channels to provide additional information about work as needed, like toy production delays or if the sleigh is undergoing maintenance. She also coordinates all elf and equipment resources for her team to optimize labor and resource use. For example, she creates guidelines and systems for best practices to help the elves do their best work every day. Finally, the Head Elf coordinates the work of her entire team. She checks their performance statistics and, when she finds an elf slipping in performance, she talks to them to find out what the problem might be. Sometimes, the elves simply need a change and need to learn a new skill, so they are reassigned to a different task. Other times, an elf might have the North Pole flu and need to stay home and drink cocoa instead of working. Or perhaps the resources to get the work done are insufficient, and the elves merely need new wheels on the hand cart. While the Head Elf in charge of Outbound Toys and Sleigh Loading manages all this work, her work is also being planned, organized, directed, coordinated, and controlled by her manager, Mr. Claus.

For fear of repeating ourselves, the essence of management is about getting work done through other people. The focus is on the work's tasks and how to maximize the effort of people performing these tasks. There are people in an organization assigned to the role of *manager* to provide this *formal* support and guidance to people doing the work, and the team or organization strives toward accomplishing a common goal. Also important to a team or organization working toward a common goal is a *leader*.

A **leader** is someone with a vision for a team or organization. The leader inspires others to follow and move into action toward a common goal. The role of a leader may be formal or informal. Leaders might be *informal* and never be assigned to a formal leadership position. Instead, their actions and words might inspire others and move them all toward a common goal. In out North Pole toy workshop, Dasher may be the Head Reindeer, but the reindeer who most inspires the team and communicates a vision that gets them all excited about working toward a common goal is Rudolph. Little Rudolph is the youngest reindeer and has no formal position of authority in the organization. However, his inspirational speeches and one-on-one chats with other reindeer, not to mention his charisma and shiny red nose, keep them all enthusiastic about their shared goal of delivering toys all over the world in one short night.

Someone with the *formal*, assigned role of manager might also fill the role of leader for many teams or organizations. When you think back to managers you have had in previous jobs, there are likely some who inspired you and made you feel part of a team, enthused to be working toward a common goal together. These managers were also leaders. However, *management* and *leadership* are two very different things, and not all good managers are good leaders and vice versa. A *manager* must focus on each individual and discover their strengths and weaknesses so that the right tasks can be assigned with the right timeframe and so that each individual has an opportunity for growth. A manager's primary concern is getting the task accomplished by optimizing each person's performance and optimizing resource utilization. A *leader* must focus on what is common to the entire group to be translated into and communicated as a vision that will ignite the whole team into action.

FIGURE 11.3 - MANAGERS VERSUS LEADERS

11.3 MANAGING OTHERS AND SELF

As you may have noticed from the previous section, management is all about getting work accomplished through other people. There is work to be completed, and a manager has a team and other resources. A manager must figure out how to plan, organize, direct, coordinate, and control both the people and the resources in an optimal way to get the work done.

When we use the term *managing people*, it is less about managing actual people and their behaviors. A manager doesn't pull people's strings and move them around like little marionettes or tell them what to do and expect them to jump to work mechanically like voice-controlled robots. Well, let's hope that there aren't any managers out there doing that! Instead, *managing people* is all about removing hurdles and providing the resources to get the job done. Therefore, managing people focuses on:

- managing their work to be done through setting work assignments, goals, deadlines, and work conditions;

- managing the work conditions and environment people experience, which includes managing employee relationships and locations, so they can get the work done and are more likely to feel focused and motivated;

- knowing each employee and their personal goals, strengths, and challenges and being aware of this when managing their work;

- understanding what conditions motivate each employee; and

- understanding how to communicate with each employee for maximum effectiveness.

Managers work with their team or department to develop skills and techniques in goal setting, time management, problem-solving, stress management, and communication. Figure 11.4 outlines a few useful techniques and resources that managers use for these topics that you might consider exploring on your own.

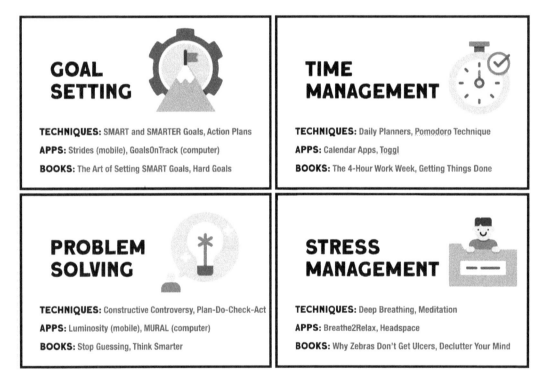

FIGURE 11.4 - RESOURCES FOR KEY MANAGEMENT SKILLS

A few communication techniques that good managers use and teach to others include:

- **Understanding and addressing body language.** Sometimes you know when communicating with certain people will be difficult before opening their mouths just by reading their body language. When people frown and stand with their arms crossed, you might take this as a clear signal that something is wrong. When they tap their feet and repeatedly look at their watch, you can tell that they are in a hurry and may not have time to talk to you. When they yawn and look at you with an expressionless face, you can guess that they are taking the time to speak with you but don't see the conversation's purpose or value.

When you observe a person's body language or tone of voice and notice that they are upset or may not be open to communication, it is best to acknowledge it and address it immediately. To the person with the frown, tightly pursed lips, and crossed arms, you might say, "I've noticed that you seem a bit upset. Is anything wrong?" Addressing negative body language provides an invitation for people to explain what might be bothering them. Once they have explained the problem, you can rectify or address it and get back to the business at hand. The problem may not even be about you. You may have misinterpreted their signals. They might be upset about something else and not even be aware of their body language or agitated state of mind. Expressing your concern or allowing them to vent shows that the interaction is important and that you value their opinion. Also, be aware of reading multiple body language signals at once. Focusing on just one signal can easily lead to misinterpretation and conflict. Notice that the five people's crossed arms in Figure 11.5 can be interpreted as five different emotions with five different messages.

FIGURE 11.5 - THE MIXED MESSAGES OF CROSSED ARMS

- **Making "I" statements.** When dealing with overly sensitive, demanding, and angry people, a particular turn-of-phrase can unintentionally appear insensitive or aggressive, providing a spark to ignite conflict with these powder-keg communicators. This dangerous language is the "You" statement. When you speak with difficult people and even not-so-difficult people, avoid starting possibly contentious statements with the word "you," because it sounds accusatory and sets you up for an immediate conflict. Instead, take ownership of your statements by starting them with the word "I" and expressing what you have felt or noticed. If a coworker is complaining but does not know that they are wrong, it would be counterproductive to make them angrier by pointing out their mistake with a "You" statement, such as, "You've got it all wrong. Look at these numbers here." A less combative way to make the same statement would be to use an "I" state-

271

ment, such as, "I noticed that the numbers in our paperwork are different from the ones you mentioned."

- **Using anticipatory statements.** When you want to make a suggestion to which you suspect a person might react negatively, using anticipatory statements is a useful technique that steers clear of conflict and may even get the person to consider your suggestion. With this technique, you anticipate a person's adverse reaction to your suggestion and incorporate it into your statement to them. An example of this would be, "I know that you had planned for me to bring cookies to the office party, but I'd like to suggest bringing a vegetable tray instead. I love vegetables and would prefer to bring a beautiful assortment of fresh vegetables instead of store-bought cookies." Anticipate and mention the person's concerns yourself before making the suggestion. They might be open to listening to your suggestion because you have demonstrated that you have considered their concerns and point of view.

- **Listening and paraphrasing.** A final communication technique useful in managing stressed and non-stressed people alike is careful listening and paraphrasing. When people know that you have taken the time to understand their point of view fully, their stress, anger, or frustration is more likely to be diffused. To listen effectively, you lean in, maintain eye contact, and nod periodically to show that you are interested in what the other person is saying. You do not interrupt. Instead, let them finish what they have to say. You then check to ensure that you have fully understood them by paraphrasing their main points. To paraphrase effectively, you restate their main ideas in your own words, using a neutral tone of voice that conveys neither approval nor disapproval of their message. The purpose of paraphrasing is to make sure that you have understood the other person because the tension between the two of you could be the result of a simple misunderstanding.

A good manager knows each unique individual working with them. They know each person's *strengths, what encourages that person to use these strengths*, and *how they can best learn new tasks and behaviors*. And before you can begin to manage other people, you must first be able to manage someone very near and dear to you. Yourself! Managing yourself is all about taking responsibility for your behavior and actions by knowing your *strengths, what encourages you to use these strengths,* and *how you can best learn new tasks and behaviors*. Sounds familiar, right?

Whether managing yourself or others, you must have a neutral, shared language for talking about commonalities and differences between yourself and others. The psychometrics.com case study, "IBM: Personality Type, The Language of International Business," describes how technology giant IBM receives a quarter of its many patents from people living outside the US. The company needed a tool to create a common language for managers and teams that cut across national boundaries to help them discuss differences and find commonalities when working together. The IBM Centre for Advanced Leadership decided to use the language of a personality test, the *MBTI*, to help its 40,000 managers speak a common language when talking about how individuals are similar and how they are different.

The **MBTI**, or **Myers Briggs Type Indicator**, is a psychological personality tool based on the theories of Carl Jung and developed by Katherine Briggs and Isabel Briggs Myers in 1942. The MBTI structure helps individuals sort their preferences and determine their unique personality type through its four categories in which people are sorted into one of two preferences. Each of these preferences is designated by a single letter. As someone is sorted according to all four categories, they are assigned four separate letters. These four letters combined reveal their **personality type**. There are sixteen different combinations of letters, as shown in Figure 11.6, which correspond to sixteen different distinct personality types.

ISTJ	ISFJ	INFJ	INTJ
ISTP	ISFP	INFP	INTP
ESTP	ESFP	ENFP	ENTP
ESTJ	ESFJ	ENFJ	ENTJ

FIGURE 11.6 - THE SIXTEEN PERSONALITY TYPES OF THE MBTI

At companies like Southwest Airlines, the MBTI is used in leadership and employee training so that employees can understand each other's differences, enabling them to understand why their coworkers approach the same challenge from a completely different perspective. In a logistics work setting, knowing the "why" behind coworkers' and suppliers' behaviors can help build trust and empathy, which are critical factors in any supply chain relationship. While the language of the MBTI is beneficial for companies like IBM and Southwest in helping people understand and manage themselves and others, the actual MBTI instrument is eschewed by research psychologists because of its inconsistent results and validity issues. Psychologists instead use a different instrument with better validity and reliability ratings called **The Big Five Personality Test**. The Big Five measures five personality traits, four of which correspond with the MBTI's four preference categories. Many companies avoid using the Big Five in corporate, management, and team settings because it is a research instrument. Its labels and language are not user-friendly and do not have the neutral nature of the MBTI. For example, someone taking the MBTI might be labeled a *Thinking* type while the same person taking the Big Five would be labeled *low in Agreeableness*.

The Big Five labels, which were designed solely for research use, can easily be misinterpreted. For the best of both worlds when managing oneself and others, it would be useful to take the Big Five Personality Test to take a deeper dive into understanding your personality. When discussing differences with others, it is helpful to know the MBTI's more value-neutral language. The case study at the end of this chapter takes a closer look at the language of the MBTI and its relationship to the personality test of the Big Five.

11.4 LEADING SELF AND OTHERS

As we mentioned in Section 11.2, leadership is all about vision. In the world of leadership, having a vision is the ability to have foresight and plan for the future with creativity and imagination. When someone in an organization has a ***vision***, it's that aspirational plan for the future of what an organization can achieve or become. A leader starts with a vision. What makes a person a leader is that this vision becomes a reality when communicating it effectively to other people in the organization. They are inspired by the leader's vision to work together toward accomplishing a common goal.

Sometimes people in an organization may have the desire to lead or have a vision they hold passionately. While some may be born leaders, others can develop the ability to lead. To lead, a person must know the uniqueness of each individual on their team and what makes them different. This is the same skill needed to manage others. However, to lead, a person must also find commonalities shared between everyone on the team. This information helps a leader develop a universal vision to rally a group and unite them toward a common goal. But that is often easier said than done!

One model that helps people develop their ability to lead others is called the Three Levels of Leadership model. Developed in 2011 by Executive Coach James Scouller, this model incorporates and expands previous leadership models into a simple format. Scouller's three levels of leadership are *public*, *private*, and *personal leadership*.

Public leadership is the action taken to influence a group or multiple people simultaneously. To achieve public leadership, Scouller outlines 34 behaviors in his book *The Three Levels of Leadership: How to Develop Your Leadership Presence, Knowhow, and Skill*. These 34 behaviors address establishing a vision and staying focused, giving power to others, making decisions, solving problems, following up, and creating a team spirit. If asked to imagine a leader, most of us would imagine one engaged in public leadership. We might imagine civil rights leader Martin Luther King, Jr delivering his powerfully visionary "I Have a Dream" speech on the steps of the Lincoln Memorial. From more recent history, we might imagine New Zealand Prime Minister Jacinda Ardern giving regular Facebook Live speeches, known for their transparency and empathy, during the COVID-19 crisis.

Private leadership relates to a leader's ability to deal with people one-on-one. Although leadership typically focuses on creating unity and cohesion in a group, all groups include individual people with different levels of experience, knowledge, confidence, and motivation. Scouller outlines fourteen behaviors to achieve private leadership, divided into two categories: (1) purpose and task, and (2) building and maintenance. The *purpose and task* category is related to setting goals, appraising performance, and discipline. The *building and maintenance* category is related to attracting new talent, knowledge, and building individual relationships. Private leadership is related to something called the *first follower*. Developed by Derek Sivers and made popular in his frequent TED Talks, the first follower is a leadership concept highlighting the importance of the first people to follow a leader. A leader has a vision and communicates it to a group. The group may be on the fence and uncertain about whether or not to follow. However, after a first follower and then second and third followers follow the leaders, others start to follow quickly because they see how to follow and that it is not as risky as they might have initially feared. These first followers are showing others how to follow. It is also essential for the leader to embrace these first followers so that they feel they are part of the leader's vision. Similarly, in private leadership, a leader needs to connect with key followers by communicating the vision and task while building a personal connection. These key followers are vital because they will influence other potential and existing followers.

FIGURE 11.7 - THE THREE LEVELS OF LEADERSHIP

Personal leadership is related to the leader's technical skills and knowledge of personal strengths and weaknesses, attitude toward others, and self-awareness coupled with self-mastery. Both personal leadership and many other leadership models stress that if you want to lead others, you must first lead yourself. **Self-leadership** is knowing and being able to clearly and immediately articulate or write down (1) *who you are*, (2) *what your strengths and weaknesses are*, and (3) *where you want to go*. Both a deep self-awareness and personal accountability are needed for this deeper dive into yourself. To master self-leadership, you can achieve knowing yourself, your strengths and weaknesses, and your vision through constructs like the *MBTI* covered in the previous section and *emotional intelligence*.

Throughout our first eighteen years or more, most of us are measured according to academic success and our *IQ, or intelligence quotient*. How well we perform in elementary school determines our course placement in secondary school. How well we perform in our secondary school courses and on our college placement tests then impacts which colleges or universities will accept us as students. Finally, the reputation of the college we attend and how we perform academically at that college has an enormous impact on which companies will hire us and how much they will pay us. Although this focus on academic performance and IQ has been the predominant model in the United States and other countries for many years, many companies believe that *emotional intelligence, or EQ*, is a better predictor of leadership success than IQ and academic success.

Before we explore the notion of emotional intelligence and EQ, let's take a quick look at the human brain. Our body experiences something through one of the five senses, such as the pain experienced when we hit ourselves on the thumb with a hammer or the wonderful smell of fresh bread baking. This information about a sensation travels to our brain by way of our nerves up the spinal column to the brain stem the base of the brain. The brainstem is the brain's intermediary, which receives and sends messages to the rest of the body. Information travels immediately from the brain stem through the brain's limbic system, the region in which we experience our emotions. Only after traveling through this emotional center does the information finally reach the brain's outer layers, including the frontal lobes of the cerebral cortex. Receiving this information assists in our rational thinking by evaluating whether our potential actions and reactions may be good or bad and perceived by others as socially acceptable or unacceptable.

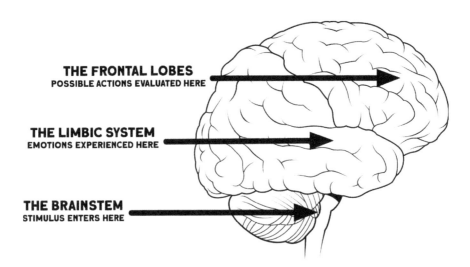

FIGURE 11.8 - THE HUMAN BRAIN: THREE REGIONS AND FUNCTIONS

Therefore, when we hit our thumb with a hammer, we first experience the emotion of extreme, blinding pain. Only after this extreme emotion do we experience the rational thought that, although we might want to scream in pain nonstop for thirty minutes, we must instead go to the hospital because our thumb looks broken. In a more pleasurable experience, when we smell fresh bread baking, we first have happy feelings and experience pangs of hunger, making us want to rip the bread from the oven and eat the entire loaf immediately. Only after do we experience the rational thought that we are not hungry, and the bread must be saved for dinner to be shared among the entire family. But what does all of this brain anatomy have to do with leadership in logistics and supply chains? Everything!

Remember our diagram of locations of people in a supply chain in Figure 11.2? People are everywhere. Therefore, to lead ourselves and others, we must have good "people skills," which puts our frontal lobes into overdrive as we try to regulate our emotions so that we don't yell at our coworkers or run screaming from the building when things go wrong. For many employers, our ability to regulate our emotions to get along and work with others, such as our coworkers and our customers, is a more highly valued commodity than pure cognitive intelligence alone. In contrast to IQ, this ability to regulate our emotions for ourselves and as we interact with others is called our *EQ* or our ***emotional intelligence***.

Science author Daniel Goleman popularized the idea of emotional intelligence in his book *Emotional Intelligence*. Goleman describes the skills of emotional intelligence as the combination of our ***personal competence*** (how self-aware we are and how well we manage ourselves) and our ***social competence*** (how socially aware we are and how well we manage relationships with others), as shown in Figure 11.9.

FIGURE 11.9 - MODEL OF THE SKILLS OF EMOTIONAL INTELLIGENCE

To develop greater emotional intelligence, we must first look inward to become aware of who we are, what we are, and the decisions we make that affect our own lives. Once we have looked inward, we must then look outward to become aware of social dynamics and the decisions we make and actions we take in our interpersonal interactions. Two concepts that can lead to greater emotional intelligence by understanding others and ourselves are *personality* and *paradigm*. In section 11.3, we introduced the concept of studying personality as a tool for self-management. In the case study at the end of this chapter, we take a closer look at how we can examine our own personality type and traits to enhance our self-leadership and utilize a neutral language to discuss personality differences. We have *personality* pretty well covered, but what is this concept of *paradigms*?

Successful relationships in both supply chains and the world at large depend on our perceptions of reality or paradigms. A **paradigm** is the set of experiences, beliefs, and values that affect how individuals perceive reality and respond to these perceptions. It is the way we see the world, not literally and visually, but within the realm of perception, understanding, and interpretation. In his best-selling management and leadership guide, *The Seven Habits of Highly Effective People*, author Stephen Covey asserts that our paradigms are a powerful influence in our lives and our ability to be effective individuals. He describes paradigms as the maps in our heads of "the way things are" (our realities) and "the way things should be" (our values). Covey states that we assume that the way we see things is the way that they are or should be. However, we see the world not as it is, but as we are conditioned to see it. Whether or not they are correct, our paradigms are the building blocks for our behaviors, attitudes, and relationships with other people.

When leading self and others, we have to understand our paradigms, their roots, and their impact on our behaviors and actions. We also have to be ready to shift our paradigms when we realize that they are wrong. In the example of Target's expansion into Canada from the beginning of this chapter, the American executives' paradigm was one of optimism. They believed that when launching stores in a new country, potential customers had few initial expectations and displayed an initial enthusiastic surge to try out the new *product*, the Target shopping experience. However, Canadians had been crossing the border and shopping in Target for years. They already had an in-depth knowledge of the Target shopping experience. Rather than enthusiasm, customers were disappointed with the Canadian Target experience because it did not match up in price or product offerings compared to the American Target. Canadian employees also warned the Target executives of serious potential distribution problems before the Canadian stores opened. This should have been the time for the corporate leaders to examine and reevaluate their paradigms, and perhaps consider a new paradigm of delaying the launch of the new store openings. However, the company executives held onto their faulty paradigms and pushed ahead with the launch of 133 stores, which were all closed in less than two years.

11.5 SUPPLY CHAIN MANAGERS AND LEADERS

Management is the act of getting work accomplished through other people. I guess we can't say it enough. In the supply chain, to get work done through other people, supply chain managers need to have three types of management competencies: *people skills, knowledge of technology*, and *analytical skills*. To manage internal and external supply chains and get work done through employees in these supply chains, managers need to communicate and work with others in an open, effective manner. They must have **people skills**. Sections 11.3 and 11.4 covered some examples of people skills, such as communication and emotional intelligence skills. Imagine a warehouse or shipyard where workers need to operate heavy machinery. In the wrong hands, misusing this machinery could result in costly mistakes or fatalities. Warehouse or shipyard managers must attention to people coming in to work and question them about and questionable body language to make sure that no-one is distracted, angry, overly preoccupied, or ill before operating any heavy machinery.

Supply chain managers must also have a **knowledge of technology** to be trusted and viewed as credible by their employees. More and more work is done through automation, robotics, and artificial intelligence. Supply chain managers must understand the strengths, limitations, and costs of technology. Not only do they manage people, but supply chain managers also manage systems and technology. For example, 3D printing, also known as **additive printing**, has become a standard part of manufacturing. Airbus, Volkswagen, Exxon-Mobil, and L'Oréal all use it in their manufacturing process. Because additive printing is used to produce items on an on-demand basis, not as many items need to be kept in inventory, especially for specialty goods, customized items, or spare parts. Also, different items take different amounts of time to be "printed." Supply chain managers need to understand technology such as additive printers and how they impact all aspects of logistics, such as warehouse inventory levels and delivery times.

FIGURE 11.10 - ADDITIVE PRINTING OF METAL PARTS IN MANUFACTURING PROCESS

Finally, supply chain managers must possess **analytical skills**. Remember back in Chapter 7 when we talked about those impossibly large sets of data called *big data*? Because of twenty-first-century computing power, supply chain managers now have tremendous amounts of data available to them for planning and decision making. Mathematical, statistical, and analytical skills are needed to help supply chain managers interpret data to make supply chains more efficient and effective. In our Target example from the beginning of this chapter, both companies may not have used data available to them to make decisions. Target Canada employees supplied company executives with data about potential distribution and supply chain problems. Target could have analyzed sales data from its American stores near Canadian border crossings to determine what items were purchased more frequently and at what price points. Supply chain managers and other executives at the company could then have analyzed all this data to determine what the Canadian stores needed in terms of what goods at what price. They could have taken the time to find suppliers and streamline the distribution system *before* opening any Canadian stores. Because either this analysis was not done or was disregarded, Target had little chance of success in Canada.

While the three management competencies above are essential, supply chains also need leadership characteristics. **_Leadership_** is having a vision for an organization and inspiring others to follow and move into action toward a common goal. Supply chain leaders must:

- **See the big picture.** Seeing the big picture and having a mind for strategy helps supply chain leaders develop a vision for the organization and its supply chain. In our KFC example from the beginning of this chapter, we learned that the chicken shortage for its England stores happened when they switched distributors. Like many distribution operations in England, the new distributor used one warehouse located in an area called the "Golden Rectangle" in the center of England. From this area, goods can reach any location in the UK within 24 hours. However, had the KFC supply chain executives been focused on the big picture of how absolutely critical chicken availability is for a chicken restaurant's operations, they might have envisioned the problems that could arise from using a distributor with a single warehouse in a single location, especially when multiple traffic accidents, bad weather, or other road-closing events occur.

- **Be fearless.** Supply chain leaders must try new things and want to learn. They must not be afraid of change in our rapidly changing technological world. Many coffee customers faced the dilemma of lacking proof that their morning jolt of java is ethically sourced. Coffee roasters partnered with IBM to provide a solution by fearlessly embracing blockchain technology. A **_blockchain_** is a growing set of digital records linked together with cryptography so that the list is protected from anyone without the key. Every time the blockchain is accessed, a new timestamp new record of that access is added to the blockchain. Cryptocurrencies such as bitcoin are examples of blockchains. Sophisticated and complex blockchain technology created by coffee roasters and IBM, called FarmerConnect, was quickly adopted by Starbucks' fearless supply chain leaders. The company, the coffee farmers, and all Starbucks customers can use the code on a bag of coffee to see exactly where the coffee beans were harvested and exactly where they were roasted. For customers, Starbucks also includes information in the blockchain on the best ways to brew the particular type of beans in the bag.

- **Have experience, be credible, and deliver results.** Supply chain leaders must have these characteristics so that others will trust them and want to follow them. Former Apple CEO Steve Jobs was a visionary, but his relationship with Apple was often a rocky one.

While suffering from a terminal illness, Jobs selected a successor who was quite different from himself. He selected Tim Cook, the company's Chief Operating Officer and supply chain leader. He was not the temperamental genius that Jobs was but was instead known for his experience and his calm, collaborative leadership style that delivered results. After taking over as CEO, Cook was able to grow Apple's market value from $348 billion in 2011 to over $2 trillion in 2020.

- **Develop others.** Finally, supply chain leaders must develop other supply chain leaders to communicate their vision to others in the organization. Many successful companies have a clear and consistent vision that is not dependent upon a single visionary leader's communication skills but upon a large network of leaders. In addition to Big Macs and its sordid history of super-sizing, McDonald's is a company known for developing its internal management teams since it opened its doors in 1955. Early McDonald's owner and its franchise model creator Ray Kroc espoused the corporate ideal that, "None of us is as good as all of us." This ideal is still part of the company's vision today. The collaborative and inclusive culture at McDonald's is also part of its supply chain leadership. Francesca DeBiase, Executive Vice President and Chief Supply Chain and Sustainability Officer for McDonald's, understands this corporate vision and the importance of developing internal supply chain leaders who can communicate this vision and inspire others. At McDonald's, the supply chain is viewed as a *we*, indicating a collaborative relationship between the company and its supplier and customers. The question "what's in it for *we*" is instilled in its leaders. As a result, McDonald's supply chain leaders are known for some of the most highly successful relationships with suppliers in its 38,000+ restaurants worldwide.

CHAPTER 11 REVIEW QUESTIONS

1. What is the relationship between *people* and the *supply chain*?

2. In your own words, how would you define a *manager*?

3. Based on a manager you have known, provide an example of each of *Fayol's five essential functions of management* that this manager did or did not display.

4. In your own words, how would you define a *leader*? How is this different from your definition of a *manager*?

5. List some of the management techniques covered in this chapter. Use an example and discuss which management techniques are the easiest for you to implement and why.

6. With examples, explain which two management techniques are the most difficult for you. What are you doing, or what can you do to improve these techniques?

7. What are Scouller's *three levels of leadership*? How are they different?

8. How are *emotional intelligence* and *leadership* connected?

9. What is a *paradigm*? Provide an example of when a leader you know did or did not change their paradigm when they needed to. What was the outcome?

10. What are three management competencies that a supply chain manager needs? Which of these competencies do you need to improve the most? How will you improve it?

CHAPTER 11 CASE STUDY

LANGUAGE & THE TRICKY SIDE OF PERSONALITY TESTS

If you want to develop both management skills and enhance your leadership characteristics, the first thing you need to do is take a deep dive into yourself. Self-management and self-leadership both require a personal review of your strengths and weaknesses. One way you can explore yourself is to examine your personality. If you are doing this on your own and don't know where to begin, a good starting point is the ***Big Five Personality Test***.

Developed over years of research into personality traits, psychologists have developed a model for understanding personality called the ***five-factor model***. The model divides the essence of a person's measurable personality traits into five categories:

- **Openness to experience.** This trait identifies how open someone is to imagination, adventure, art, and various experiences.

- **Conscientiousness.** This trait identifies how much a person displays or values self-discipline, dutifulness, and achievement.

- **Extraversion.** This trait identifies how much someone gains energy from the external environment and pursues a breadth rather than a depth of activities.

- **Agreeableness.** This trait identifies how much someone values social harmony and the well-being of others.

- **Neuroticism.** This trait identifies someone's tendency to experience or display negative emotions, such as depression, anger, and anxiety.

The various tests available to measure the five-factor model are useful and provide valid and reliable results. One such test is the Big Five Personality Test, which is available free online at https://openpsychometrics.org/tests/IPIP-BFFM/.

However, the challenge with all five-factor tests is the labels, and language associate with the five-factor model all appear to be laden with judgment or bias. When you read more about the model and read the test's in-depth results, the language is more neutral. However, it sounds bad from the start to read that your results are "low on agreeableness" or "low on openness to experience." Conversely, you may get an inflated sense of self and incorrectly think that you aced the test if you scored "high on conscientiousness" or "high on agreeableness." As a result, the Big Five Personality Test is used primarily for psychological research and by a few MBA students studying organizational behavior. So what personality tests do companies use to help employees develop themselves as managers and leaders?

Earlier in this chapter, we introduced the ***MBTI***, or ***Myers Briggs Type Indicator***. The MBTI helps individuals sort their personality preferences through a series of questions. It determines their unique personality type through its four categories, which sorts people into one of two preferences. Each of these preferences is designated by a single letter. As someone is sorted according to all four categories, they are assigned four separate letters. These four letters combined reveal one of sixteen possible ***personality types***.

Even though the instrument has low validity and reliability scores, approximately 80-90% of Fortune 500 companies use the MBTI for team building, leadership training, and mentoring. People love it, and the internet is full of funny memes for each of the sixteen types. But why use a test that doesn't consistently measure what it is supposed to? The broad appeal of the MBTI appears to be in its labels and language. While the Big Five uses labels with unintended negative connotations, the MBTI labels are all neutral and straightforward to understand. On the Big Five Personality Test, you can score either *high in Extraversion* or *low in Extraversion*, which sounds like either good or bad results. On the MBTI, your result would instead be either *extravert* or *introvert*, which are more value-neutral and not perceived as either good or bad. Since so many companies love it, let's take a look under the hood at the MBTI.

The MBTI's structure helps individuals sort their preferences and determine their unique personality type through its four categories in which people are sorted into one of two preferences. Each of these preferences is designated by a single letter. As someone is sorted according to all four categories, they are assigned four separate letters. These four letters combined reveal their ***personality type***. There are sixteen different combinations of letters and, correspondingly, sixteen different distinct personality types. As we cover the four preference pair categories, determine and write down which letter more aptly describes you.

The first of the four preference pair categories sorts people according to how they *gain energy*. If you become more energized from the outside world, you have a preference for ***Extraversion*** and are given the letter ***E*** as the first letter of your four-letter personality type. If you become more energized from your inner resources, you have a preference for ***Introversion***. You are given the letter ***I*** as the first letter of your four-letter personality type. For example, if you prefer to spend more of your free time with people or "out and about," you may have a preference for Extraversion. If, however, you prefer to spend your free time alone or working on independent pursuits, you may have a preference for Introversion.

The second of the four preference categories sorts people according to how they *take in information*. If you prefer to deal with individual, specific facts, you have a preference for ***Sensing*** and are given the letter ***S*** as the second letter of your four-letter personality type. If you prefer to deal with the "big picture," you have a preference for ***Intuition*** and are given the letter ***N*** as the second letter of your four-letter personality type. Intuition is given N instead of I to avoid confusion because I has already been assigned to Introversion. For example, in the crime and mystery genre of popular television shows, the detail-oriented forensic researchers on *CSI* demonstrate a preference for Sensing, while the guesswork and intuitive reasoning of the classic detective show *Columbo* demonstrate a preference for Intuition.

The third of the four preference categories sorts people according to how they *make decisions*. If you more often make decisions using logic and critical analysis, you have a preference for ***Thinking***. You are given the letter ***T*** as the third letter of your four-letter personality type. If you more frequently decide based on your values and take other people into account, you have a preference for **Feeling**. You are given the letter **F** as the third letter of your four-letter personality type. Often, those with a preference for Thinking would prefer others to view them as right or competent, while those with a preference for Feeling would prefer for others to like or care about them.

The fourth and final of the four preference categories sorts people according to how they *approach life*. If you prefer order and structure, you have a preference for **Judging** and are given the letter **J** as the final letter of your four-letter personality type. If you prefer flexibility and spontaneity, you have a preference for **Perceiving** and are given the letter **P** as the final letter of your four-letter personality type. For example, if you enjoy making "to do" lists, you may have a preference for Judging. If you prefer instead to "go with the flow," you may have a preference for Perceiving.

ISTJ	ISFJ	INFJ	INTJ
ISTP	ISFP	INFP	INTP
ESTP	ESFP	ENFP	ENTP
ESTJ	ESFJ	ENFJ	ENTJ

After you have been sorted into each of the four preference categories, you have four letters. When written together, these four letters represent your MBTI personality type. Each of the sixteen possible MBTI types is unique and has unique means of communicating, learning, handling conflict, working with others, and relaxing. Typically, people of one given type will have an easier time communicating with and understanding people of the same or similar types. They have a more difficult time with those of very different types. Unlike that of the Big Five, the language of the MBTI is a fun and easy one to use. In the workplace, it can become a shorthand for people to describe particular things about themselves in a neutral language without positive or negative connotations. For example, at an Alaska telecommunications company that taught the language of the MBTI to its employees, one manager put a sign outside their door that read "ENTJ, but working on my F." This sign lets others know that they may not be as good at the Feeling skills but that they were consciously making an effort to improve these valuable people skills, like displays of caring and empathy.

By learning about ourselves and others' personality type preferences, we can adjust our behavior to improve communication and enhance understanding. It can help you adjust your paradigm (*remember: the map in your head*) to better understand and communicate with others. Knowing about personality type theory allows you to understand better your own paradigm, the paradigms of others, and how these maps in our heads influence our actions. At companies like Southwest Airlines, the MBTI is used in leadership and employee training to understand each other's differences, enabling them to appreciate why their coworkers approach the same challenge from a completely different perspective. In a corporate setting, knowing the "why" behind coworkers' and suppliers' behaviors can help you build trust and empathy with each other, which are critical factors in any supply chain relationship.

But we have a tricky situation with personality tests in the workplace. One test is good at what it assesses but uses a language that does not accurately and neutrally convey personality differences. The other test is not so good at what it assesses but uses a highly useful and neutral language to describe personality differences that people understand and utilize easily. Therefore, some companies are beginning to use the MBTI language but not the MBTI test for team building and discussing personality differences with others. Then, for a more in-depth look at one's own personality traits and the development of self-management and self-leadership skills, other instruments such as the Big Five are an option.

Despite the positives and negatives of the Big Five and the MBTI, both measure similar things. A study by Furnham, Moutafi, and Crump in 2003 in the journal *Social Behavior and Personality* found a correlation between four of the Big Five traits and the four MBTI preference pairs. The Big Five *Extraversion* trait correlated strongly to the *Extraversion-Introversion* MBTI preference pair. Although to a lesser degree, the same was true for:

- the *Openness to Experience* trait and the *Sensing-Intuition* preference pair,

- the *Agreeableness* trait and the *Thinking-Feeling* preference pair, and

- the *Conscientiousness* trait and the *Judging-Perceiving* pair.

No matter what route you choose to explore your personality and communicate with others about personality differences, it's always useful to know yourself before you begin to manage and lead others.

Chapter 12
Strategy and Supply Chain Management

You've made it to the final chapter of *Looking at Logistics*! Queue the fanfare and ticker-tape parade. After finishing the first eleven chapters, you've learned all there could possibly be to learn for a career in logistics and supply chain management, right? That's what Toni and Pia thought when they made it to this stage of the book. The two lifelong friends and logistics students are the stars of this chapter's introductory story who discovered that they needed this last chapter of the book and its strategic management tools before embarking on their careers in logistics.

For their entire lives, Toni and Pia dreamed of owning their own business. When they worked together for a moving company one summer, the two friends knew what they wanted to do. They loved trucks, helping people, and getting exercise while they worked, so they decided that they wanted to own their own moving company. They lived in a large university town and thought it might be fun to help college students move in and out of their living accommodations. For years, they talked about calling their business "Truck U" because it would reference the fact that they catered to their university town. They even thought it would be fun to allow students to pay for their moving services in pizza and beer.

Before going to the bank to apply for a business loan for Truck U, the two friends read Chapter 12 and were glad they did! They realized what a colossal mistake many of their ideas would have been without developing a strategic plan and using strategy tools. As we will see in the examples throughout this chapter, Toni and Pia's abysmally bad idea of Truck U to move university students in and out of accommodation in exchange for pizza and beer evolved into a different concept, SecuriClean Transportation, which catered to the huge regional medical supply market. Not only were they able to secure a business loan, but the two friends were able to grow a highly profitable business with 20 trucks in a short five-year span, all thanks to an understanding of strategic management and implementing strategy tools.

12.1 STRATEGIC MANAGEMENT

Companies are like ships at sea. They have a desired destination they are striving to reach in an ocean of uncertainty. A well established local orange juice producer might strive to reach a specific, consistent level of profitability every year. A newly formed kazoo manufacturing company might be striving to achieve a certain level of sales in an additional eight regional markets per year for the first five years of its operations. Or a favorite local sandwich shop might be trying to reach a modest level of profitability while paying employees enough to retain them year after year and maintaining the food quality standards that loyal customers have come to expect. Although their destinations may differ, all companies have one. And like ships at sea, companies have challenging waters to navigate. Like the mariners of old who looked to the stars or today's ship captains who use sophisticated satellite navigational systems, company executives need something to guide them toward their desired destination. The maps companies use are called **strategic plans**, and the process of creating and utilizing these maps is called *strategic management*.

Strategic management occurs when a company uses its resources in a planned and informed way to achieve its goals. It is carried out by the executive-level leadership in a company, often as a team representing the breadth of company operations. A strategic management team might look like the *supply chain management team* from way back in Chapter 2, typically including the heads of a company's core departments, such as marketing, finance, manufacturing, human resource management, and logistics. Instead of the supply chain management team's task of focusing on the flow of goods into and out from the company, the **strategic management team** works together to develop and implement a *strategic plan* to help the company meet its goals and get to its desired destination.

In the business world, a **strategic plan** is a company's roadmap to help it stay focused and best use its resources as it works to meet predetermined goals. It keeps everyone on the same page and answers questions that a company's employees and stakeholders have: *What* are we doing? *Why* are we doing it? And *how* will we get it done? A typical strategic plan addresses and includes:

- the **company's intent**. This section of a strategic plan explains its intention and desired destination to ensure that everyone understands the essence of the company. It often occurs in the form of a *mission statement* and a *vision statement*. Often in only a single sentence, a **mission statement** expresses why a company exists, what it does, whom it serves, and how it serves them. Most companies have additional sentences tor paragraphs following a mission statement to explain what it means. Highly successful larger companies ofter train employees in their mission statement, so employees will remember the *why* of what they are doing at work every day. A **vision statement** explains where the company is heading. Also often expressed in one sentence, a vision statement is aspirational and summarizes the company's dreams, sometimes focusing on the greater good or what they are doing to bring change to the world. Some companies combine elements of the mission and vision statements into a single statement, while others clearly outline both separately. No matter how a company represents it, the strategic plan begins by expressing the company's intentions. Figure 12.1 lists the mission and vision statements of a few well-known national and global companies.

COMPANY	MISSION STATEMENT	VISION STATEMENT
STARBUCKS	To inspire and nurture the human spirit – one person, one cup and one neighborhood at a time.	To establish Starbucks as the premier purveyor of the finest coffee in the world while maintaining our uncompromising principles as we grow.
TESLA	Tesla's mission is to accelerate the world's transition to sustainable energy.	Create the most compelling car company of the 21st century by driving the world's transition to electric vehicles.
TWITTER	The mission we serve as Twitter, Inc. is to give everyone the power to create and share ideas and information instantly without barriers. Our business and revenue will always follow that mission in ways that improve – and do not detract from – a free and global conversation.	Reach the largest daily audience in the world by connecting everyone to their world via our information sharing and distribution platform products and be one of the top revenue generating Internet companies in the world.
BP	Our purpose is reimagining energy for people and our planet.	We want to help the world reach net zero and improve people's lives.
GOOGLE	Our mission is to organize the world's information and make it universally accessible and useful.	To provide access to the world's information in one click.
CATERPILLAR	Our mission is to enable economic growth through infrastructure and energy development, and to provide solutions that support communities and protect the planet.	Our vision is a world in which all people's basic needs — such as shelter, clean water, sanitation, food and reliable power — are fulfilled in an environmentally sustainable way and a company that improves the quality of the environment and the communities where we live and work.
PEPSICO	Create more smiles with every sip and every bite.	Be the global leader in convenient foods and beverages by winning with purpose.

FIGURE 12.1 - MISSION AND VISION STATEMENTS FOR WELL-KNOWN COMPANIES

- **corporate goals** . Corporate goals outline where the company wants to go and what it wants to do to achieve its mission. These goals are broader, bigger picture ones that focus on the company and its performance. Company websites and external reports to stakeholders often list these goals. For example, on the FedEx website, the company lists its six long-term corporate goals, such as "Increase EPS [earnings per share] 10%-15% per year," with five strategies to support these goals, such as "Grow our supply chain capabilities."

- **department-level goals and objectives** . These goals and objectives are the next step down from the corporate goals. They are written for individual departments in the company, outlining their part in helping a company achieve its corporate goals and fulfill its mission. They include the resources needed to achieve these department-specific goals and meet objectives with money, equipment, and human resources. They also help employees see the big picture and understand where their work fits in achieving its goals.

Companies develop their strategic plans by looking at what's happening both *inside* the company and *outside* in the external environment. When developing and implementing a strategic plan, companies move through the following stages:

FIGURE 12.2 - STAGES OF DEVELOPING A STRATEGIC PLAN

- **Analysis.** During the analysis stage, a company looks inward to collect information about itself. It looks at what is working and what isn't working. It also assesses internal factors from inside the company that influence its operations and success. During the analysis state, a company also looks outward to scan the external environment in which it operates. It assesses the industry it is in, its location of operations, and its competition.

- **Formation.** During the formation stage, a company makes decisions regarding how it will define itself to its employees and the rest of the world and how it wants to look and operate in the future. To reach this desired future, the company then creates a strategic plan based on what it learned from the analysis stage. Executives from many departments, such as the Logistics Department, work together for this formation stage, address strategic decisions, and set goals throughout the organization. They also create scorecards and other means of measuring success in meeting goals.

- **Implementation.** During the implementation stage, a company makes its strategy come to life by putting the strategic plan into action. It begins following steps to achieve the goals and objectives outlined in the strategic plan. The company may also change its organizational structure and policies if required by the plan. It will also likely need to educate employees and other stakeholders, highlighting the different departments' roles and responsibilities under the plan.

- **Evaluation.** During the evaluation stage, a company determines whether the strategic plan is working to meet its goals and objectives. It gets feedback from those working the plan and those impacted externally and internally, like suppliers and customers. This feedback can come in the form of scorecards, surveys, or other means of evaluation. The company determines if it needs to change anything in the plan to meet its corporate and department-level goals better.

After finishing the four stages of developing and implementing a strategic plan, a company starts the process again with the analysis stage, taking in information to see if there have been any changes in the internal or external environment impacting its mission and vision. Many companies revisit these four stages annually, often connected to annual scorecard reviews for the evaluation stage.

In the sections to follow, we will introduce a few of the strategy tools used in the analysis stage of strategic management and planning. These tools are used for *external analysis*, taking a macro look at the company's external operating environment and industry, and *internal analysis*, which takes a micro look at its inner workings. In these sections on strategy tools, we will also revisit the case of the two friends from the beginning of the chapter and their dream of owning a transportation and moving business called Truck U. We'll see how their business concept changed drastically from Truck U to SecuriClean Transport after using some of these tools for both their external and internal analysis when developing their strategic plan.

A WORD OF CAUTION

Recommended in a 2014 article in the *Harvard Business Review* called "The Big Lie of Strategic Planning," a **strategic plan** can also be called a **strategy statement**. The author, Roger Martin, says that many companies get a false sense of comfort from highly detailed strategic plans with pages and pages of analysis. For employees and other stakeholders, he instead recommends having a streamlined and simplified strategy statement. It should focus on which customers to target and how to compel them to select its products or services. Even though the company would do lots of analysis beforehand, this analysis doesn't need to be in the document shared with employees and stakeholders. Instead, the strategy statement can be a single page of simple words and simple concepts and clearly outlined logic, which serves as a simpler way to keep everyone on the same page.

12.2 STRATEGY TOOLS: REFINING THE VISION

When companies are crafting their mission and vision statements, they put their purpose and desired future into words. It helps when they can refine their vision. Even large, profitable companies with well-developed mission and vision statements can falter when they have not revisited the analysis stage for their mission and vision statements. For example, the maker of Lego toys, Lego Systems A/S, has been around since 1932. The company grew and expanded to become a global company over many decades. As the brand grew, Lego began to offer an increasingly diverse range of non-toy products, such as clothing, theme parks, and other non-brick style toys. In 1998, the company experienced a significant loss and decided to cut 1000 jobs the next year.

After a few years of losses, Lego hired a new CEO, Jørgen Knudstorp. He revisited Lego's original mission, abandoned in a chase for profit through diverse offerings such as clothing and summarized in five words: creativity, imagination, unlimited, discovery, and constructionism. Essentially, for years the focus had been all about children releasing their creativity and imagination through building with Lego brick toys. Knudstorp and other executives at Lego returned to the company's original mission and vision. He divested the company of offerings that were not related to its core mission and reduced the complexity of its product lines by 50%. As a result, after a couple of short years, Lego returned to a company of increasing annual profits because it got the company refocused on its original mission and vision.

When companies create or revise their mission and vision statements, two strategy tools that help provide structure and focus to this part of the analysis stage are *Porter's generic strategies* and *integration strategies*. Harvard Business School professor and business strategy expert Michael Porter developed a framework for companies to consider how they would like to position themselves in the market. The framework, known as ***Porter's generic strategies***, has companies define their place in the market in terms of their **strategic advantage** among their competitors and the **strategic target** of customers to pursue.

In terms of strategic advantage, a company decides whether it will achieve its goals through *cost leadership* or *market differentiation*. A company decides whether it wants to win customers over by offering goods at lower prices than its competitors to be a cost leader or to offer something different from its competitors that sets it apart. For example, in the car market, Kia has selected a cost leadership strategy, while Mercedes has selected a differentiation strategy.

In terms of strategic targets, a company defines its target market. The company selects whether it will attempt to sell its goods or services to all possible customers or a smaller segment of the total market of customers known as a *niche market*. In the world of breakfast cereals, many cereal brands target the total market of customers, like Cornflakes and Chex. Conversely, other cereal brands have narrowed the spectrum of customers they are trying to reach. Examples include Kashi brand cereals for the health and environmentally focused customer and the General Mills cereals, Count Chocula and Franken Berry, for young customers that love monsters and Halloween.

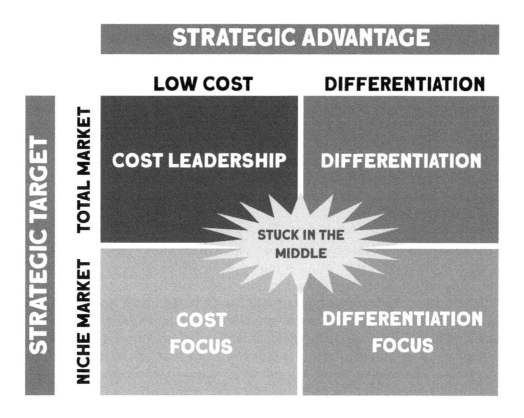

FIGURE 12.3 - PORTER'S GENERIC STRATEGIES

Porter's generic strategies framework can help a company establish its mission and vision, prompting the company to define its customer and its strategic advantage in either cost or differentiation. Porter argued that if companies did not do this, they would be "stuck in the middle" of all of their competitors with nothing to make them stand out to potential customers. In the case of our two friends, Toni and Pia, who wanted to start a moving and transportation business called Truck U in their university town, they began to rethink their strategy when they used Porter's generic strategies. At first, they hadn't considered their strategic advantage or strategic target. When considering their competition, they discovered that there were already quite a few cost leaders in their town, including a few independent operators and a couple of franchises such as College Hunks Moving Junk and Two Men & a Truck. They knew they would have to differentiate and offer something unique to stand out.

Toni and Pia wanted to find something that was needed in their town but wasn't currently offered. They asked their friends, family, and everyone they met, "When hiring companies for your moving or transportation needs, what is your biggest challenge? Is there a service that's hard to find in our town?" Most had no challenges to report because their university town was full of affordable and reliable moving companies. However, a few who worked in hospitals or the medical industry had the same thing to report. There was no reliable, secure, or even hygienic transportation service in town for medical equipment and supplies. The town's three hospitals, two large universities with medical research facilities, and multiple independent research facilities had to rely on transportation companies from a few towns away, who all charged an additional distance rate to provide their services. The two friends realized they might need to consider changing the Truck U concept, which risked getting "stuck in the middle" of competitors. They instead began to consider the niche market of hospitals and research facilities and to differential their services by focusing on the transportation of medical equipment and supplies.

A second strategy tool for providing structure and focus when companies are refining their vision is a consideration of *integration strategies*, which help a company define how it will grow its operations and its supply chain. Companies can increase the scope of and control over their logistics and supply chain operations using two strategies: *vertical integration* and *horizontal integration*.

Vertical integration is a strategy a company uses to gain more control over its supply chain by acquiring or merging with other companies already in its external supply chain. As a result, the company grows its logistics operations and controls most of its supply chain for a product. For example, the Swedish big-box and low-price furniture store IKEA has grown its logistics control and operations through vertical integration. IKEA acquires their suppliers and their suppliers' suppliers, such as Romanian lumber providers and the Romanian forests themselves. IKEA also controls its supply chain downstream by using a strategy of vertical integration. The company does not sell its products to wholesalers or retailers but instead sells directly to end users in its stores and on its regionally based website. The company even controls the supply chain after it delivers goods to end users' homes. In 2017, IKEA acquired TaskRabbit, an American online service marketplace, which matches local freelance service providers with customers. IKEA has built TaskRabbit into its in-store and online ordering so that customers can immediately order furniture assembly service when purchasing their unassembled furniture. The Swedish furniture giant now controls the supply chain for some of its products from a tree in a Romanian forest to in-home assembly in customers' homes across the US, Canada, and the UK.

While vertical integration focuses on a company's logistics growth upstream and downstream, ***horizontal integration*** is a strategy a company uses to grow its logistics control and operations by increasing its production at the same point in the supply chain. Horizontal integration can be achieved through internal or external expansion. *Internal expansion* occurs when a company sells to a broader range of customers or offers an expanded range of products. *External expansion* occurs when a company acquires or merges with other companies selling products in the same industry, allowing the same manufacturing facilities to be used for more products. Over the past two decades, the number of beverage companies worldwide has steadily decreased to a small handful of beverage giants. This decrease is due to horizontal integration through mergers and acquisitions of beverage producers. PepsiCo, one of the world's largest beverage producers, began as the Pepsi Cola Company. It grew as it expanded its product lines and steadily acquired other beverage companies, including Mountain Dew, Tropicana Products, SodaStream, and various Russian milk and fruit juice producers. Beverage producers such as PepsiCo utilize horizontal integration to grow logistics control and operations because they leverage the same bottling equipment, packaging, and distribution networks as new beverage brands are acquired and added.

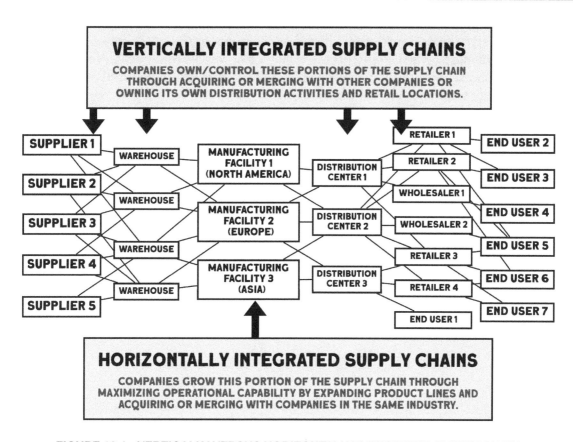

FIGURE 12.4 - VERTICALLY VERSUS HORIZONTALLY INTEGRATED SUPPLY CHAIN

Companies can grow their logistics operations and control their supply chains by utilizing *both* vertical and horizontal integration strategies. For example, while PepsiCo acquired and merged with other beverage providers for horizontal integration, the company also used vertical integration by acquiring suppliers in some markets, such as purchasing dairy suppliers in Russia for its milk-based beverages. Consideration of integration strategies helps a company envision and plan its future, which is reflected in its vision statement.

12.3 STRATEGY TOOLS: EXTERNAL ANALYSIS

An essential part of the strategic analysis stage is taking a broad look at the external environment in which the company operates. As it plans for the future and sets its goals and objectives, a company needs to look around and know what is happening locally, nationally, internationally, and within its industry. Our example of Target's expansion from Chapter 11 highlights a company that might not have completed a broad analysis of the international Canadian market into which it was moving. Sam's Club, a membership-based warehouse store, is another example of a company that might not have completed a broad analysis of regional national markets. The Sam's chain closed 63 US stores in 2018, many of which were in the Pacific Northwest. Thirty-five years earlier, Costco was founded in Seattle, the heart of the Pacific Northwest, and continues to have a strong foothold in the region's hearts, minds, and wallets. Costco was too entrenched in the region's economic and social systems to allow room for the Walmart-owned competitor. In Chapter 9, we saw other examples of why external analysis is vital for entering a new global market. We even introduced a strategy tool before the "Strategy and Supply Chain Management" chapter: *the PESTEL framework*.

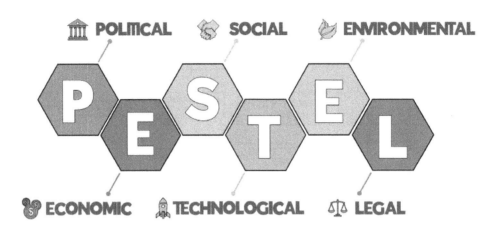

FIGURE 12.5 - THE PESTEL MARKET ANALYSIS FRAMEWORK

A **PESTEL framework** outlines environmental factors that can impact business operations and decisions. PESTEL is an abbreviation for the six factors examined using the tool: *political, economic, social, technological, environmental*, and *legal*. All six factors can influence a company's supply chain operations and management when operating in a specific environment. The PESTEL framework we explored in Chapter 9 was in the context of international business operations. However, the PESTEL strategy tool can be used by a company in any operating environment, including a small business operating only in a local region. The important thing to remember is to seek information about all six areas of the PESTEL in your current or desired market location. In the case of our two friends who want to start a transportation business, they would perform a PESTEL analysis on their university town and local operations area. As the business grows, they would expand the analysis to include the national or international expansion area, likely performing a unique PESTEL analysis on each new region of operations.

While the PESTEL analysis can help a company look at the external operating environment locally, nationally, or internationally, *Porter's five forces* is another strategy tool that can help a company examine the environment within its industry or an industry it may be considering entering. Michael Porter, the Harvard Business School professor who developed the generic strategies framework, also created a strategy tool called the **five forces**, which examines five factors that impact an industry and determine its strengths and weaknesses. In this context, an **industry** is the total group of companies that operate to manufacture or produce the same type or category of products, such as the dairy industry or the household appliances industry.

The five forces that shape each competitive industry in the world and the questions a company might pose for each are:

- **Industry Rivalry.** How many competing companies are in the industry, and how strong are they? Would any of the companies be direct competition for our company, offering the same products or services in the same market?

- **Power of Suppliers.** How many suppliers are available? Is it easy for suppliers to increase their prices? Is it easy to switch suppliers or to find less expensive alternatives? For service industry companies, what is the size of the local labor force to supply workforce?

- **Power of Buyers.** How many potential customers are in the market? Would their orders be large or small? Would their orders be recurring or one-off? Are the buyers powerful enough to dictate terms or force companies to decrease prices?

- **Threat of Substitutes.** Can customers easily find competing companies that could replace our products or services? Can customers easily find alternatives to our products or services?

- **Threat of New Entrants.** Is it easy for competitors to enter the market? Do companies incur any costs or regulations when entering the market that may prevent them from entering? What is the history of competing companies entering the market?

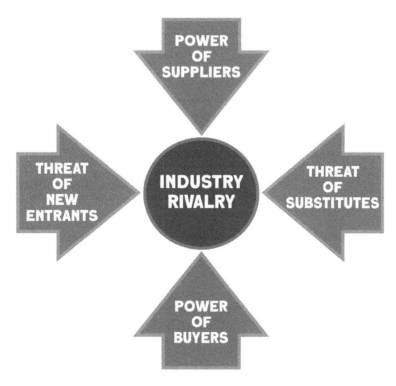

FIGURE 12.6 - PORTER'S FIVE FORCES

In the case of our two friends who want to start a moving and transportation business in a university town, Toni and Pia completed a five forces analysis for their original Truck U moving company idea and the newly discovered idea of a medical supplies and equipment transportation company. From the results shown in Figure 12.7, the two friends now see that there may be a lot more room for profitability and growth in the medical supplies and equipment transportation industry than in the general household goods moving industry, especially one catered to college students. They decide that the low cost of entering the household moving market is not worth the risk posed by the high industry rivalry, threat of substitutes and threat of new entrants. They believe that their long-term prospects could be better in the medical transportation industry, which has low industry rivalry, power of buyers, threat of substitutes, and threat of new entrants.

FIVE FORCES	TRUCK U HOUSEHOLD MOVING COMPANY	UNNAMED MEDICAL TRANSPORTATION CO.
INDUSTRY RIVALRY	• At least twenty competing companies • Two large low-cost, well-known franchise operations • **HIGH INDUSTRY RIVALRY**	• No local competition • Higher cost competing companies in other locations in the state • **LOW INDUSTRY RIVALRY**
POWER OF SUPPLIERS	• Truck, gasoline, and moving supplies readily available from multiple suppliers • Large local labor force of college students available • **LOW POWER OF SUPPLIERS**	• Truck, gasoline, and moving supplies readily available from multiple suppliers • Specialized labor force expensive and challenging to attain • **MEDIUM POWER OF SUPPLIERS**
POWER OF BUYERS	• Many potential customers in market • Customer orders typically small (two-hour to four-hour jobs) • Customers orders typically one-off • **MEDIUM POWER OF BUYERS**	• Many potential customers in market who have a difficult time finding suppliers • Customer orders typically large or recurring ones • **LOW POWER OF BUYERS**
THREAT OF SUBSTITUTES	• Customers have easy time finding household moving companies • Many companies offer discounts • Customers could hire a rental truck and move household goods themselves • **HIGH THREAT OF SUBSTITUTES**	• Customers cannot find similar companies in the local market • Customers forced to use companies with distance transportation surcharges • Customers can't move equipment themselves • **LOW THREAT OF SUBSTITUTES**
THREAT OF NEW ENTRANTS	• Not difficult for competitors to enter market • Minimal regulations for companies entering market • **HIGH THREAT OF NEW ENTRANTS**	• Initially costly to enter market - specialty equipment and training is needed • FDA labeling regulations for medical and radiation-emitting devices • **LOW THREAT OF NEW ENTRANTS**

FIGURE 12.7 - FIVE FORCES ANALYSIS OF TWO INDUSTRIES FOR TRANSPORTATION COMPANIES

12.4 STRATEGY TOOLS: INTERNAL ANALYSIS

Just as a company looks outward to the external environment during the strategic analysis stage, it also looks inward at itself and its internal operations as it plans for the future and sets goals and objectives. Two strategy tools used for internal analysis are the *value chain analysis* and the *life cycle analysis.*

Chapter 1 introduces the value chain as another way of looking at the supply chain through the current and potential value added throughout each of the chain's stages. Another strategy tool developed by Harvard business professor Michael Porter, the **value chain** outlines the chain of primary and support activities found in all companies that deal with goods, as shown in Figure 12.8. Companies can analyze all the stages in the value chain to look for opportunities to add more value to goods or reduce current costs. Because of its many actions with lots of opportunities for in-depth analysis, many companies rely on software templates, programs, and apps for value chain analysis.

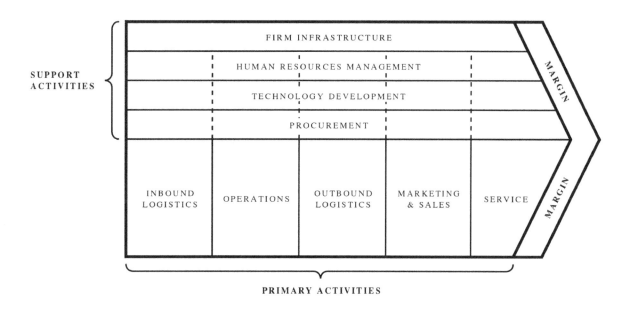

FIGURE 12.8 - PORTER'S VALUE CHAIN

Another strategy tool used for internal analysis is the **life cycle model**, a framework that illustrates the stages of growth of a product, company, or industry to guide decision-making. For this stage of internal analysis in developing or refining a company's strategic plan, it is useful for a company to investigate where it is within its company life cycle. A company's life cycle has four stages: *introduction*, *growth*, *maturity*, and *decline*. During the **introduction stage**, a company is new to the market. Everyone at the company is learning, new structures are being created, and enthusiasm is at its peak. Unfortunately, this is the stage at which many new companies fail because they are still so new that they do not generate enough sales to pay for all of the employees or support needed. Mistakes can also be made because companies may not have found or developed good relationships with suppliers and customers. During the **growth stage**, systems are starting to solidify, and the company has worked out its vision, mission, and strategic plan. Everyone is working hard. Resources are required to pay them and bring in expertise and technical systems to continue growing the company. In this stage, supply chains begin to solidify, and companies can begin to look for value in supply chains through Porter's value chain analysis. During the **maturity stage**, companies may grow but at a much lower rate. Business earnings are somewhat predictable, which may put some companies at risk because complacency can set in. Companies must continue to use strategic analysis tools regularly to evaluate how they are doing and to look for growth opportunities and threats needed to be managed to keep the maturity stage going as long as possible. This stage is a time for companies to continue to look for opportunities for updating and streamlining their supply chains. Finally, during the **decline stage**, companies business begins to drop off. If they do not regularly perform strategic analysis using strategy tools, companies may have no idea why they are faltering. At this stage, companies may either fail or take significant innovative steps to renew themselves.

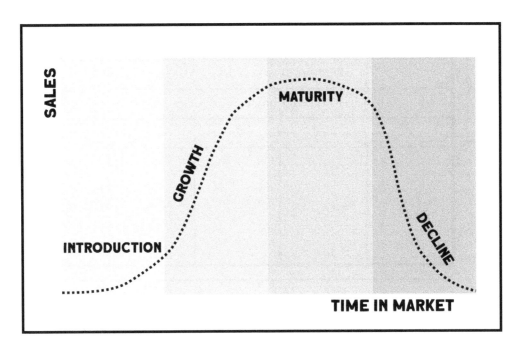

FIGURE 12.9 - COMPANY LIFE CYCLE

The purpose of a life cycle analysis is to determine where the company is in its life cycle and use this information to prolong its life at that stage or successfully transition to the next stage. For example, suppose a company is in the decline stage. It must plan to continue prolonged profitability at this stage while also planning for renewal or reinvention of the company, which starts the company life cycle over again. Netflix accomplished this when it was in decline as a DVD mail-order rental company. It reinvented itself to become one of the top on-demand video streaming services and original video content creators.

If a company is in its introduction stage, it needs to plan to set up the business and establish internal processes. At the same time, it also needs to prepare for the growth stage while developing its strategic plan so that it does not collapse at the initial tenuous stage in its development where many businesses fail. Some companies get so bogged down in setting themselves up to do business that they lose sight of how they will quickly grow and earn money to pay their employees and reinvest in the business. In the case of the two friends and their new transportation company, they know that they must include goals and objectives in their strategic plan. It must address both set-up and initial growth, ensuring they secure a loan that will allow them to pay key employees for the first three years.

12.5 STRATEGY TOOLS: INITIAL AND ONGOING ANALYSIS

One useful strategy tool that combines internal and external analysis is the **SWOT matrix**. Companies can use it to examine what is happening both inside and outside the company and outline what is helpful and harmful to the company. Companies use the SWOT matrix often throughout strategic planning to help develop initial strategic plans, support ongoing annual reviews of company strategy, or gain information and insight when working on specific projects. Individuals can also use the SWOT matrix to help in personal or professional decision-making.

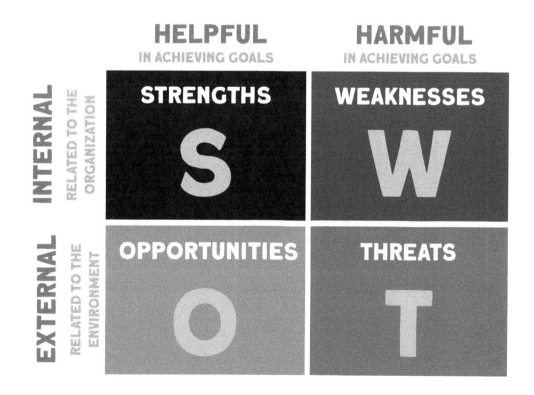

FIGURE 12.10 - THE SWOT MATRIX

SWOT is an abbreviation for strengths, weaknesses, opportunities, and threats. In a SWOT matrix analysis, a company examines each of these four categories:

- **Strengths:** What are our company's elements or characteristics that give it an advantage or a competitive edge over others? *This category looks at the internal environment inside the company to see what is helpful.*

- **Weaknesses:** What are our company's elements or characteristics that put it at a disadvantage compared to its competition? *This category looks at the internal environment inside the company to see what is harmful.*

- **Opportunities:** What are the elements or characteristics outside of our company in the external environment that we could use to give it an advantage or a competitive edge over others? *This category looks at the external environment outside the company to see what is helpful.*

- **Threats:** What elements or characteristics in the external environment could put our company at a disadvantage compared to its competition? *This category looks at the external environment outside the company to see what is harmful.*

Remember the two friends, Toni and Pia, who wanted to open a moving and transportation company? The entrepreneurial pair decided to perform a SWOT analysis on their original idea for Truck U, a moving company in a university town that lets students pay them in pizza and beer. Figure 12.11 shows the results of their SWOT.

HELPFUL
IN ACHIEVING GOALS

HARMFUL
IN ACHIEVING GOALS

INTERNAL RELATED TO THE ORGANIZATION

STRENGTHS

- The business owners are very enthusiastic about the idea
- The business owners have some experience in the industry as employees and customers

WEAKNESSES

- The business owners do not have management experience
- The business will have no name recognition or existing contacts in the market
- The pizza and beer element in the business logo might be confusing

EXTERNAL RELATED TO THE ENVIRONMENT

OPPORTUNITIES

- The local area has two large universities with students moving in and out in large numbers twice a year
- The business owners can borrow a family member's truck for one month

THREATS

- There are two large franchise competitors with sales promotions
- Including beer in the logo or marketing might make a negative connection to drinking and driving
- The name of the business sounds like a profanity-laced insult

12.11 - SWOT ANALYSIS FOR TRUCK U

Although Toni and Pia are incredibly enthusiastic about the concept of Truck U, after performing a SWOT analysis, they see that there are weaknesses and threats to their idea. Because of the many red flags that they cannot ignore, the two friends decide to perform a SWOT analysis on the new idea that has evolved since completing the generic strategies and five forces analyses, a transportation company for medical equipment and supplies. Because they have worked small transportation jobs during college breaks for multiple relatives who work locally in various aspects of the medical equipment and medical research industries, they have easy access to information about the external environment for their SWOT analysis, as shown in Figure 12.12.

FIGURE 12.12 - SWOT ANALYSIS FOR SECURICLEAN TRANSPORTATION

Based on the SWOT analysis results, the two friends abandoned their colossally bad idea of Truck U. They ended up forming SecuriClean Transportation, a specialized transportation company for medical equipment and supplies, with a plan to develop a model to be franchised for operations in other cities. The bank was so impressed with their strategic plan and analysis that the friends could secure a loan for employees, equipment, and training for the first three years of their operations.

CHAPTER 12 REVIEW QUESTIONS

1. What is the connection between supply chain management and *strategic management*?

2. What is a *strategic plan*? Describe each of its components and purpose.

3. Why might a strategic plan be useful to a logistics or supply chain manager in an organization?

4. What is the difference between a *mission statement* and a *vision statement*?

5. Describe the stages to develop a strategic plan.

6. Think of a company you know well and describe where it would fall in *Porter's generic strategies* framework. Explain your answer.

7. Describe *Porter's five forces* analysis and a situation in which it would be useful.

8. Complete a five forces analysis for a company you know well.

9. Describe the concept of *life cycle* analysis. Why would it be useful for a logistics or supply chain manager to know where their company is in its life cycle?

10. What is the purpose of a *SWOT* analysis? Conduct a SWOT analysis based on your current job or career goals, outlining the strengths, weaknesses, opportunities, and threats related to you and your career.

CHAPTER 12 CASE STUDY

THE SUPPLY CHAIN MANAGEMENT HERO

We began our chapter case studies with a fairy tale, but we will conclude our end-of-chapter case studies with the story of a brave hero venturing out into the wild world of logistics and supply chain management. You may ask, "Who is this brave hero?" Well, this brave supply chain hero is YOU! You now have the knowledge to unravel the most complex of supply chains, plunge into the perils of purchasing, withstand the worries of warehousing, and tackle the troubles of transportation. You have a bag of tricks ready at your side, including information systems, customer service skills, strategic management tools, and a knowledge of finance and the global environment.

What are the next steps to help send you on your way into the daunting world of customers, suppliers, and everyone in between before you begin to slay the dragons of the bullwhip effect, the RFX process, and international trade documentation? Below are five easy and not-so-easy steps to take to continue your journey to becoming a logistics and supply chain management hero.

1. **Analyze Your Career Goals**

   If you are considering a career in logistics and supply chain management or are already heading down that path, make sure this is the right path for you! Take a personality test like the Big Five to delve into who you are and see if a logistics career is a good fit for you. After taking a good look at your personality and what motivates you, dig a bit deeper and conduct a SWOT analysis of yourself. Consider your professional strengths and the career opportunities available to you and weigh them against your professional weaknesses and the threats lurking on your career horizon. Plan for ways to bolster your strengths, take advantage of the opportunities, eliminate your weaknesses, and minimize the threats. Once you have completed this, roll up your sleeves to draft your career path goals and objectives.

2. **Read Regularly about Logistics Topics**

   To confront, tackle, and gain the most significant competitive advantage from a rapidly changing present and future in logistics and supply chain management, good logistics managers arm themselves with the most potent weapon available: knowledge! Logistics and supply chains are in the news every day. Look for articles related to supply chain management in your usual news sources and expand your horizons by reading logistics magazines, journals, and blogs that interest you. Websites for various interesting articles and blogs on logistics and supply chain management include logisticsmanagement.com, supplychainmanagementreview.com, supplychaindive.com, logisticsviewpoints.com, inboundlogistics.com, 3PLwire.com, foodlogistics.com, and supplychainbrain.com. If you are interested in reading something with a more research-oriented or academic approach, consider academic journals. A few journals worth checking out are the *Journal of Business Logistics*, the *Journal of Supply Chain Management*, the *International Journal of Physical Distribution and Logistics Management*, and the *Journal of Purchasing and Supply Management*.

3. Network on Social Media

If you are looking to begin or further your logistics and supply chain management career, LinkedIn is a great way to start. LinkedIn is a social media website and app used primarily for professional networking. Although there are some fee-based functions, anyone can join LinkedIn for free. On the site, there are hundreds of groups for those interested in supply chain management. Some of the largest are the "Logistics and Supply Chain Professionals" group and the "Supply Chain Management (SCM)" group. You can use these groups to link and communicate with logistics professionals from around the world. You can also use the site to find job opportunities and educational content. Finally, professional social media sites like LinkedIn are not just for finding people and content. They are also your virtual professional face to the supply chain management world. You should make sure your profile is essentially the *you* who would show up for a job interview. Companies often use LinkedIn to find or check out job candidates' profiles, so make sure yours shows the true supply chain management hero in you!

4. Join Supply Chain Management Professional Organizations

To keep abreast of advances in supply chains and network with others in the profession, consider joining a professional logistics and supply chain management organization. These organizations typically hold annual conferences and issue both trade and academic publications covering the latest theoretical and practical advances in their fields. Their websites also provide a wealth of up-to-date information and useful links related to their areas, including various free e-learning opportunities. If you are currently a student, many of these organizations have free or reduced-price student memberships, so it might be worth joining a few of them now to see which ones might best suit your career development needs in the future.

Core professional organizations in the US utilized by logistics and supply chain managers and practitioners include:

- **The Council of Supply Chain Management Professionals (CSCMP)**, the largest professional organization in the United States whose members represent those working and studying within the field of supply chain management;

- **The Association for Supply Chain Management (APICS)**, a professional association for those interested in end-to-end supply chain management, which also offers a variety of options for professional certification;

- **The Institute for Supply Management (ISM)**, a professional organization devoted to supply management and its related standards of excellence, research, promotional activities, and education;

- **The Warehousing Education and Research Council (WERC)**, a professional organization devoted to warehouse management and its place in the supply chain;

- **The Material Handling Industry of America (MHIA)**, a professional association for those who provide materials handling and logistics services; and

- **The American Trucking Associations (ATA)**, a professional organization devoted to promoting truckers and legislative, judicial, and press trucking issues.

5. Share Your Knowledge

One of the best ways to reinforce your knowledge is to teach and share your knowledge with others. If you are currently working in the logistics and supply chain management field, seek opportunities in work, professional organization, and educational settings to share what you have learned and share your experiences. This sharing could range from talking about what you read to posting original content on LinkedIn about your experiences to becoming a supply chain mentor to someone with less experience. Not only will you become a logistics and supply chain management hero, but you will help other heroes grow, too.

Photo and Image Attributions

Figure 1.1 through Figure 1.8: ©Access Education.

Figure 1.9: "Titanic at the Docks of Southampton," by unknown, under public domain, cropped from original. https://commons.wikimedia.org/wiki/File:Titanic_in_Southampton.jpg.

Figure 1.10: "Rivet Patterns in the Hull of RMS Queen Mary," by carlfbagge, licensed under CC by 2.0. https://www.flickr.com/photos/12535240@N05/6135289845.

Figure 2.1 through Figure 2.5: ©Access Education.

Figure 2.6: "Boeing 787 U.S. Air Force Photo," by Samuel King Jr, under public domain.

Chapter 2 Case Study Figure 1: "Major Commodities and Trade Routes of the Silk Road in Approximately 1200 CE," by G. Moss and A. Ekinci, licensed under CC by SA 4.0.

Chapter 2 Case Study Figure 2: "Map of the Russian Campaign 1812," by J. Hart, under public domain.

Chapter 3 Intro Image: "Toddler Eats While Watching Movies on the Mobile Phone," by Antonio Gravante, under Envato Elements commercial license. Modified with icons and text by Access Education.

Figure 3.1: ©Access Education.

Figure 3.2: Public Domain.

Figure 3.3 through Figure 3.7: ©Access Education.

Figure 3.8: "Create Purchase Requisition," by SAP, licensed under CC by SA 2.0.

Figure 3.9: "ERFX System," by SAP, licensed under CC by SA 2.0.

Figure 3.10: "Coke Freestyle Machines at AMC Theaters in Palisades Mall," by TMBLover, licensed under CC by SA 3.0. Cropped by author.

Figure 3.11: "Purchase Order," by SAP, licensed under CC by SA 2.0.

Figure 3.12: ©Access Education.

Figure 5.11: Image under Envato Elements commercial license.

Figure 5.12 through Figure 5.13: ©Access Education.

Chapter 5 Case Study Figure 1: ©Access Education.

Chapter 6 Intro Image: Three combined images under Envato Elements commercial license.

Figure 6.1: ©Access Education.

Figure 6.2: Image and cover from US Bureau of Transportation Statistics *2020 Pocket Guide to Transportation*, under public domain.

Figure 6.3 through Figure 6.5: ©Access Education.

Figure 6.6 (left): "Rail Network of Israel," by Maximilian Dörrbecker, licensed under CC by SA 2.5. https://en.m.wikipedia.org/wiki/File:Israel_Railways_Map_(en).png

Figure 6.6 (right) through Figure 6.7: ©Access Education.

Figure 6.8: From U.S. Department of Transportation Federal Highway Administration, under public domain.

Figure 6.9 (left): "Weight Limit Signs," by Keith Evans, licensed under CC by SA 2.0. https://commons.wikimedia.org/wiki/File:Weight_Limit_Signs_-_geograph.org.uk_-_1806541.jpg. Cropped by author.

Figure 6.9 (middle): "Speed Limits in Poland," by Mike101, under public domain. https://commons.wikimedia.org/wiki/File:Znak_D-39._Ograniczenia_prędkości_w_Polsce_od_2011.svg

Figure 6.9 (right): "Japanese Road Sig," by Kiyok, licensed under CC by SA 3.0. https://en.m.wikipedia.org/wiki/File:Japanese_Road_Sign_118-3_and_118-4_(Ease_the_Limit_of_GVW_and_Height).jpg. Cropped by author.

Figure 6.10 through Figure Figure 6.13 (top left and right and bottom left): ©Access Education.

Figure 6.13 (bottom right): "Barge à Charbon," by LPLT, licensed under CC by SA 3.0. https://commons.wikimedia.org/wiki/File:Barge_à_charbon.jpg

Figure 6.14 (top): "Mars 2020 Project," by NASA, under public domain. https://www.jpl.nasa.gov/spaceimages/details.php?id=PIA23917. Cropped by author.

Figure 7.8 (left): "Till Shot Retail," by CyberTill HQ, licensed under CC by SA 4.0. https://commons.wikimedia.org/wiki/File:Till_Shot_retail.jpg. Cropped by author.

Figure 7.8 (right): Photo under Envato Elements commercial license.

Figure 7.9: "Office Supply Vending Machine," by Danielle Gregory, under public domain. https://www.tinker.af.mil/News/Photos/igphoto/2000606124/.

Figure 7.10: ©Access Education.

Figure 7.11: Label and tag images under public domain. Images combined with border and text by Access Education.

Figure 7.12 (left and right): Photos under Envato Elements commercial license.

Figure 7.12 (middle): "QR Code Streamlines Work Order Submittals," by Senior Airman Timothy Moore, US Air Force, under public domain. https://www.dm.af.mil/Media/Photos/igphoto/2000918823/. Cropped by author.

Figure 7.13 (left): "RFID Scanner," by Oscar111, under public domain. https://commons.wikimedia.org/wiki/File:Rfid-scanner.jpg.

Figure 7.13 (right): "Handspring Springboard Scanner Modules," by Waldohreule, licensed under CC by SA 3.0. https://en.wikipedia.org/wiki/File:Handspring_Springboard_Scanner_modules-.jpg.

Figure 7.14: Images from US 9,900,061 B1 and 10,546,204 B1, US Patent Office, under public domain.

Figure 7.15: Photo under Envato Elements commercial license.

Figure 7.16: "Mobile Industrial Robots," by FFOliver, licensed under CC by SA 4.0. https://commons.wikimedia.org/wiki/File:MiR_Robots.jpg.

Figure 7.17: ©Access Education.

Chapter 8 Intro Image: ©Access Education.

Figure 8.1: "Certificate of Purchase Class A Stock for 20 Shares of The Coca Cola Company," by Unbekannte Autoren und Grafiker; Scan vom EDHAC e.V., under public domain. https://commons.wikimedia.org/wiki/File:Coca_Cola_1929.JPG.

Figure 8.2 through Figure 8.20: ©Access Education.

Chapter 9 Intro Image: Photos under Envato Elements commercial license. Modified with text, cropping, and borders by Access Education.

Figure 9.1: "World Population Percentages," by Wikideas1, licensed under CC by SA 4.0. https://commons.wikimedia.org/wiki/File:World_population_percentage.png. Cropped by author.

Figure 9.2 through Figure 9.3: Multiple images under Envato Elements commercial license. Arranged and modified with text and graphic elements by Access Education.

Figure 9.4: "Billboard in Newcastle by Anti-Brexit Campaign Group Led-by-Donkeys," by Paul Harrop, licensed under CC by SA 2.0. https://commons.wikimedia.org/wiki/File:Billboard_in_Newcastle_by_anti-Brexit_campaign_group_Led_By_Donkeys.jpg.

Figure 9.5: Photo under iStockPhoto commercial license. Cropped by author.

Figure 9.6: "Ashram Recycling Campaign," by Jay Galvin, licensed under CC by SA 2.0. https://www.flickr.com/photos/jaygalvin/16996256031. Cropped by author.

Figure 9.7: "CPTPP Countries," by Australian Government Department of Foreign Affairs and Trade, under public domain. https://blog.dfat.gov.au/2019/02/27/five-reasons-why-the-cptpp-is-a-good-deal-for-australia/. Modified with text by Access Education.

Figure 9.8: "Colón Free Trade Zone," by Administración de la Zona Libre de Colón, under public domain. https://commons.wikimedia.org/wiki/File:Aerial_view_Colón_Free_-Trade_Zone.jpg.

Figure 9.9: "Form B for International Trade," by Edmond8674, under public domain. https://commons.wikimedia.org/wiki/File:Form_B_for_international_trade.jpg.

Figure 9.10: "Single Administrative Document," by United Nations, under public domain. https://unstats.un.org/wiki/pages/viewpage.action?pageId=6324525.

Figure 9.11: "Janesville GM Assembly Plant - ISO 9001 Certified Sign," by Cliff, licensed under CC by SA 2.0. https://commons.wikimedia.org/wiki/File:Janesville_GM_Assembly_-Plant_-_ISO_9001_Certified_sign_(3549915451).jpg. Cropped by author.

Figure 9.12: "ISO 9001 Certification," by generalising, licensed under CC by SA 2.0. https://commons.wikimedia.org/wiki/File:ISO_9001_certification_(6609209769).jpg. Cropped by author.

Figure 9.13: "ISO 9001 Tsukiji," by Chris 73, licensed under CC by SA 3.0. https://commons.wikimedia.org/wiki/File:ISO_9001_in_Tsukiji.jpg. Cropped by author.

Chapter 9 Case Study Photo 1: ©Access Education.

Chapter 9 Case Study Photo 2: "Distillery-Made Alcohol Sanitizers," by Paulo O, licensed under CC by SA 2.0. https://www.flickr.com/photos/brownpau/50001547058.

Chapter 10 Intro Image: ©Access Education.

Figure 10.1 through Figure 10.2: ©Access Education.

Figure 10.3: "A Customer Journey Map," by Rosenfeld Media, licensed under CC by SA 2.0. https://commons.wikimedia.org/wiki/File:SD053-_Figure_5.14_(8462249080).jpg. Cropped by author.

Figure 10.4: ©Access Education.

Figure 10.5: Image under iStockPhoto commercial license. Cropped and modified by Access Education.

Figure 10.6 through Figure 10.7: ©Access Education.

Figure 10.8: "7 Ps of Services Marketing," by BronHiggs, licensed under CC by SA 4.0. https://commons.wikimedia.org/wiki/File:7_ps_of_services_marketing.jpg. Cropped by author.

Figure 10.9: ©Access Education.

Chapter 10 Case Study Photo 1: "Self-Service Checkout at Meny Supermarket at Bergen Storsenter Shopping Mall in Bergen, Norway," by wolfmann, licensed under CC by SA 4.0. https://commons.wikimedia.org/wiki/File:Self-service_checkout_at_supermarket_in_Bergen,_Norway_(selvbetjente_kasser,_selvskanning_i_Meny_i_Bergen_Storsenter)_2017-10-23_a.jpg.

Chapter 10 Case Study Photo 2: "Amazon Go - Seattle," by Sikander Iqbal, licensed under CC by SA 4.0. https://commons.wikimedia.org/wiki/File:Amazon_Go_-_Seattle_(20180804111407).jpg. Cropped by author.

Chapter 10 Case Study Photo 3: ©Access Education.

Chapter 11 Intro Image: "KFC UK Crisis Management," by Ged Carroll, licensed under CC by SA 2.0. https://www.flickr.com/photos/renaissancechambara/40522484191.

Figure 11.1 through Figure 11.4: ©Access Education.

Figure 11.5: Photos under Envato Elements commercial license. Cropped, arranged, and modified borders by Access Education.

Figure 11.6 though Figure 11.9: ©Access Education.

Figure 11.10: Photo free for commercial use. https://www.pxfuel.com/en/free-photo-xfqzx. Cropped by author.

Chapter 12 Intro Image: Images under Envato Elements commercial license. Arranged and text added by Access Education.

Figure 12.1 through Figure 12.4: ©Access Education.

Figure 12.5: Images under Envato Elements commercial license. Modified with text elements by Access Education.

Figure 12.6 through Figure 12.8: ©Access Education.

Figure 12.9: "Michael Porter's Value Chain," by Denis Fadeev, licensed under CC by SA 3.0. https://commons.wikimedia.org/wiki/File:Michael_Porter%27s_Value_Chain.svg.

Figure 12.10 through Figure 12.12: ©Access Education.

Index

3PLP	141	batch picking	104, 105
3PL	141	bid	56, 58
ABC analysis	90	big data	155, 164
acquisition	36	Big Five personality test	273, 284, 285
active RFID tag	169	bilateral	222
additive printing	279	bill of lading	227
AI	165	binding	53
AIDC	160	blanket purchase order	60
air	136, 137	bonded warehouse	76
aircraft	127	BPO	60
artificial intelligence	165	bulk carriers	135
asset turnover	193, 194	bullwhip effect	157-160, 236, 237
assets	186		
automated warehouse	74, 75	business to business	48
automatic identification and communication equipment	88	business to consumer	48
		business to government	48
automatic inventory replacement	44	buying to requirements	43, 44
autonomous mobile robot	172	capital goods	39
autonomous technology	171	cargo port	135
autonomous truck	173	carrier	138-141
B2B	48, 162	carrier documents	227
B2C	48, 162	carrier's insurance certificate	227
B2G	48	carrying cost	92
back end	12	centralized purchasing	40-43
balance sheet	186-192	certificate of origin	226, 227
banking documents	228, 229	CFC	76
barcode scanner	166	claims on assets	186, 189
barges	136	Class I railroads	133

climate-controlled warehouse	75, 76	customer service process	247-249
closing inventory	183	CX	243
cloud-based	47	D2C	110, 260
cluster picking	104, 105	dangerous goods warehouse	76
collaborative robot	172	data	152, 155
commercial invoice	225	data mining	155
commodities	39	decentralized purchasing	41-43
common carrier	139	demand chain	10
competitive bidding	56-58	Department of Transportation	144
consolidated warehouse	77, 78	deregulation	144
consumer	4	DFN	164
container	86, 87	digital freight network	164
container ships	135	direct channel distribution	109, 110
continuous inventory checking	91	direct exporting	214
cooperative purchasing	43	direct to consumer	110, 260
cooperative warehouse	78	discrete picking	104
corporate finance	181	dispatch area	82
cost accounting	200-205	distribution center	3, 4, 76
cost proposal	53	distribution channel	103, 109, 249
cross-docking facility	77	distribution resource planning	90, 162
CSS	242	DOT	144
current assets	188-190	downstream	9, 10
current liabilities	189-191	DRP	162
customer	4, 240, 241	DRP II	90
customer experience	242, 243	DSS	161
customer fulfillment center	76	DuPont model	195-199
customer journey	244, 245	e-auctions	162
customer relationship manage-ment	242	e-commerce	48, 162
		e-procurement	48
customer service	240-242	e-tailing	162
customer service policy	242, 243		

EC Treaty	223	financial statements	181-187
economic order quantity	90, 204	finished goods	39
EDI	48, 160	fiscal year	183
electronic data interchange	48, 160	five forces	298-300
electronic records management	160	five-factor model	284
emotional intelligence	275-278	fixed assets	188-190
end user	4	fixed liabilities	190-192
enterprise software	50	FMCSA	144
EOQ	90, 204	forecast	44
EPOS	119, 162	foreign trade zone	225
EQ	276, 277	form utility	28, 246
eRFX system	54	forward buying	44, 45, 235
ERM	160, 161	four Ps of marketing	250
ERP	67, 160	free trade agreement	222
expedite	61	free trade zone	225
export declaration	227	freight consolidator	140
export documents	225-227	freight forwarder	141
export license	226	frictionless shopping	259
export processing zone	225	front end	12
extended marketing mix	252, 253	FTZ	225
external customer	240	fulfillment center	76, 77
external inventory yard	78, 79	goods	2, 39, 40
external supply chain	10, 11, 24	goods-specific documents	227
extranet	48	government warehouse	78
FAA	144	GPS	169
Federal Aviation Administration	144	gross income	184
finance	26, 181	gross profit margin	183-185
financial accounting	200	handheld device	169
financial leverage	194	handheld scanner picking	106
financial ratio	192-195	hazardous materials warehouse	76

hazmat warehouse	76	intranet	48
horizontal integration	296, 297	inventory	89
hub	130	inventory carrying cost	184
hybrid distribution channels	113	inventory control	90, 102, 114
hybrid purchasing	42, 43	inventory holding cost	92, 202
ICT infrastructure	219	inventory management	89
IFB	53	inventory management systems	89
import documents	227	inventory turnover ratio	198, 199
imports	222	inventory visibility	114, 115, 248
inbound logistics	21, 71	invitation to bid	53
inbound supply chain	5, 6, 19	ISO	230
income statement	181-186	ISO 9001 series	230
INCOTERMS	229-232	ITB	53
indirect channel distribution	110	JIT	90, 164
indirect exporting	213, 214	joint venture	214
industry	298	just-in-time	90, 164
information	152, 153	last-mile delivery	172
information communication technology infrastructure	219	leader	268, 269
information systems	159	leadership	266, 269, 274, 275, 280
information technology	159	liabilities	186, 187, 190, 191
information utility	29	licensing	214
infrastructure	127, 128, 220	life cycle model	301-303
insourcing	52	light-aided technology	170
intermediate goods	39	link	128
intermodal transportation	142, 143	LIS	159
internal customer	240	loading bay	80
internal supply chain	11, 20	loading dock	80
International Organization for Standardization	230	local line-haul railroads	133, 134
international trade	212	logistics	11, 19, 26
intramodal transportation	142	logistics information systems	159

logistics management	20, 25	multilateral	222
maintenance, repair, and operating supplies	39	multimodal transportation	142, 143
make or buy decision	51	multiple source purchase	58
Malcom McLean	148, 149	negotiation	56
management	266	net profit margin	193
manager	266	net sales	183
managerial accounting	200	new competitive purchase	55
manual handling	84	NHTSA	145
manufacturer	3	node	128
manufacturing resource planning	90	O2C	101
maquiladora	224	omnichannel retail strategy	113
MARAD	145	one level channel	110
market entry strategy	213-216	one-off purchase	44
market operating strategy	213-216	online sales	214
marketing mix	250-252	opening inventory	183
materials handling	84, 85	optimization systems	164
materials handling equipment	87, 88	order cycle	101-103
materials management	22, 60	order cycle time	101-103, 252
materials requirement planning	48, 90	order picking	81, 102
MBTI	272-274, 284-287	order picking area	81
McLean, Malcom	148, 149	order receipt	102
mechanical handling	84, 85	order-to-cash	101
mission statement	290	OTC	101
mode of transportation	130	outbound supply chain	6
modified purchase	55	outdoor storage area	78
motor vehicle	127	outgoings	182
MRO supplies	39, 40	outsourcing	52
MRP	48, 90	outstanding	183
MRP II	90	overage	158
multichannel distribution	113	overseas trade	222

packaging	107	profit and loss	181
packing and unitization area	82	proposal	53
pallet	85	public leadership	274
paradigm	278	public warehouse	74
passive RFID tag	168	publicly traded	180
people skills	277	purchase agreement	59
performance metrics	61	purchase order	59
periodic inventory checking	91	purchase requisition	50-52
personality type	273, 285	purchasing	35, 36
PESTEL framework	216, 298	purchasing process	49
physical count	91	put-to-light	170
physical distribution management	23, 98	QR code	167
physical inventory	90, 91	quotation	53
physical inventory check	91	quote	53
pick-to-light	170	rail	132-134
picker	106	railed vehicle	127
pipeline	138	ratio	192
place utility	29, 124, 246	raw data	155
PO	59	raw materials	39, 89
Porter's generic strategies	294	real-time visibility	164
positioning equipment	88	receiving area	81
possession utility	29, 246	reception area	81
preferred supplier	51	reciprocity	45
print and apply labeling	166	recycling	220
private carrier	139	regional railroads	133
private leadership	275	regional trade agreement	223
private warehouse	74	regulation	144-146
procurement	36	request for information	52
producer	3	request for offer	53
profit	180	request for proposal	53

request for quotation	53	shareholders	180
retailer	4	shortline railroads	133
retained earnings	190, 191	simple supply chain	2-4
return on assets	194	single administrative document	227
return on equity	195	single order picking	104
return on net worth	195	single source purchase	57
reverse auction	58	smart warehouse	75
reverse logistics	115, 116, 249	sole source purchase	57
reverse supply chain	8, 115	SOW	50
RFI	52, 53	special economic zone	224
RFID	167-169	specifications	50
RFO	53	spot buying	43
RFP	53	spot checking	91
RFQ	53	staging area	82
RFX process	52	statement of work	50
road	130-132	storage area	78,81
robot	172	storage equipment	88
roll-on/roll-off ships	135	straight purchase	55
RoRo ships	135	straight repurchase	55
route	129	strategic management	290
routine order release	60	strategic management team	290
safety stock inventory	90	strategic plans	290, 293
self-driving truck	173	strategic profit model	195, 196
self-leadership	275	strategic sourcing	37
semifinished goods	39	strategy statement	293
service area	82	supplier	2
service utility	29, 30	supplier relationship management	37
services	40	supply chain	1-2
SEZ	224	supply chain management	25
shareholder equity	187, 191	supply chain management team	25-27

supply chain network	128	value added area	81
supply chain network optimization	128	value chain	10, 28, 301
supply management	37	vehicle	126
supply management approach	37	vendor	2, 48, 163
switching and terminal (S&T) carriers	134	vendor managed inventory	48, 90, 163
SWOT matrix	303, 304	vertical integration	296
technical proposal	53	vessel	127
terminal	129	video conference	48
TEU	135	virtual meeting	48
third-party logistics service provider	3, 141	vision statement	290
three level channel	110	VMI	48, 90, 163
three-way match	62	voice picking	107, 170
time utility	29, 124, 246	voice-aided technology	165, 170
TMS	161	warehouse	3, 70, 74, 157
total cost of goods sold	183	warehouse management	71
TPLs	141	warehousing	70
trade agreement	222	water	134-136
trade bloc	223	watercraft	127
trade pact	222	wave picking	104, 105
tradeoff principle	28, 124	wearable technology	165, 169
transaction documents	225	wholesaler	4
transport equipment	88	wholly owned subsidiary	215
transportation	2, 114, 122	WMS	161
transportation network	128, 129	work-in-process	89
two level channel	110	World Trade Organization	223
underage	158	WTO	223
unit load	84	yard	78
unit load formation equipment	88	zero level channel	109, 113
upstream	9, 10	zone picking	104, 105
utility	28, 123, 246		

Printed in the USA
CPSIA information can be obtained
at www.ICGtesting.com
CBHW080902310724
12473CB00014BA/516